Postcolonial Conrad

Across the twentieth century Joseph Conrad's colonial novels were read from radically different perspectives and interpreted through a wide range of discourses. By the century's end these fictions, which record the encounters between Europe and Europe's 'Other' at the moment of high imperialism, had become key texts in the burgeoning field of postcolonial studies. In this study Terry Collits tackles what is now a central question in both postcolonial studies and Conrad scholarship: what happens when Conrad's novels are read from the perspective of the colonized?

Drawing on many years of research and a rich body of critical approaches, including psychoanalysis, feminism and discourse analysis, *Postcolonial Conrad* not only offers fresh readings of Conrad's novels of imperialism but also maps and analyses the interpretative tradition they have generated. Terry Collits begins by examining the reception of Conrad's work in terms of the history of ideas, traditional literary criticism, concepts of 'Englishness', Marxism and postcolonialism. The novels he then selects for detailed re-evaluation are *Heart of Darkness*, *Lord Jim*, *Nostromo* and *Victory*.

Collits' incisive, wide-ranging volume re-examines a century of literary history, analysing the ways in which changing political, pedagogical and theoretical conditions have generated an interpretative tradition of extraordinary density. *Postcolonial Conrad* concludes by identifying lines of political criticism that are emerging in the twenty-first century and thus asks anew in what terms we might understand these powerful and intriguing novels.

Terry Collits is Head of Chisholm College at La Trobe University in Melbourne, Australia, and a Senior Associate of the English departments of both La Trobe and the University of Melbourne. His teaching and research ranges from Greek tragedy and contemporary theory to the novels of Joseph Conrad and their postcolonial transformations and Indian writings in English.

Postcolonial Literatures

Edited in collaboration with the Centre for Colonial and Postcolonial Studies, University of Kent at Canterbury, this series presents a wide range of research into postcolonial literatures by specialists in the field. Volumes will concentrate on writers and writing originating in previously (or presently) colonized areas, and will include material from non-Anglophone as well as Anglophone colonies and literatures. The series will also include collections of important essays from older journals, and re-issues of classic texts on postcolonial subjects. Routledge is pleased to invite proposals for new books in the series. Interested authors should contact Lyn Innes or Rod Edmond at the Centre for Colonial and Postcolonial Studies, University of Kent at Canterbury, or Routledge's Commissioning Editor for Literature.

The series comprises three strands.

Routledge Research in Postcolonial Literatures is a forum for innovative new research intended for a specialist readership. Published in hardback, titles include:

Postcolonial Literatures makes available in paperback important work in the field. Hardback editions of these titles are also available, some published earlier in the *Routledge Research* strand of the series. Titles in paperback include:

Readings in Postcolonial Literatures offers collections of important essays from journals or classic texts in the field. Titles include:

Postcolonial Conrad
Paradoxes of Empire

Terry Collits

Routledge
Taylor & Francis Group

LONDON AND NEW YORK

First published 2005
by Routledge
2 Park Square, Milton Park, Abingdon, Oxon, OX14 4RN

Simultaneously published in the USA and Canada
by Routledge
270 Madison Ave, New York, NY 10016

Routledge is an imprint of the Taylor & Francis Group

Typeset in Baskerville by
Rosemount Typing Services, Auldgirth, Dumfriesshire

Printed and bound in Great Britain by
Antony Rowe Ltd, Chippenham, Wiltshire

British Library Cataloguing in Publication Data
A catalogue record for this book is available from the British Library

Library of Congress Cataloging in Publication Data
A catalog record for this book has been requested

ISBN 0–415–35575–3

For George Russell

In gratitude for support long ago

Contents

Epilogue: Conrad and the new world order   **189**

Preface

I have spent the past four years writing this book. At the millennium a centenary study of Joseph Conrad's colonial novels seemed not only appropriate but also a way for me to bring together thoughts accumulated over many years. These had often been formed, I realized, in response to changing conditions both in the world and in the ways in which literary texts were discussed in universities.

The process of writing this book, I discovered, was both complex and collective, and took two particular forms. First I enjoyed generous encouragement and input from colleagues and friends. Then in revisiting now remote times and places, I remembered various discussions, debates, seminars and supervisions – some pleasurable, others annoying, all passionate. These interacted productively with more recent comments on my work from critical readers and conference respondents.

The first three people I want to thank were all products of that 'Cambridge English' which occupies a substantial part of the book. They provided me with a vicarious experience of that influential institution. Very soon after undertaking this project I received strong support and advice from Terry Eagleton, with whom I have long had fine points of agreement and disagreement about Conrad. He read and commented in detail on two early drafts, and provided substantial input that was warm, constructive and sometimes exacting. Perhaps sympathetic to a diffident would-be writer, Howard Jacobson insisted that I should go ahead with the book, and gave me help and advice for making it a palpable reality. Much earlier, when I was an undergraduate of his at the University of Sydney in the 'Sixties', Howard had introduced me to the sheer pleasure of reading Conrad's writing. Another close friend and peerless reader of Jane Austen, John Wiltshire, had come (like Howard) straight from Downing College, Cambridge to a lecturing appointment in Sydney in the 1960s. His influence in my undergraduate career was decisive. One of the pleasant side-effects of writing this book was the opportunity it gave me to enjoy once more with John serious discussions about literature, this time at La Trobe University in Melbourne.

The form of the book, however, derives mainly from my experiences in the English Department of the University of Melbourne in the 1980s. Like many students and colleagues at Melbourne in that decade, I benefited from the encouragement, advice and knowledge of Simon During, who joined that Department in 1982. We needed confidence to negotiate those new discourses that were beginning to impinge on the humanities. Teachers and students alike had to completely rethink the terms of their discipline, and often abandon or radically change proven and successful habits of talking and thinking about books and ideas. In 1978, Howard Felperin had been appointed to the Robert Wallace Chair of English at Melbourne previously occupied by the Leavisite S. L. Goldberg. As a result of Howard's appointment, the University of Melbourne housed the first 'traditional' English Department in Australia to engage seriously with critical theory. Much of my discussion of Conrad's novels of imperialism is shadowed by the narrative of the disciplinary changes, at once threatening and exciting, that happened at Melbourne.

More recently, Leela Gandhi and Pauline Nestor joined the group of people who – quite independently of one another – told me I should 'write more'. Along with Dick Freadman and Jenny Gribble, who were my first Australian readers, they helped to instil the self-belief I needed in order to sustain this project. Since then I have enjoyed the disinterested encouragement and advice of Conradian and postcolonial scholars further afield. They make up a kind of international club I hope to belong to. Their UK members include, first and foremost, Keith Carrabine, as well as Robert Hampson, Allan Simmons, Rajeswari Sunder Rajan, and Gurminder Bhambra; in France, Anne Luyat above all, and then (partly through her firmly persuasive 'interventions'), Jacques Darras, Josiane Paccaud-Huguet, Nathalie Martinière, and Véronique Pauly; in the United States, Peter Mallios, who showed me that at least one American shares my warm affection for *Victory*; and in India, Udaya Kumar, Sambudha Sen, C. Vijayashree and M. Asaduddin, in whose company I have rehearsed sections of the book over the past three years, and who (with many others) have provided the most stimulating milieu for academic exchange I have enjoyed for a long time. I would particularly like to thank my son, Brendan Muller, not only for helping me to navigate Paris but also for hours of conversation about new world orders and related matters.

My biggest intellectual debt is to the wonderful students I have taught. Postgraduate supervisions and undergraduate classes both at Melbourne and at La Trobe have generated most of the ideas in this book. Sometimes when reading their written work I begrudged the fact that my students had more time than I did to keep abreast of theory. Secretly harbouring a desire to have a go myself, I would occasionally resent giving them feedback. In overcoming those frustrations, I recognized that two postgraduate students in particular taught me more about postcolonialism than I managed to teach them. In their different ways, Andrew McCann at Melbourne and Ira Raja at La Trobe also took me to India, and opened up the imperial horizon that I needed to comprehend properly the field I was venturing into.

No one has contributed as directly to the making of this book as my former colleague at Melbourne, Ken Ruthven. I have been fortunate to receive the tireless attention and eagle-eyed intelligence of the best sub-editor I could think of. Through the gruelling last stages of the book, Ken became much more than an editor: he was my ideal reader, teacher and moral supporter at those moments when the project might have stalled.

My greatest debt of gratitude is to my wife and partner, Tessa Jones, and not only for the obvious reasons why writers often thank those closest to them. I have certainly learnt just how much domestic forbearance, support and joint commitment it takes for a sizeable book to be written. But I also owe Tessa thanks for a very special favour. From her own professional base as a psychologist, she introduced me to Jacques Lacan by once encouraging me to attend a seminar given by Russell Grigg. Lasting the best part of a year, it was devoted to reading slowly Lacan's seminar on the *Ethics of Psychoanalysis*. That brought me into contact with the Melbourne-based Australian Centre for Psychoanalysis. After that, Tessa regularly provided me with intriguing suggestions in response to such questions as why, in *Lord Jim*, Brierly commits suicide but Jim doesn't. This book would not have taken the directions it has without those interventions. Its shortcomings – of which I am acutely aware – are entirely my own responsibility.

Acknowledgements

Earlier versions of parts of some of the chapters appeared in the following journals or books: Chapter 4 in *Arena* (70, 1985); Chapters 4 and 9 in *Textual Practice* (volume 3, number 3, 1989); Chapter 4 in *Southern Review* (volume 22, number 2, 1989); Chapter 5 in C. Tiffin and A. Lawson, editors, *De-Scribing Empire* (1994); Introduction and Chapter 6 in *L'Époque Conradienne* (volume 29, 2003); Chapter 6 in *International Journal of the Humanities* (volume 1, 2003); Chapter 7 in *L'Époque Conradienne* (volume 30, 2004); Chapter 8 in *The Conradian* (volume 29, number 2, 2004). I would like to thank the editors and/or publishers for permission to draw on this material.

Unless otherwise indicated, all citations from Joseph Conrad's writings are from the Collected Edition (1946–55) and indicated simply by page numbers. Those from Sigmund Freud are from the Standard Edition (1953–74) and indicated by SE and the appropriate volume and page numbers.

Introduction
The Conradian moment

In 1948 Bertolt Brecht urged us to 'drop our habit of taking the different social structures of past periods, then stripping them of everything that makes them different; so that they all look more or less like our own' (Brecht 1964: 190). Nearly half a century later, however, Slavoj Žižek was to declare that 'there is more truth in the later efficacy of a text, in the series of its subsequent readings, than in its supposedly "original" meaning' (Žižek 1989: 214). This book will address the hermeneutic problem framed by these two statements: from our perspective in the present, what is the best way of relating to writings from the past? More specifically, it will engage with some serious problems of literary interpretation and evaluation that have arisen in postcolonial studies. This seemingly straightforward enterprise, however, quickly encounters difficulties. For a start, 'interpretation' and 'evaluation' have been intensely, even bitterly, contested categories for at least eighty years, which is virtually the whole time during which 'English' has purported to be an academic discipline. And 'postcolonialism' itself is already stricken with a definitional and ethical self-consciousness – about its aims, methods and locations – that could prove permanently disabling. Nor is the task made easier by focusing on Joseph Conrad, who not only wrote in the colonial period (and was thus subject to all of its unresolved contradictions), but is also one of the West's canonical authors. More seriously, one of Africa's most famous postcolonial novelists, Chinua Achebe, has plausibly labelled him a racist. In this respect, the very notion of a 'postcolonial Conrad' sounds paradoxical in the extreme.

In the early stages of what came to be called postcolonialism, Conrad was continuously invoked, either for praise or blame, as central to the enterprise. For a time *Heart of Darkness* was treated almost as an ur-text in the new disciplinary field. Conrad's canonical status was probably enhanced rather than damaged by those controversies, though nowadays he is not cited quite so often in postcolonial criticism. Postcolonial studies, on the other hand, continues to generate voluminous publications. Yet it drifts a little unsteadily, anxious about the authenticity and relevance of its presumed 'politics'.

This book does not pretend to resolve all those problems. Its more modest aim is to survey the shifting contexts in which Conrad has been read for more than a century. By relocating his novels of imperialism in the discursive field of postcolonial studies we can review the terms and conditions of political criticism in our own time. We now know that a different place awaited Conrad after F. R. Leavis had located him in *The Great Tradition* (1948). It seems a good time to ask what kind of life awaits Conrad beyond the cultural politics of the late twentieth century.

The first impression conveyed in everyday uses of the term 'moment' is of something ephemeral, fleeting and elusive – however poignant or potent it might also happen to be. Literary historians use the term to name a significant turning point marked by a grand design and a particular figure who is the agent of change. An early example of this now fashionable usage is Patrick Cruttwell's *The Shakespearean Moment* (1954) whose subtitle (*and its place in the poetry of the 17th century*) captures perfectly this dual function (Cruttwell 1960: 1). Cruttwell's Shakespeare is not merely a great poet but the one who made a difference to the literary and cultural possibilities of the century that followed. A century after Conrad's novels first appeared, it is now possible to assign to their author a place in twentieth-century literature which is structurally similar to the one Cruttwell granted Shakespeare in the seventeenth – leaving aside for the purposes of this exercise the evaluative question of their relative stature.

Cruttwell's mid-century book on Shakespeare sharply reminds us of those institutional and cultural changes that have radically affected the ways in which canonical writers are currently read in universities. Those seismic shifts have so altered the conditions of reading and interpretation that no centenary study of Conrad's colonial novels can avoid the problem posed by different interpretations of his fictions at radically different moments. We can no longer assume, as Cruttwell did, that the novels 'themselves' are the natural focus of study. Both the historicism of Brecht and Žižek's hermeneutic inclusiveness arise from a common recognition that texts change over time, so that we have long since lost the unitary notion of 'the text itself'. Texts too have their moments, and however variegated are the patterns these changes have left, their accumulation gradually comes to constitute an interpretative tradition. The present study therefore will not only re-read Conrad's colonial novels ('themselves') but also map and analyse the interpretative tradition they have generated. By deploying all the meanings and ambiguities in current uses of the term 'moment', it will argue the importance of being critically aware of other and sometimes neglected moments in the reception of Conrad's fiction.

Like other writers whose literary reputations extended significantly beyond their own lives, Conrad has been read so radically differently at different times that it is tempting to talk of different Conrads. The differences may derive as much from the reader's angle of perception as from intrinsic qualities of the novels. One way of dealing with such hermeneutic challenges is to situate Conrad's intriguing texts in other histories of reception and interventionist reading. No other novelist of his time was affected so drastically as Conrad was by those shifting academic, literary, political, cultural and global changes across the twentieth century. His colonial novels represent – at the very moment of high imperialism – the most significant encounter recorded in canonical literature between Europe and Europe's Other.

The elusive object

Rather than attempting a comprehensive and chronological survey of Conrad's reputation in the twentieth century, I intend to examine four distinct moments in the reception of his fiction which are arguably four different aspects of the Conradian moment, more widely understood. The first is the originary moment, the time when the novels were first published. As Žižek reminds us, however, to seek the imagined pure communication between pristine text and perfectly placed first reader is, to say the least, a problematical endeavour. Strictly speaking, such a moment either does not exist or, if it does, cannot be recovered. Nevertheless, the historicizing ambition of most Conrad studies, this one included, is to recover that lost time. The second moment to be considered is Conrad's canonization as one of England's great writers. Championed from the late 1930s by F. R. Leavis, who was to become by mid-century the most influential literary critic in the English-speaking world, Conrad achieved posthumous academic recognition at a time when his reputation in the places where 'serious literature' was valued was beginning to wane. The third moment was an effect of the cultural turmoil of the 'Sixties', which was characterized by wars of National Liberation, revolutionary hope (sexual in the West, political/cultural in the East), and a French-inspired epistemology known as critical theory. These were just some of the 'events' that produced the postcolonial moment of a writer now perceived to be ambivalent about colonialism: was Conrad for or against European imperialism, and in his representation of non-European peoples was he even-handed or in fact deeply racist? Finally there is the shadowy and reflective present moment, marked by attempts like my own to absorb the accumulated discoveries of the interpretative tradition and to negotiate Conrad anew.

If the mutually contradictory remarks of Brecht and Žižek are read dialectically (against one another rather than as cancelling one another out), they present complementary perspectives on a single problem: namely, the status of different meanings assigned at different times to the same literary text.[1] It raises questions of validity and truth while acknowledging that a range of plausible meanings might be assigned to a particular text. Brecht is arguing (perhaps surprisingly) *against* a fashion for modernizing productions of older dramas, on the grounds that they occlude one of the chief pleasures of such works, which derive from the differences produced by their historical distance from us. Žižek, on the other hand, invokes Hans-Georg Gadamer in order to release that plenitude of meaning and truth in a writer's work that is proscribed by a hermeneutic tradition that prioritizes some original and irretrievable truth.

This is clearly not a recent problem. Located in different halves of the twentieth century, both writers raise questions of historicity that did not require the theoretical revolution of the 1960s for their enunciation. They were present, for example, in T. S. Eliot's famous observation in 1919 about the 'historical sense', a faculty which 'involves a perception, not only of the pastness of the past, but of its presence' (T. S. Eliot 1932: 14). Unavoidably, they will dog my own project. If we were to hold strictly to Žižek's dictum we might expect to discover more important truths in postcolonial interpretations of Conrad than his novels could have exhibited in their imagined originary moments – or even (dare we say) than Conrad himself could have dreamed of. Brecht, on the other hand, might then make us wonder whether postcolonial critiques of Conrad are merely a recent but no less disturbing instance of that relentless erasure of the pastness of the past which weakens our historical sense and leads to a dangerous blandness. For readers of Conrad nowadays the difficulty is compounded by the rapid changes during the twentieth century to the discourses in which the dialectics of past and present were debated. These touched the root of Conradian thematics.

In the very last year of the century, a remarkable event occurred that neatly illustrates this difficulty. This was the screening of a veritable postcolonial film of Jane Austen's classic novel, *Mansfield Park* (1814). Theoretically, the simplest problem posed by the movie is the old chestnut about whether or not the film is 'true to' Austen's novel. This question, however, does not assume a rigid notion of truth. Literary critics have long recognized that *Mansfield Park* deals with complex shifts in the class formation of Britain on the eve of its imperial greatness. It even came to address the fact that the Antiguan estates owned by Sir Thomas Bertram and worked by slaves constitute the stubbornly material foundations of all those anxieties about morals and manners that preoccupy the novel.[2] The interpretative tradition of Austen's novel was thus not radically affected by the important shift in the 1960s from historically and politically neutral discussions of moral values in Jane

Austen (the F. R. Leavis tradition) to the historically specific analysis of values advocated by Raymond Williams.[3] For a start, each approach could claim to be justified by the novel 'itself'. *Mansfield Park* certainly alludes to such controversial contemporary problems as the slave trade; on the other hand, the fact that these references are perfunctory and marginal might be seen to validate older and less avowedly political readings, which aim at fidelity to the novel's own perceived balance of forces. From their different points of view, both historicists and idealists could claim to be avoiding the distortions of anachronism.[4]

What is certain is that neither Leavis' nor Williams' discussions of Austen in any way foreshadowed the 1999 film's interpretation of *Mansfield Park*. It is notoriously difficult to compare a novel with the film version of it. But even allowing for the fact that the sexual revolution made visible what Austen merely alluded to – though, importantly, she did so: Austen was no Victorian – the film's two climactic scenes are so shocking as to take interpretation to the edge of plausibility. That is provided we regard the movie as a version of Austen's novel and not something else. The first of these scenes is Fanny Price's discovery of obscene sketches made by her cousin Tom of his own and his father's experiences with black women in Antigua: is this the dark underside to the strict and normative moral code of Mansfield Park? The second is Fanny's personal encounter with the trauma of sex, when she inadvertently opens a bedroom door and gets a back view of her wooer, Henry Crawford, bonking – no other word quite catches the effect – her married cousin, Maria Bertram.[5] My verbal summary of these scenes produces, of course, a further distancing, not only from the novel 'itself' (which records neither of them) but also from interpretations supportive of the view that this film is decidedly *not* 'Jane Austen'. For one thing, talk about 'dark undersides' and 'the trauma of sex' evokes anachronistically the psychoanalytic literature of the twentieth century. Such terms raise the question of what value there can be in positing the existence of a textual unconscious in a novel written nearly one hundred years before Sigmund Freud produced that category of thought. Without invoking Freud's own metaphorical allusions to the 'dark continent' of feminine sexuality, it might still be possible to argue that what the movie of *Mansfield Park* reveals as the dark and obscene underside of Austen's novel is none other than Conrad's 'heart of darkness', whose central metaphor entered twentieth-century culture world-wide. Such a bizarre reading would unexpectedly support Leavis' claim that the great tradition of the English novel stretches from Austen to Conrad.

One critic who did entertain such thoughts about Austen's novel was Edward Said, whose writings instigated the third Conradian moment. Said regards the Atlantic slave trade as directly relevant to Austen. In pursuit of 'a fascinatingly expanded dimension' to *Mansfield Park*, Said takes his historical bearings from the colonial context of Austen's England, and his cultural critique from what came to be known as postcolonialism (Said 1993: 100). He makes explicit the political implications of such re-readings: 'Perhaps then Austen, and pre-imperialist novels generally, will appear to be more implicated in the rationale for imperialistic expansion than at first sight they have been' (ibid.). Those 'implications' would eventually dominate the third phase of Conrad's twentieth-century journey, and determine his place in the postcolonial world.

Such matters create major problems for literary historians at the turn of the millennium. That my chosen author is not Austen but Conrad – the yoking of whose name to imperialist expansion is no longer even remotely controversial – does not settle the hermeneutic problem raised by Žižek. Literary scholars have long been divided on the status of the 'text itself'. In 1864 Matthew Arnold opened his famous essay on 'The Function of Criticism at the Present Time' by naming as the most basic aim of criticism and of most other knowledge 'to see the object as in itself it really is' (Arnold 1964: 9). The extreme essentialism of this stance may now seem breathtaking. Yet Arnold's belief that the proper object of critical contemplation is the literary text in its integrity still determines most empirical studies of Conrad's work and, more negatively, encourages the growling conservative impatience with newfangledness of every kind.[6]

The American Marxist Fredric Jameson is a literary theorist and historian whose writings exhibit an extraordinary openness to new discourses, whether they are political, aesthetic, or academic. Conveniently for my purposes, Jameson has also written one of the most impressive essays on Conrad. He argues that the question of literary history and interpretation involves choosing between two options. 'As the traditional dialectic teaches us', he writes,

> the historicizing operation can follow two distinct paths, which only ultimately meet in the same place: the path of the object and the path of the subject, the historical origins of the things themselves and that more tangible historicity of the concepts and categories by which we attempt to understand those things.
>
> (Jameson 1981: 9)

Here the hermeneutic difficulty is not so much resolved as put to one side by Jameson's tactic. Because *The Political Unconscious* chooses the 'path of the subject', it seeks to understand Conrad by working its way through those dense filters of interpretative practices and ideological discourses in whose swirls the novels 'themselves' are endlessly caught. Yet for all his deftness in admitting that his selection of categories and materials is somewhat arbitrary, Jameson neatly sidesteps the problem of the ontological status of Conrad's novels as objects for analysis.

For Žižek, the irresolvable problem created by Jameson's distinction highlights the need for a radical realignment of those objects that are designated literary works. In terms of the Lacanian orientation Žižek writes from, the adjustment he proposes corresponds with the shift from an Enlightenment conception of the object of knowledge to the new 'subject-object' of psychoanalysis. He counters the supposedly 'naïve reading' which claims 'immediate access to the true meaning' of a text by arguing that such a moment does not exist (Žižek 1989: 213–15). The fact is that, right from the start, 'a number of mutually exclusive readings claiming access to the true meaning' always co-exist. He does not simply deny the existence of an original true meaning; he goes on to argue that the interpretative tradition itself offers a way through the impasse of mutually exclusive possibilities. His formulation is worth quoting in full:

> [T]his problem of the 'true', 'original' meaning of Antigone – that is, the status of *Antigone*-'in-itself', independent of the string of its historical efficacy – is ultimately a pseudo-problem: to resume the fundamental principle of Gadamer's hermeneutics, there is more truth in the later efficacy of a text, in the series of its subsequent readings, than in its supposedly 'original' meaning.
>
> (ibid.: 214)

A happy inconsistency about Jameson complicates the debate that I have represented somewhat misleadingly as a matter of opposite sides. For one of the best examples of Žižek's proposition is none other than Jameson's own comprehensive 'metacommentary' on *Lord Jim* in *The Political Unconscious*. By any measure, Conrad's text is here the primary object of analysis, although not as something that lies outside history. He discusses *Lord Jim* in terms of categories that were contemporaneous with the moment of the novel's composition, such as Max Weber's analysis of reification. But his interpretative repertoire also includes other discourses unavailable to Conrad's first readers, such as the narratological theories of A. J. Greimas (Greimas 1987). Jameson does not exactly aim to see the object (Conrad's novel) 'as in itself it really is'; nor does he ignore the historicity of Conrad's text in order to make it the occasion of a freewheeling meditation on the nature of things. Jameson's rigorous method requires him to historicize not only the text but also the interpretative codes and methodologies that inform its reading. Those codes themselves thereby become objects for critique, resulting in an ever more inclusive practice of cultural hermeneutics. My construction of Conrad has been deeply influenced by the methodology of Jameson's project in *The Political Unconscious*.

Žižek's restatement of Gadamer's proposition concerning the nature of textual interpretation also incorporates a structure of analysis derived from the French Freudian, Jacques Lacan. From a Lacanian perspective, that elusive and always-out-of-reach moment of pristine meaning which still entices literary scholars is uncannily like the lost object of desire, which is driven into the unconscious when the Oedipal conflict is resolved. That resolution (which is also a repression) is in Freud's account our moment of access into language, meaning and culture. As Žižek argues, the idea of a pre-existent and pristine meaning that escapes the vicissitudes of interpretation, like that other object of desire, lingers only as a lost illusion.[7]

One way of testing this theory is to examine Conrad's record of his own early experience of authorship with the Lacanian account in mind. A significant anecdote in this respect is recorded in Conrad's autobiographical *A Personal Record* (1912) touching these very problematics (15–18). It is the story of his first reader, who appears to be that impossibly naïve (yet percipient) reader Žižek thinks does not exist. Conrad relates how, for a number of years, he had carted the manuscript of his first novel, *Almayer's Folly*, around with him, even on the famous Congo journey that provided the material for *Heart of Darkness*. But not until he voyages to Australia as Captain of the *Torrens* does he find among the passengers his first reader of the novel: a somewhat spectral 'young Cambridge man' to whom Conrad had nervously shown his manuscript. The would-be writer of fiction had to wait several days for the judgement that would confirm or deny his literary ambition. Eventually the manuscript is returned:

> He tendered it to me with a steady look but without a word. I took it in silence. He sat down on the couch and still said nothing. I opened and shut a drawer under my desk, on which a filled-up log-slate lay wide open in its wooden frame waiting to be copied into the sort of book I was accustomed to write with care, the ship's log-book. I turned my back squarely on the desk. And even then Jacques never offered a word. "Well, what do you say?" I asked at last. "Is it worth finishing?" This question expressed exactly the whole of my thoughts.
>
> "Distinctly," he answered in his sedate veiled voice, and then coughed a little.
>
> "Were you interested?" I inquired further, almost in a whisper.
>
> "Very much!"
>
> (16–17)

That's all we are given. Like the Freudian unconscious, or 'falling in love', this pristine first reading remains opaque. Conrad's well-chosen reader articulates nothing more than encouragement, and even that is relatively unreadable because the respondent's words appear strangely toneless. Nevertheless, Conrad's invocation of Novalis in the same context suggests that this evanescent moment powerfully reinforced his drive to become a writer: ' " It is certain my conviction gains infinitely the moment another soul will believe in it" '(15).

We do not know whether Conrad actually recalled the quotation from Novalis on receiving the Cambridge man's approval, or added it to his reconstruction of the episode in 1912. Either way, he certainly used it as the epigraph for *Lord Jim*. That novel takes the form of a narrative meditation on Marlow's refusal to allow objective evidence to shake his belief in Jim. Like Conrad's own ambition, Jim's self-belief involves both a fiction and a believer in it. It parallels the interpretative act of reading, which brings the text into the world in a reciprocal and indissoluble relationship. That relationship necessitates the awkward procedure of attempting to follow two paths at once: the path of the object and that of the subject. The fact that such an approach is hopelessly unscientific does not make the enterprise either quixotic or arbitrary. Instead, it takes place in the realm of the provisional and the persuasive, where literature, theory and politics are at home.

The theme of a 'secret sharer' (like the Cambridge man) recurs throughout Conrad's writing, although not usually in connection with writing itself. Conrad's account of how a virtually anonymous first reader confirmed his desire to become a writer partially enacts Lacan's famous paradox, that 'Man's desire is the desire of the Other' (Lacan 1977: 235). Conrad represents himself in this exchange as a diffident lover who has long preserved the secret of his love. On the point of declaring it, however, he clings anxiously to the defence-mechanism that his foray into fiction is not nearly as important as the 'serious' matter of the ship's log-book – 'the sort of book', he gruffly adds, 'I was accustomed to write with care'. The tension in this simple narrative reveals a libidinal charge, which belies that posture and reconfigures it significantly as a moment of painful self-exposure. This meaning is not stated in the words, but implied in the pauses of the telling. Such are the limitations of writing that we cannot even guess what thoughts – if any – lay behind that momentous act of reading and critical judgement.

Both Freud and Lacan recognized that their insights into the nature and existence of the unconscious had been anticipated by the poets, if only as intimations. That is one reason why it is not necessarily inappropriate to interpret older texts with the benefit of modes of knowledge developed subsequently. In this respect, psychoanalysis might illuminate the poetry of fiction, and vice versa, and its categories closely match the poetry of the text. This is not to privilege psychoanalysis as an interpretative practice: the same can be said for other discourses of knowledge, such as Marxism, feminism, or the broadly encompassing poststructuralism. This strengthens Žižek's claim that textual meaning is discoverable through the interpretative tradition. It also involves acknowledging that the categories of psychoanalysis, Marxism and feminism have entered the language of late-twentieth-century critical thought as well as circulating in the wider culture. As such, they need to be constantly renegotiated, since the meanings they carry, like the politics they provoke, will remain contestable. The hermeneutic process knows no closure.

In this study of Conrad's novels of imperialism and their twentieth-century journeys I attempt to maintain a dual perspective by engaging both the novels themselves and the interpretative traditions they have inspired. Theoretical advances in the twentieth century changed critical fashion and produced newer if not better Conrads. His novels of imperialism continue to exert a transferential power over their analysts and historians. My task is to describe how Conrad, a Polish-born witness of the effects of British and European imperialism around the turn of the twentieth century, and a writer whose perspective was broadly Eurocentric, proved to be the one whose novels of empire would continue to be read by changing their significance. To keep the project manageable, and to prevent this 'dual perspective' from collapsing into eclecticism, the book is arranged in two parts. The first is a meditation on the problematic of Conradian textuality, which is exposed at various stages in the interpretative tradition. The second presents readings of Conrad's principal novels of imperialism, and does so by situating them among some of the books and ideas that might foster new traditions of post-imperial fiction. The major advantage afforded by this dually retrospective gaze is the possibility of surveying a moment of presence in the past not just with a sense of its continuing presentness but with a knowledge of its future which is only available to hindsight.

Two of the most significant books published at the very turning point of the twentieth century were Conrad's *Heart of Darkness* and Freud's *The Interpretation of Dreams*. We are now in a position to consider that moment in relation to what happened subsequently – not just events, but the discourses that influence and are influenced by them. Some of these have fed into our collective consciousness, and affected the ways in which we read and think the world. They include the production of psychoanalytic theories and practices; the ascendancy and decline of Marxism both as a politics and a discourse of knowledge; the transition from literary realism to modernism and postmodernism; the protracted struggles which preceded the eclipse of the old European empires, and the rise of new nation states as former 'colonies' became the 'Third World'; the invention of the volatile and increasingly hybrid academic discipline known as 'English', together with the desire (which eventually waned) for a university-guaranteed canon of great writers; the changing balance of power and focus of desire in that rich amalgam of discourses loosely described as 'orientalism'; the 'linguistic turn' or 'theoretical revolution' in the humanities; and, perhaps the most far-reaching of all, revolutionary changes to the place of women in societies.

This list of cultural developments is not exhaustive, and some feature more than others in twentieth-century criticism of Conrad. Until recently, for example, feminism had impacted much less on Conrad studies than on other fields of academic inquiry. That absence prompts the discussion of gender in Conrad which brings this book to its incomplete conclusion. The purpose of this list is to indicate some of the recurring themes in the book, which are grouped into two major categories. One is orientalism, understood broadly to include all cultural and epistemological transactions between Europe and its others and between modernity and non-modernity, as well as mismatches between the old colonial world order and its twentieth-century consequences. The other is imperialism, whose older meanings are extended to include those material and cultural inequalities and controls in our contemporary world which derive from the inherited politics of European domination. I treat these two categories as interdependent, and examine them by way of the novels in which they are incorporated rather than the real histories to which they supposedly allude. In emphasizing the nexus with modernity in the story of Europe (and by extension the United States) I unashamedly revive an unfashionable master narrative, announcements of whose demise continue to seem premature. A world imperial system is just appearing on Conrad's horizon. That has issued in the late-twentieth-century vision of a new world order based on inexorable processes of globalization, which tend to erase or otherwise incorporate all difference. In this context, the most rigorous judgements are likely to be attentively indeterminate. Conrad remains one of the best writers to work with on questions of indeterminacy.

The first Conradian moment

'Moment' is a key term for my retrospective appraisal of Conrad because its contradictory connotations ('period', 'event', 'ephemerality', 'impact') make it usefully open-ended. 'Moment' appeals to flexible chronologies and significant happenings. While evoking a sense of ripeness and rightness it also insists on the conjuncture of historical possibility and potent intervention. Its hint of inevitability dimly recalls the ancient concept of Necessity – another term which, for all its religious gravitas, was no less problematic.

What is the justification for labelling the appearance of Conrad's novels 'the Conradian moment'? When Conrad gave up his seaman's career and became a novelist, he 'colonized' a new territory for English fiction by capitalizing on his few months' direct experience of Southeast Asia. In those days, literary and imperialistic achievements seem to have been strangely enmeshed. An early notice of *Almayer's Folly* (1895), for example, announced that Conrad had 'annexed the island of Borneo', while one reviewer dubbed Conrad 'the Kipling of the Malay Archipelago'. Such labels, however, soon needed adjusting. The publication of *The Nigger of the 'Narcissus'* (1897), with its shift of locale from the jungles of Borneo to ship-board life, produced the unexciting cliché of Conrad as 'Prose Laureate of the Merchant Service' (Sherry 1973: 47, 61). The consistent strand in these various notices is that Conrad's novels first attracted attention on account of the exotic nature of their content.

The life span of this new and serious novelist of the far-flung places of empire – as opposed to a writer of mere adventure stories for boys – coincided with a crisis in British imperialism. Józef Teodor Konrad Korzeniowski was born in 1857, the year in which the so-called 'mutiny' of the Indian army took place.[8] This event was an early sign that the greatest empire the world had ever seen might not be invincible after all. He died in 1924, the year that saw the publication of E. M. Forster's classic colonial novel, *A Passage to India*. From the perspective of the longer view of history we now have, Forster's story of the Raj can be read as foreshadowing the imperial crises to come, announcing the beginning of the end of British imperialism. The coincidence of Conrad's life with the crisis of empire is the first justification for calling this epoch 'the Conradian moment'. It encapsulates the time when the flood-mark of European imperialism was matched by the writing career of imperialism's greatest 'poet', the novelist Conrad.

The distinctively Conradian perspective on empire was revealed around the turn of the new century with the publication of two powerful complementary narratives, *Heart of Darkness* and *Lord Jim*. This makes 1900 (rather than 1890, the year following Conrad's transforming Congo voyage when he began his first novel) the appropriate beginning date for the period on which we are focusing. The moment might be said to end with the Great War of 1914–18. Those two dates situate Conrad's major writings in the middle of what historians routinely call either 'the age of imperialism' or 'the new imperialism'. A world-changing cataclysm was thus bound up indirectly with the production and destiny of the Conradian *oeuvre*. How was it constructed at the time, and how does it come to us today? Conrad's great classics of a dying colonialism were published throughout this period: *Heart of Darkness* (1899), *Lord Jim* (1900), *Nostromo* (1904) and *Victory* (1915). Collectively representing

Conrad's sustained meditation on European imperialism, they are his major literary achievement and helped to shape the ways in which the twentieth century came to understand and evaluate imperialism.

These novels, however, cannot be said to celebrate the achievements of imperialism. A more appropriate candidate than Conrad for the title 'laureate' is his older contemporary, Rudyard Kipling, most of whose tales of empire were more comfortable with the actualities of imperialism than were those of the awkward foreigner Conrad. But it was the work of the ironical foreigner which proved to be not only the more durable but also more iterable, throughout the twentieth century.[9] Conrad's novels have been able to assume new meanings in different times and places because of their problematical relationship to imperialism. One of their important insights was that the highest point of Europe's imperial success might also be its lowest in terms of moral authority. In retrospect, that contradiction appears to foreshadow the demise of the European empires. In their angular relationship to empire, these novels mull over cracks in the edifice of imperial ideology instead of celebrating its magnificence. Others gradually found their way through those cracks, individually at first, and eventually in battalions. They included producers of high literature and middlebrow fiction, Hollywood makers of movies and a welter of travel writers, latter-day Western adventurers and Third-World champions of Liberation, postcolonial intellectuals and some of the most renowned writers of the twentieth century. All invoked Conrad as their guide.[10]

More traditional literary historians have seen these novels as occupying a transitional space in English writing, because they embody a breakdown of faith in both nineteenth-century literary realism and its humanist underpinnings. Realism staked its claim to represent 'the real' with a social contract that came under increasing threat in the second half of the nineteenth century.[11] A significant stage in the breakdown of that contract was what Jameson has called 'the peculiar heterogeneity of the moment of Conrad', which opened the way to literary modernism (Jameson 1981: 280). Literary and cultural histories, of course, also have their moments. Discrete and semi-autonomous, they generate in turn their own significant movements.

Other events in the year of Conrad's birth help us to situate this complex writer. The publication in 1857 of Gustave Flaubert's *Madame Bovary* and the legal challenge it provoked were a watershed moment not only in the history of realist representation but also in relations between serious writers and their public. Conrad was an exact contemporary of Freud (born just one year earlier), which reminds us that the novel's transitions from realism to modernism involved revolutionary turns in both narrative method and authorial point of view, as well as in the very diction used to figure human subjectivity (the 'character-effect'). We broaden our perspective on the Conradian moment by including in it not just the climax of European imperialism but the revolutionary names of Flaubert and Freud. Although a sense of cultural crisis at that time was ubiquitous, it was accompanied paradoxically by extraordinary intellectual and artistic productivity throughout Europe, which occupied those gaps that had appeared in the language of cultural confidence, the grounds of scientific knowledge, and the moral basis of imperial domination. Responsive to the excitement as well as the threat of this crisis, Conrad's novels articulated the underlying conditions of its indeterminacy.[12]

The politics of literature

The strange presence of the *émigré* Conrad in the literary milieu of England was sharply registered by his contemporaries. Its far-reaching effects would continue to be discovered throughout a century of world-historical changes. These included massive alterations to the readership of Conrad's fictions. Most significantly, by the end of the century the descendants of those colonized 'natives' on the periphery of Conrad's narratives came to constitute a new class of postcolonial intellectuals and writers.

Before considering these developments, we need to recall those cultural processes that produced a Conrad almost totally devoid of political significance, a writer whose novels of imperialism were felt to be best appreciated without reference to their politics, a process that Conrad himself did not entirely resist. In England, a minor side-effect of the Great War was to encourage a particular kind of cultural censorship and appropriation. The 'Englishing' of Konrad Korzeniowski was achieved partly by eradicating political considerations from analyses of his work. As a prominent adopted son of England, and a writer whose own son was fighting at the front, the ageing Conrad was closely involved in the conflict. He often presented himself in public roles that simplified his own profound understanding from first-hand experience of the dislocations produced by European imperialism. Not unlike one of his spiritual heirs, George Orwell, who repressed his socialist tendencies at the outbreak of the Second World War and 'opted for England',[13] Conrad publicly aligned himself with the British war effort. By doing so he became a willing conscript in the reductive process that prepared his writing for its post-war moment of consumption.

Borys Conrad's military service at the front led his father to dedicate his one important wartime novel, *The Shadow-Line* (1915), to human solidarity:

To
Borys and all others
who like himself have crossed in early youth the shadow-line
of their generation
With Love.

But the disruptions of war affected Conrad in ways not revealed by this moving dedication. By ushering in the final and least productive phase of his writing life, they enabled the Polish-born writer to identify himself more closely than had hitherto been possible with the trappings of Englishness. But while publicly lending his presence and his pen to the war effort, privately Conrad remained preoccupied with the implications of the war for the 'Polish question'.

Also serving at the front was another young man who would shape Conrad's mid-century reputation, after achieving academic fame and notoriety as Dr F. R. Leavis of Downing College, Cambridge. Through his journal *Scrutiny*, Leavis decisively influenced the formation of the new academic discipline of literary studies known simply as 'English'.[14] Traces of wartime nationalism are discernible in its rapid growth after the war. In Leavis' version of English, individual and social values were to be contemplated in a discourse emptied of political considerations. The *Scrutiny* group claimed to be concerned with the 'essentially human'. Like the nineteenth-century liberal humanism of John Stuart Mill, however, it maintained a restrictive notion of humanity. In-groupish and elitist, it refused interrogation in terms other than its own. To put the matter bluntly: Leavis constructed a 'great tradition' of the English novel that contained a George Eliot without her feminism, a Henry James who was not an aesthete, a Conrad indifferent to the politics of imperialism, and a D. H. Lawrence without the sex. European (especially French and German) connections were minimized. Meanwhile, the dispersed and hybrid cultures generated in the wider world by centuries of British imperialism remained unspeakable.[15]

The enlistment of Conrad as a foundation member of the Great Tradition of the English Novel involved two major adjustments to the Conrad everyone thought they knew. First, the foreigner had to be made into a true-blue Englishman. Leavis admitted outsiders such as James and Conrad into his great tradition by stressing the essential 'Englishness' of what was of value in their writings. The tradition Leavis invoked and celebrated was almost as organic as a natural phenomenon: *Wuthering Heights*, for example, is described as 'kind of sport', in the horticultural sense of an almost unnatural mutation (F. R. Leavis 1948: 27). Clearly, before Conrad could be identified as belonging to the parent stock, a considerable amount of ideological work had to be done on all that was foreign in him. But a further adjustment was required. In order to embed Conrad in a lineage that invoked the broadly humanist values of the English liberal tradition, the 'merely' political had to be evacuated from appraisals of his novels.

Although Leavisian criticism consolidated its influence in Cambridge and beyond during the 1930s, its effectiveness in redrawing the map of English literature was felt chiefly in another period of national reconstruction after the Second World War. It is more than coincidental that tensions heightened in the 1920s and 1930s over the question of empire, and especially over British India. The academy's desire to keep its pedagogy free of politics was encouraged by a national need to dampen enthusiasm for epochal changes taking place elsewhere in the world.[16] Constitutive in this context were the famous battles in the 1930s between Leavisism and British Marxism.[17] At that time, Leavisites managed to withstand challenges to their fundamentally humanist assumptions. But changing conditions in the post-war period prompted a new interest in the political dimensions of Conrad's fictions. This academic reorientation was itself powered by the renewed challenges to empire, which culminated in the great movements of national liberation.

Conrad studies became politicized and internationalized in the 1960s just as imperialism was given new currency as a term for describing exploitative capitalism. In this time of anti-colonial struggles, intellectuals from the former colonies of Europe insisted on being heard. The first political readings of Conrad by academics came from the United States, not England.[18] Critiques from Third-World writers followed, some of them admiring, others hostile. The most famous was a scandalous intervention by the Nigerian novelist, Chinua Achebe, who on one memorable occasion called Conrad a racist.[19]

While voices from the former colonies were transforming the academy by generating new theories and setting fresh agendas, both literary and cultural studies began moving beyond the old imperialist geometry of centre and margins. These changes, which have taken Conrad studies in new directions, go under the collective name of postcolonialism. Since its history includes some of the most nightmarish experiences in the twentieth-century world, its understanding of what matters cannot be confined within the great traditions of England. Postcolonialism is an academic development that is not restricted to the academy. Its complex and ever-changing forms of cross-cultural critique describe the socio-political experiences of peoples all around the world. Its achievements already include restoring the manifold density of Conrad's own times and revising their history.[20]

The most powerful intervention in Conrad criticism since its Leavisite moment has been Fredric Jameson's. His magisterial reading of *Lord Jim* in *The Political Unconscious* (1981) synthesizes the major developments in literary studies that followed the eclipse of both Leavisian humanism (in Britain and British Commonwealth countries) and New Criticism in the United States. The Conrad so patiently constructed in *The Political Unconscious* is culturally and historically cosmopolitan. As a European consciousness at the turn of the century, Jameson's Conrad contemplates the ambiguities of that moment of high imperialism, which encompasses both the zenith of colonial expansion and the nadir of moral confidence. His fiction combines the adventurer's desire to conquer unknown parts of the earth with real-life experience of its pre-capitalist zones. Intellectually, Jameson's Conrad is highly credentialled, and informed by the literary traditions of continental Europe as well as those of Britain. He is the spiritual *confrère* not only of Friedrich Nietzsche, the philosopher-poet of the representative *fin-de-siècle* category of *ressentiment*, but also of Max Weber, the diagnostician of how *ressentiment* was structured by both economic rationalization and social reification. However unexpected, such affiliations are more or less contemporaneous. But Jameson also finds in Conrad intimations of Sartrean existentialism and equally (*avant la lettre*) a full-blown postmodernist practice of *écriture*. This Conrad is not only a prescient commentator on world-historical convulsions in his own time – such as the crises of imperialism and the Great War – but also prophesies that moment of colonial *revanche* marked by the wars of national liberation. He thus appears to substantiate the global claims in Henry James' praise of Conrad in a letter of 1906 as 'the artist of the whole matter' (James 1987: 368).

Most of Conrad's novels about ship-board life focus on relationships among the crew, and not on what he often sees as the 'sordid' enterprise of colonial trade that was the *raison d'être* of such voyages. In these novels, both imperial commerce and the non-European life of those marginal communities whose labour and commodities fed it figure only as mute backgrounds. Questions about the politics and ethics of such a hierarchy were regarded as 'sordid' in Leavisian readings of Conrad, if only because they threatened his reputation as a writer whose values are universal because they transcend mere politics. Those questions were first asked from the imperial margins. They slowly entered mainstream academic criticism in the West through the powerful influence of politicizing critics such as Raymond Williams, Terry Eagleton, Edward Said and Fredric Jameson. They now dominate contemporary readings of Conrad, and have helped to constitute a new ethics – that incorporates difference – in literary studies.

A note on methodology

My chief object in this book is to reconsider Conrad's meditations on European imperialism in a handful of remarkable novels set in non-

European parts of the world, and to do so with reference to significant moments in the discussion they have provided during the past hundred years. That complex body of commentary constitutes the genealogy of what amounts to an interpretative tradition. This centenary study is not constrained by an exclusive notion of the political. It may reasonably be located, however, among other post-1989 attempts to revise Marxist traditions of cultural analysis in the light of 'world-historical' collapses of regimes around that date. Even within such limits, it does not aspire to be comprehensive, but focuses instead on certain local specificities. While drawing mainly on the interpretative tradition generated by Conrad's novels, it also includes the insights of writers who are outside 'Conrad studies' but have impacted nevertheless on the ways in which we now think about his work. I situate Conrad partly (as remains fitting) in Leavis' Great Tradition and partly among recent writers and other artistic creators who come from very different traditions but nevertheless seem to continue the Conradian legacy. Finally, my transatlantic academic style accommodates some of the slogans of globalization and may occasionally expose antipodean interests and emphases.[21]

Two of the most prominent non-Marxists to appear in these pages are Jacques Lacan and Michel Foucault – neither of whom, as far as I know, has ever mentioned Conrad's name. But my approach is no more a Lacanian or a Foucaultian than a neo-Marxist analysis of literature and imperialism. Nor do I attempt to amalgamate all three into a new post-Marxist methodology. I simply draw extensively on their distinctive and influential bodies of knowledge as well as their interpretative methods, which deepen the possibilities for political critique.

No overview of discursive changes in the twentieth century can avoid psychoanalysis, although its inclusion raises difficult problems of choice. This is because the many post-Freudian 'schools' focus on different things, and consequently have varying degrees of relevance for practices of reading. The most illuminating for my purposes is the 're-reading of Freud' of the French psychoanalyst, Jacques Lacan, whose psychoanalytic categories I draw on at different points of the discussion. Given the proliferation of mutually exclusive Lacanian schools, even this attempt to specify the field is questionable – although it is not just arbitrary. Apart from its contagious influence in the intellectual ferment of Paris since the 1960s, Lacan's work inspired original insights into postcolonial subjectivity. Attentive to these interventions, I use Lacan's shifting categories in an open-ended way to elucidate meanings not only in Conrad's novels but also (and reciprocally) in Lacan's own categorical complexities. But I do not engage with this controversial figure in order to produce what in literary studies are called 'Lacanian readings'. My justification for using Lacan in this piecemeal way (instead of treating his work as a totalizing system) is that he himself stubbornly resisted the appropriation and commodification of his project into a coherent set of 'teachings':

> If I were not to have taught you anything more than an implacable method for the analysis of signifiers, then it would not have been in vain . . . If it is true that what I teach represents a body of thought, I will not leave behind me any of those handles which will enable you to append a suffix in the form of an "-ism".
>
> (Lacan 1992: 251)

Like literary studies in general, this book on Conrad has been influenced by Foucault's method rather than the content of his work. In juxtaposing Conrad's creative moment at the turn of the twentieth century with the post-1968 revolution in the human sciences, and viewing both from the perspective of the present, I am both encouraged by Foucault's liberation of the modes of producing history and disciplined by his relentless and inconclusive interrogation of the problems encountered in such projects. Although the kind of mapping I attempt bears some resemblance to Foucault's archaeologies or genealogies, and accepts his warnings against foreclosure, it is un-Foucaultian in a number of ways. My field is nowhere near as inclusive as his 'archive', and my interpretative style is nearer to Anglophone traditions of close textual reading than to Foucaultian analysis. My choices often rest on stated or implied judgements of literary value, in which Foucault showed little interest. He wanted to account for phenomena without using traditional (Marxist) narratives of history and to discover methods of reading texts politically that did not rely on a priori assumptions (in the case of Conrad, these might include assumptions about the inequities of European imperialism and its place in history). Above all, Foucault sought to understand the subtle complicities between systems of knowledge and the circulation of power.

* * *

The principal concern of this study is to answer the question of how – given the complexity of the issues it examines – we may read and understand Conrad nowadays. If, as is possible, it appears to present a particular image of Conrad, as a man or a writer, that will be merely a secondary effect in a book which attempts neither portraiture nor final definition. As is perhaps fitting. For while some elusive lost object we know as 'Conrad' is no doubt 'out there', its existence is felt here only as the motivating force and impossible goal which drive my analysis. No less for us now than for Conrad's contemporaries, the figure who emerges from time to time as an effect of his writings remains unfathomable. That surely befits a writer who found language a frustratingly inadequate means of penetrating the unknowableness of a Kurtz, a Jim, or a Heyst.

Part I
Locations

1 Conrad in the history of ideas

In 1906, Henry James wrote to Conrad: 'No-one has *known* – for intellectual use – the things you know . . . [Y]ou have, as the artist of the whole matter, an authority that no-one has approached' (James 1987: 368).[1] What kind of knowledge did James think Conrad had? Was it intuitive knowledge, for example, like D. H. Lawrence's 'blood consciousness', or an intellectual version of 'carnal knowledge', if that is imaginable? James' Sibylline utterance seems to refer to the rich material for fiction that Conrad's exotic experiences gave him. And while it may not represent the Master's final appraisal of Conrad's *oeuvre*, its terms are both striking and excessive: Conrad earns the accolade of being 'the artist of the whole matter' on account of his *knowledge*.

To put the question more fancifully: in James' respect for Conrad's work cannot echoes be heard of older and fatal desires for forbidden knowledge such as the Faustian quest or the impulse which drove the artisan Daedalus to delve (like the modern explorer or anthropologist) into unknown places? Perhaps it conjures up the mythical seer Teiresias, who – changed by the gods into a woman and then back again into a man – was well placed to answer one of the unanswerable human conundrums: does the man or the woman have the greater pleasure in heterosexual intercourse?[2] Those old narratives recall elements of futility and human limitation more suggestive of tragedy than militant enlightenment. Yet that need not diminish their relevance to Conrad. The modern counterpart of such ancient quests to know the Other took the form of scientific anthropology, whose triumph elided their tragic overtones. I do not intend to link Conrad directly with the famous ethnographers of the following generation, since that has been done already.[3] Instead, I will focus on the aura he presented to many of his contemporaries, which is best evoked by describing him as a man who (in the Nietzschean or Dostoyevskyan phrase) had *crossed over*.

The extraordinary growth and spread of the capitalist world order emanated from (and is still centred in) what has been variously called Europe, the West, the Free World, or more recently the North.

Consequently, the most prominent form of that age-old desire in this period has been the quest to know Europe's Other. While sharing that desire, Conrad maintained an ironical relationship towards it. He recognized, for example, that the 'opening-up' of the whole world through exploration and conquest would destroy the conditions that preserved the Other as exotic. As Marlow puts it in *Heart of Darkness*, 'the glamour's off' (52). Conrad's deepest knowledge derives not so much from authentic life experiences as from despair at the impossibility of achieving them. This edge of despair aligns him with the great tragedians, who also have complicated relationships to formal knowledge.

Crises of knowledge, doubts about authority

It may seem bizarre to make 'knowledge' a key term for approaching Conrad's work and even more so to locate him within a history of ideas. From a philosophical perspective, his fictions and other writings contain little original thought and his direct contributions to institutionally endorsed knowledge are negligible. The appearance of Conrad's novels, however, coincided with an epistemological crisis as well as a crisis of empire. It is therefore fruitful to ask whether the two are linked.

Academic developments that followed the discursive turmoil of the 1960s stimulate such an inquiry. That intellectual ferment partly resulted from new crises in both imperialism and the forms of knowledge. In examining the cultural role played by Conrad's novels of imperialism during these two moments of discursive crisis, I will argue that the period between them constitutes a significant turning point in Europe's self-understanding. In each case, a re-adjustment of the relations between Europe and non-Europe produced changes whose effects have lasted to the present time. It is now acknowledged that the scientific revolution of the Enlightenment conjoined with colonial expansion to produce the global agenda of modernity. By the end of the twentieth century, however, new constituencies – defined in terms of race, gender and cultural diversity – had completely discredited European humanism's claims to universality. Modernity now came to include possibilities never countenanced in its Western version.

The first problem encountered by an epistemological approach to Conrad is this: what kind of meanings do his novels contain? Hans-Georg Gadamer succinctly formulates the relationship between a work of art and the constituents of knowledge:

> [W]hen we say that the work of art *says* something to us and that it thus belongs to the matrix of things we have to understand, our

assertion is not a metaphor, but has a valid and demonstrable meaning. Thus the work of art is an object of hermeneutics.

(Gadamer 1976: 98)

By Conrad's time, French and late-Victorian aestheticism had distanced art from both knowledge and politics. By the end of the twentieth century, that tendency had been reversed. Scholars in search of historical truth routinely treated works of fiction, paintings and music as part of their documentary archive. Significant changes of perspective and methodology resulted from the recognition that if different kinds of texts are to yield their meanings they must be handled differently.

Another and more difficult problem arises when we attempt to situate Conrad within a discursive field. In *The Archaeology of Knowledge* (1972) Michel Foucault developed a lexicon for dealing reasonably with such a project. It was controversial partly because it engages with a cluster of received categories ('science', 'knowledge', 'truth', 'meaning' and 'interpretation') whose semantics and value were hotly contested throughout the twentieth century.[4] In order to specify the nature of Conradian knowledge and situate it discursively, I will draw on a range of disciplines with overlapping concerns, especially epistemology, politics and history. The resultant spread of texts corresponds roughly with Foucault's notion of the 'archaeological field' of an ideological formation.

I start with the hypothesis that Conrad's turn-of-the-century fictions were written in a time of epistemological crisis. As older discourses came under threat, and newer ones were yet to be established, accredited knowledge experienced a moment of hiatus. In periods such as this, both confidence in the grounds of truth and agreement about what constitutes knowledge appear to lapse. Because the notion of an epistemic gap or crisis is usually attributed to Foucault, it is important to remember his own provisional and nuanced descriptions not only of these matters but also of the forces which might act on a particular field:

> My problem was . . . to pose the question, "How is it that at certain moments and in certain orders of knowledge, there are these sudden take-offs, these hastenings of evolution, these transformations which fail to correspond to the calm, continuist image that is normally accredited?" But the important thing here is not that such changes can be rapid and extensive . . . [I]t is that this extent and rapidity are only the sign of something else: a modification in the rules of formation of statements which are accepted as scientifically true . . . It is a question of what *governs* statements, and the way in which they *govern* each other so as to constitute a set of propositions which are scientifically acceptable . . . In short, there is a problem of the regime, the politics of the scientific statement . . . of what effects of power

circulate among scientific statements, what constitutes, as it were, their internal regime of power, and how and why at certain times and at certain moments that regime undergoes a global modification.

(Foucault 1984: 54–5)

To achieve insight into the networks within which knowledge circulates, Foucault first broadens the range of archival texts for analysis. He thus avoids reiterating canonical narratives. He further seeks to disturb those teleological 'grand narratives' of history that both depend upon and sustain a narrow selection from records of what happened. In order to reveal the nexus between knowledge and power, he subjects his cluttered 'archaeological' field to an analytical process that interprets history in terms of discontinuities as well as received (Marxist) narratives. I draw on these Foucaultian strategies to re-evaluate Conrad's place in literary and cultural history. If the 'new imperialism' of the late nineteenth century coincides with intellectual developments that consolidate the human sciences, it is important to determine the impact on Conrad of both the politics of imperialism and the formation of new kinds of knowledge.

In attempting to situate Conrad within a Foucaultian genealogy of knowledge we can turn once more to Gadamer, whose 'philosophical hermeneutics' resists science's exclusive claims to authority. An untrained and uncensored 'hermeneutical consciousness', Gadamer argues, is capable of grasping what is worth knowing in the first place, and thereby asking questions that generate *significant* knowledge. While not seeking to reinstate the culturally regressive function of a certain notion of 'common sense', Gadamer credits this faculty with the production of knowledge (Gadamer 1976: 3–17).[5]

The holistic category of 'the human' became a problem in the course of the nineteenth century, when different styles of learned investigation colonized different aspects of a fragmented humanity. The constitution of new disciplines such as sociology, psychology and anthropology (all of which had their own particular antecedents) involved more than simply adding them to the post-Enlightenment list of natural sciences, which focused largely on non-human entities. Until quite recently the practice and theory of these disciplines either mimicked or remained subservient to the authority of the natural sciences. In their earlier and more heroic moments, however, the human sciences had sought to transcend the objective and rationalistic basis of the natural sciences by introducing methods derived from humanism, and valuing 'artistic-instinctive induction' as highly as scientific logic.[6] Twentieth-century developments of the human sciences (including the hybrid subject called 'English') led to recognitions and methodologies that paradoxically undermined the certainties of humanism.

During the so-called epistemological revolution of the 1960s, traditional humanism appeared too narrow to deal with the major problems of the time.[7] This second-stage knowledge-explosion put into question the very foundation of scientific authority: namely, the Cartesian split between a knowing (human) subject and an (inert) object of knowledge. Enlightenment intellectuals had also divided the world into spheres homologous with the Cartesian distinctions between (active) subject and (passive) object. The colonialist separation of an advanced Europe from its backward dependencies could be regarded as either natural or at least a true description of current reality. As long as it was accepted, the distinction between those with true knowledge and those without it did not need to be stated. European truth was universal truth. From the latter half of the nineteenth century, however, the gradual constitution of the human subject as an object of new forms of inquiry eventually undermined Enlightenment confidence in the mission of modernity.

Conrad occupies a median place not only in the trajectory from early European expansionism to the break-up of Europe's empires but also in the epistemological development from Cartesianism to twentieth-century assaults on its basic tenets. Terry Eagleton points out significant ideological contradictions in the England which welcomed Conrad:

> [N]ineteenth-century imperialism demanded the production of a corporate, messianic, idealist ideology: but it demanded this at precisely the point where mid-Victorian faith in progress was being eroded into pessimism, subjectivism and irrationalism . . . [I]t also bred an awareness of cultural relativism at precisely the point where the absolute cultural hegemony of the imperialist nations needed to be affirmed.
>
> (Eagleton 1975: 134–5)

Here Eagleton defines ideology as a social or cultural force that, in the interests of consolidating specific power groups, uses discursive subtlety to project ideal resolutions to unresolved contradictions and incompatible tensions in 'lived reality'. In this sense, 'ideological struggle' may involve political philosophies, parties or slogans but is never contained by them. Eagleton reveals the strategies (some of which are unconscious) that, in setting the terms for such struggles, determine what might be sayable or even thinkable. By discussing epistemological crises in terms of ideology we can see how literature functions within those discourses which both effect and are affected by such crises.

Significantly, the most familiar descriptions of the *Zeitgeist* in late Victorian England were not cast in the language of crisis. The turn of the century was more commonly perceived as inaugurating an era of optimism. In 1904 – the year *Nostromo* was published – a triumphal Lord Acton instructed the contributors to the *Cambridge Modern History* to regard 'the scientific demand for completeness and certainty' as an attainable standard for this monumental publication:

> In our own time, within the last few years, most of the official collections in Europe have been made public, and nearly all the evidence that will ever appear is accessible now.
>
> As archives are meant to be explored, and are not meant to be printed, we approach the final stage in the conditions of historical learning.
>
> (Stern 1956: 247)

Clearly, the 'end of history' did not have for Lord Acton the apocalyptic resonance it would acquire in the dying decades of the twentieth century.[8] Edwardian England was a period of public confidence, when both the successful carve-up of Africa and the Western control of most of Asia engendered national pride. That persisted despite the fact that a new round of colonial conquest threatened the idea of 'liberal imperialism'. The world seemed to be on the verge of being integrated into a common system. Like the nationalistic melodies composed by Sir Edward Elgar for an empire on which the sun never set, the epistemological certainty of Lord Acton caught the very spirit of the age before the cataclysm.

The appearance of the great trans-Atlantic ocean liners, culminating in the *Titanic*, exemplifies both British optimism and Conrad's disengagement from it. Conrad wrote two articles for *The English Review* about the inquiry into the sinking of the *Titanic* which he regarded as a monumental instance of human fatuity (*Notes on Life and Letters* 213–48). He avoided sounding wise after the event by adopting instead a tone that enabled him to 'say all [he] felt [he] would have to say in scorn as well as in pity', as he would later describe the 'ironic method' of *The Secret Agent* (Author's Preface xiii). His response to the *Titanic* affair sprang not from his habitual negativity to the rhetoric of progress but from darker convictions.

I start with the proposition that Conrad experienced his own times as situated perilously across a gap in history. A vivid metaphor in *Victory* depicts this 'transitional' period as an 'age in which we are camped like bewildered travellers in a garish, unrestful hotel' (3), a description adopted by James Clifford as characterizing perfectly the age in which we still live (Clifford 1988: 275). The Conrad I wish to assess is primarily and pre-eminently the writer of that gap. The gap I refer to is the epistemological crisis around 1900, which (like the one in 1968) manifested itself on many fronts. To narrow the task and establish a link between these two dates, I will focus on a field of knowledge whose subject matter and methods are particularly relevant for Conrad. His moment coincides with what Clifford characterizes as a crisis of 'ethnographic authority' (ibid.: 21–54).

Conrad and some contemporaries

Despite his ingrained scepticism, Conrad was respectful whenever he thought about science. In a somewhat old-fashioned manner he adopts the standpoint of the interested amateur. He links modern scientific discovery with the voyages of those great explorers of the enlightened and idealistic age that succeeded the crude acquisitiveness of the early buccaneers:

> Cook's three voyages are free from any taint of that sort. His aims needed no disguise. They were scientific. His deeds speak for themselves with the masterly simplicity of a hard-won success. In that respect he seems to belong to the single-minded explorers of the nineteenth century, the late fathers of militant geography whose only object was the search for truth.
>
> (*Last Essays* 10)

Conrad sees the world of science as both mutable and susceptible to failure and corruption like other human endeavours. Not unlike Gandhi in this respect, Conrad resists modernity's representation of its authority as not only natural and universal but instantly acceptable. While consigning the golden age of global and scientific discovery to a rapidly disappearing past, his attitude to the new sciences often seems amused and sceptical. *Heart of Darkness* includes a veritable 'head-shrinker' in the form of the doctor Marlow consults before his journey into darkest Africa. Ominously, this amateur psychologist – or 'alienist', to use Marlow's archaic term for this new breed of medical practitioner – seeks permission to measure Marlow's head. The doctor's paradoxical reason for doing so is that 'the changes' take place not to the size of the cranium but 'inside, you know' (58). He thereby shows himself to be indeed a forerunner of Sigmund Freud.

Typically, Conrad is modest about his own knowledge. That modesty, however, is often expressed in a detached tone and accompanied by extraordinary independence of judgement. Both modesty and independence are displayed in terse exchanges he sometimes had with famous friends, especially when an issue of principle or commitment was at stake. For instance, in his friendship with Sir Hugh Clifford he respectfully deferred to the superior knowledge the old Malaya-hand had acquired during years spent in the foreign service. Duly accepting this obeisance, Clifford in turn acknowledged Conrad's superiority as a writer of colonial fictions. Their mutual acceptance of the idea that true knowledge and literary artistry belong to separate spheres obscured an important tension between them.

Clifford spent most of his lifetime in the colonies as an administrator. He 'knew' intimately both the people and language of the Malay Archipelago, and wrote 'Malay' fictions in English. If 'identification' is the desideratum of modern ethnography, Clifford had far more ethnographic knowledge than Conrad could have acquired in his few months' experience of 'the East'.[9] Clifford, moreover, had reviewed *Almayer's Folly* for the *Singapore Free Press* before he met its author. Seizing on its inauthentic portrayal of Malay life, he bluntly attacked Conrad's 'complete ignorance of Malays and their habits and customs' (Sherry 1971: 139–40). Conrad was piqued by this review. In a letter to Blackwood he attributes his errors to the authors of those secondary sources he claims to have checked scrupulously, and then questions the authority of the reviewer. At this stage of his writing career, Conrad seems to have thought it reasonable enough that fiction be judged by the tenets of Zolaesque naturalism. A few years later, when reviewing Clifford's own Malay tales, Conrad praised the writer's 'effective sureness of knowledge' while remaining mute about their success as fiction:

[T]o apply artistic standards to this book would be a fundamental error in appreciation. Like faith, enthusiasm, or heroism, art veils part of the truth of life to make the rest appear more splendid, inspiring, or sinister. And this book is only truth, interesting and futile, truth unadorned, simple and straightforward.

(Notes on Life and Letters 24)

Conrad's careful discrimination between the concealments of art and the straightforward simplicity of truth (reductively described as 'interesting and futile') is a further warning against assuming that the novelist of exotic places shared the veridical aspirations of contemporary ethnographers.

Conrad subsequently suggests that the distinction between knowledge of a subject and the artistic power to make it vivid is less clear-cut. In a letter to Blackwood in the following year, he still seems preoccupied with Clifford's criticism. He praises a story by Clifford that had appeared in a recent number of *Maga*: 'His last thing . . . was rather good – I mean as a piece of writing. His knowledge is unique. If I only knew one hundre[d]th part of what he knows I would move a mountain or two' (*Letters* 2: 194). This casual comment again raises the question of what kind of knowledge fiction purveys, and anticipates the terms in which James would describe Conrad as 'the artist of the whole matter'.

Much later in life, Conrad wrote to Bertrand Russell in a similar vein, after reading his book, *The Problem of China* (1922):

> I have always liked the Chinese, even those that tried to kill me (and some other people) in the yard of a private house in Chantabun, even (but not so much) the fellow who stole all my money one night in Bankok, but brushed and folded my clothes neatly for me to dress in the morning, before vanishing into the depths of Siam. I also received many kindnesses at the hands of various Chinese. This with the addition of an evening's conversation with the secretary of His Excellency Tseng on the verandah of an hotel and a perfunctory study of a poem, The Heathen Chinee, is all I know about Chinese. But after reading your extremely interesting view of the Chinese Problem I take a gloomy view of the future of their country.
>
> (Russell 1975: 396)

Conrad's address to the distinguished intellectual is marked by self-deprecating ironics and a self-parodying presentation of himself as amateur orientalist. The playfulness again masks a different attitude. He uses those intriguing glimpses of his exotic life experiences, and the sharply observed details that conjure up these stereotypical Orientals as both alien and familiar, to support a polemic strategy that pits one way of knowing against another. He contrasts the illuminations of a writer-artist with the conceptual framings of a philosopher-savant. In this way, what Russell confidently treats as certainties are drawn into the penumbral region of a Teiresias-like traveller: Conrad's duplicitous stance and ironic tone enable perceptions that unsettle the kind of knowledge Russell presents. In proving to be as arrogant as it is modest, his letter exhibits the famous Janus-face of Conradian irony before trenchantly rejecting Russell's liberal-socialist hope for a solution to the 'Chinese Problem':

> He who does not see the truth of your deductions can only be he who does not want to see. They strike a chill into one's soul especially when you deal with the American element. That would indeed be a dreadful fate for China or any other country. I feel your book the more because the only ray of hope you allow is the advent of international socialism, the sort of thing to which I cannot attach any sort of definite meaning. I have never been able to find in any man's book or any man's talk anything convincing enough to stand up for a moment against my deep-seated sense of fatality governing this man-inhabited world. After all it is but a system, not very recondite and not very plausible. As a mere reverie it is not of a very high order and wears a strange resemblance to a hungry man's dream of a gorgeous feast guarded by a lot of beadles in cocked hats. But I know

you wouldn't expect me to put faith in any system. The only remedy for Chinamen and for the rest of us is the change of hearts, but looking at the history of the last 2000 years there is not much reason to expect that thing, even if man has taken to flying – a great 'uplift', no doubt, but no great change. He doesn't fly like an eagle; he flies like a beetle. And you must have noticed how ugly, ridiculous and fatuous is the flight of a beetle.

(ibid.)

Conrad's disavowal of optimism is breathtaking in its scope and intensity. He not only refuses to commit himself to a political solution but also contemptuously rejects the most futuristic invention of the new age. In accepting Russell's critique he renders the political meaning of his novels both contentious and baffling. Equally relevant to my argument is the effortless way in which Conrad negotiates the nexus between knowledge and ideas on the one hand, and politics and power on the other.

I will return later to the matter of Conrad's politics and how they relate to ideas expressed in his writing. Here I want to use the glancing insights afforded by Conrad's exchanges with contemporaries as a way of examining his fictional treatment of science. While science is not a pervasive theme in Conrad's fiction, it makes an early and memorable appearance in *Lord Jim* in the form of Stein, the German adventurer and naturalist. Stein's function in the plot is to effect a transition from the disgraced Jim of the *Patna* to the rehabilitated 'Tuan Jim' of Patusan. But in helping us to understand the nature of Jim's case, he also performs an important function in the novel's pre-scientific project of knowing 'the whole matter' of Jim. Stein's utterances provide insights into the problems facing the representation in realist fiction of psychology and character at that time. He points at the same time to the way in which imaginative fiction overlaps with the field of science.

After Marlow's visit to Stein, 'Tuan Jim' gets his opportunity to achieve a heroic destiny after all. But the novel's narrative drive has already moved Conrad along a different trajectory, on account of the aleatory attempts by Marlow and others to come to terms with something in Jim which is also at the heart of European colonialism: the germ of corruption. In attempting his complex analysis of Jim, Stein behaves like an old-fashioned scientist, romantically driven as he is and dedicated to the analysis of his impaled butterflies. For neither his positivistic methods of classifying the myriad species of lepidoptera nor his wonderment at their natural perfection helps him to know Jim:

" 'Man is amazing, but he is not a masterpiece,' he said, keeping his eye fixed on the glass case. 'Perhaps the artist was a little mad. Eh?

What do you think? Sometimes it seems to me that man is come where he is not wanted, where there is no place for him; for if not, why should he want all the place . . . ' "

(208)

Stein's agnosticism seems less applicable to the universal Man he invokes than to acquisitive European man, who has certainly 'come where he is not wanted'. Yet the Hamlet-like musings throughout this episode and the great flourish of Jim's heroic death show that the conventions of tragedy also feed into the novel's meditations on its protagonist. Its most striking link to Shakespearean tragedy, however, is its insight that Jim is *unknowable*, which reproduces Shakespeare's presentation of a world caught in a discursive impasse.[10] Whereas Marlow insists that Jim is one of us, Conrad is more interested in the degree to which he is not, which is why this novel is about indeterminacy rather than definition. As a man still 'under a cloud' at the end of the novel (416), Jim presents a case study too complicated for contemporary methods of diagnosis.

At the level of content, Stein's intervention links the novel to tragedy by introducing something that permeates *Heart of Darkness*, which is the notion of a dispersed evil or will to (self-)destructiveness:

" 'Yes! Very funny this terrible thing is. A man that is born falls into a dream like a man who falls into the sea . . . The way is to the destructive element submit yourself, and with the exertions of your hands and feet in the water make the deep, deep sea keep you up. So if you ask me – how to be?'

"His voice leaped up extraordinarily strong, as though away there in the dusk he had been inspired by some whisper of knowledge."

(214)

As a romantic and proto-existentialist, Stein foregrounds the problem of knowledge, and in doing so reveals the epistemological leap Conrad took when he abandoned *The Rescue* to write *Heart of Darkness* and *Lord Jim*. In thereby jettisoning certain modes of realist representation, Conrad undertook the bleaker task of producing characters and narratives in the knowledge that such an enterprise was impossible. An important corollary to that recognition was that Conrad's change of focus significantly affected his representation of non-European characters. Although Jim appeared to be an ideal product of British imperialist ideology, and an obvious candidate for the Service, he became instead a symptom of impending crisis. A comparable sign is that in *Heart of Darkness* Conrad renounces those 'sympathetic' portrayals of 'native' life found in his earlier fiction. Marlow and his audience can know black Africans only through the stereotyped and (necessarily) racist deformations embedded in the language of the colonizer.

Conradian vision and ethnographic authority

Conrad's famous Preface to *The Nigger of the 'Narcissus'* (1898) constitutes a manifesto of the new author's aesthetic: 'My task which I am trying to achieve is, by the power of the written word to make you hear, to make you feel – it is, before all, to make you *see*. That – and no more – and it is everything' (x). This was Conrad's first published piece of literary criticism. It begins by focusing on the way in which fiction works and is related to other forms of knowledge. In emphasizing that art is concerned above all with the sensuous it grants pride of place to the visual. Conrad distinguishes art not only from philosophy but also from science, whose work is seen as 'weighty' but ephemeral because it appeals only 'to our credulity'. If art cannot justify itself as cognitive knowledge, it nevertheless brings to light a kind of 'truth'. But in this context, what is the nature of 'vision' and 'truth', and how do they relate to other ways of knowing Europe's Other?

Those who have attempted the task of classifying the nature of Conradian knowledge often begin with this question of his peculiar *vision*. 'I felt', Edward Said records,

> first coming across Conrad when I was a teenager, that in a certain sense I was reading, not so much my own story, but a story written out of bits of my life and put together in a haunting and fantastically obsessive way . . . He has a particular kind of vision which increases in intensity every time I read him, so that now it's almost unbearable for me to read him.
>
> (Salusinszky 1987: 133)

Said is the late-twentieth-century prototype of an *engagé* intellectual. He was also the chief provocateur in that second crisis of ethnographic authority that resulted in the academic formation of postcolonial studies. By no means the first to name Conrad as his spiritual ancestor, he sustained this affinity throughout his life. His Conrad is first of all a story – in some sense of Said's own life (or parts of it) but composed as it were before the event. The story Said connects with is imagined not as a text (the narratives of specific novels) but as a vision. That vision is set in a colonial world, whose synchronic pervasiveness enables Said to imagine that some of his own life experiences went into the composition of Conrad's story. What matters here to Said cannot be reduced to either chronological difference or colonial similarity. As indicated by the title of his autobiography, *Out of Place* (1999), Said aligns himself with Conrad and a growing band of writers who speak *between* cultures. In addressing what I have called the condition of indeterminacy, they write from a space that was opened up in modern times mainly by colonial encounters between Europe and non-Europe. It is now the site of many other life experiences, such as decolonization, uprootedness, migration and neo-colonialism, all of which are seen as aspects of the postcolonial condition. Conrad enabled Said and others to 'see' their world differently, and by doing so helped to create new ways of knowing the world that would require the invention of new heuristic tools.

A turning point in the journey towards such knowledge was Said's remarkably timely book, *Orientalism* (1978). This pioneering work was so successful that its central proposition now seems remarkably simple. Said assembled a mountain of evidence to show how three centuries of Western presuppositions had skewed the production of knowledge of 'the East'. He disturbed that branch of Western scholarship known as 'Orientalist studies' by challenging its practitioners to recognize that their apparently disinterested researches contained a hidden politics. In short, both knowledge of the Orient (lovingly accumulated through centuries of impressive scholarship) and supposedly innocent love-affairs with the East described by poets, novelists and travellers were shown to be produced and sustained by the power structures of the imperial system.

Orientalism's Foucaultian enterprise is to reconstruct the genealogy of representations of the Orient by European writers, artists and scholars. Their enterprise is not merely to depict the 'Orient'; in fact, they bring 'the Orient' into being. They thereby set in place and sustain certain assumptions that subject the 'East' to cultural (and material) dominance by the 'West'.[11] In patiently describing the internal consistency of orientalist discourse, Said is less concerned with either the accuracy of its representations or the fairness of its implied value judgements. The refusal by Said to engage with those questions certainly shocks: writers and scholars of different stature and varying respectability are all lumped together and implicated in maintaining existing power relations in a common structure of knowledge. Scholars who devoted their lives to 'oriental' cultures and the peoples they worked with in relations of mutual respect and affection are treated no differently from the most arrogant politicians of empire. The binary opposition reconstructed by Said was designed to keep the East under Western eyes. It transcends such differences as those between earlier British/Indian relations based on orientalist respect for cultural difference and later 'anglicizing' policies that were often frankly demeaning to colonized peoples. The structure persists whether the East is labelled benignly as the 'mysterious east' or denigrated as 'barbaric'. Its profound political implications lead Said to a somewhat perfunctory dismissal of Karl Marx.[12]

As late as 1984, Said claimed that anthropology and ethnography had still failed to come to terms with their origins in power relations established by European colonization (Said 1984: 14–27). Whether stimulated by this assault on the basis of orientalist learning, or in reaction against it, contemporary ethnographers and postcolonial critics have debated the authenticity of ethnographic narratives. The orientalist structure which is revealed as having governed their narratives is now seen to go back at least as far as Herodotus. More modern narratives are typically the product of anthropological researches into strange and distant peoples, written for consumption by Western academics and intellectuals. One current version of this problem – aggravated by identity politics – focuses on anxiety about the 'subject position' of postcolonial literary critics. Entwined with the later history of European colonialism, it registers the fact that, in claiming to represent an authentic knowledge of non-Western or 'primitive' people, Western science has been hard pressed to survive challenges to its supposed objectivity.

The most distinguished anthropologist to respond to these challenges was Clifford Geertz, who engaged late in his career with the contemporary critique of ethnographic writing (Geertz 1988: 1–24). He attributed its current crisis of both epistemology and narrative to the breakdown of European colonialism. The work of older anthropologists depended on the 'power asymmetries' of the colonial world so that anthropology's 'subjects and its audience were not only separable but morally disconnected' (ibid.: 132). The gradual breaking down of those boundaries in various ways weakened the scientific certitude enjoyed by the impressive group of anthropological writers who had consolidated the new discipline in the early and middle decades of the century. The ensuing crisis, however, had a positive outcome: the dissolution of older taxonomies opened a space for the production of new knowledges.

A basic element in ethnographic narrative, Geertz observes, is the subjectivity and desire of the fieldworker. He finds it significant that one of those who constitute his 'great tradition' of twentieth-century anthropologists, Bronislaw Malinowski, was, like Conrad, a 'wandering Pole'. Both the life experiences of ethnographers and their narrative skills are now considered to contribute to the cogency and authenticity of ethnographic writing. 'Writerliness' is thus as important as empirical evidence in convincing readers that *this* person was really *there*, and that this story (however strange) is to be believed. In establishing common ground between ethnographic narratives and literary fictions, Geertz recalls the way in which science constructs its truth-effects. In addition to regarding literary analysis as an appropriate model for understanding ethnographic writing, Geertz repositions the knowing subject. His blurring of the subject–object distinction, for example, is in some respects homologous with the psychoanalytic phenomenon of the transference.

For Jacques Lacan, the 'desire of the analyst' is paramount in the production of both insight and narrative in psychoanalytic practice (Lacan 1977: 9–10).

James Clifford elaborates these questions in a powerful discussion that also links the two 'wandering Poles' (Clifford 1988: 92–113). Like Malinowski, Conrad spent the first half of his adult life roaming among peoples considered strange by Europeans, and the second half writing up the experience. Clifford's comparison of these two *émigré* careers requires some temporal adjustment, because the work of the older writer – Conrad – turns out to be the more modern, and so much so that '[a]nthropology is still waiting for its Conrad' (ibid.: 96). Adopting a term from Stephen Greenblatt (1980), Clifford parallels Conrad's method of 'life-fashioning' with the fieldwork model of ethnography:

> [E]thnographic fieldwork remains an unusually sensitive method. Participant observation obliges its practitioners to experience, at a bodily as well as an intellectual level, the vicissitudes of translation. It requires arduous language learning, some degree of direct involvement and conversation, and often a derangement of personal and cultural expectations.
>
> (Clifford 1988: 23–4)

While acknowledging that ethnographic authority is in crisis, Clifford reaffirms his commitment to the fieldwork model. Instead of being enshrined under the sign of scientific truth and academic authenticity, he argues, it should see itself more modestly as a particular practice that relies on *participation* as a way of escaping, however partially and unevenly, the limitations of the familiar self. This process involves translation (in a strong sense), vicissitudes (in a non-moral sense) and (with a psychoanalytic overtone) 'derangement'. It begins by reconfiguring the Cartesian division between subject and object. Poststructuralist psychoanalysis repositions the 'object' of analysis (the analysand) as the subject, just as the modernist novel relinquishes authorial omniscience by reducing the narrator to a component of the story. Absorbing the lessons of both narratology and poststructuralism, Clifford argues that postcolonial ethnography accesses less 'objective' truths than those claimed by nineteenth-century science and historiography, which require the rigorous transformation of 'unruly experience . . . into an authoritative written account' (ibid.: 25). By partially relinquishing the stability and prestige of the knowing subject, contemporary ethnographers come to resemble a Conradian narrator. In an appropriately nautical metaphor, they are 'continuous[ly] tacking between the "inside" and "outside" of events: on the one hand grasping the sense of specific occurrences and gestures empathetically, on the other stepping back to situate these meanings in wider contexts' (ibid.: 34).

The major turning point in the history of modern ethnography is thus none other than our own 'Conradian moment'. Clifford describes it as 'a complex decade of choice, the 1890s, beginning with the African voyage and ending with its narration. The choice involved career, language, and cultural attachment' (ibid.: 96–7). *Heart of Darkness* disrupts the traditions of both the Service and novel writing by breaching narratological and ideological contracts. Conrad's bad faith in these matters results in a novel that, centring the scene of writing and treating it as the primary problem to address, is 'a paradigm of ethnographic subjectivity' (ibid.: 100). Clifford's *Heart of Darkness* is closer to a postcolonial consciousness than the writings of Malinowski, which sought merely to consolidate new academic structures within the guiding assumptions of Western modernity. The institution of modern anthropology initially required the reassuring familiarity of classical realism and the validation provided by scientific status. That is why Clifford describes it as 'still waiting for its Conrad'.

The Conradian moment, however, is unrepeatable. Its resonant intimations are not facts or objects capable of being reproduced by a sheer act of will in the self-conscious era of postmodernity. The idea that anthropology still awaits its Conrad places author and discipline in a false relationship to one another. The knowledge Conrad had could be expressed only through his kind of writing. Its moment was neither the one when modern anthropology flourished nor the more self-conscious era of poststructuralist sophistication and postmodern inclusiveness. As we shall see, Conrad's dark vision can be recalled, in the form of pastiche, by a stylish writer such as Bruce Chatwin – or 'completed' by other writers whose very different perceptions of imperial subjugation and its aftermaths enable them to recreate the experiences of the colonized. But no 'Conrad' can be slotted into such an imaginary continuum.

2 Conrad in literary history

In attempting to specify the nature of Conrad's knowledge, I have focused so far partly on matters of content and partly on the institutional processes which sanction a noetic field. That procedure leaves out the possibility, proposed by Gadamer and others, that literary forms themselves constitute modes of knowledge, and have played significant roles in the early history of science. Nineteenth-century polemicists such as Matthew Arnold argued that poetry embodies a special kind of truth.[1] Belatedly echoing such claims, even Conrad prefaces *The Nigger of the 'Narcissus'* by contrasting scientific with artistic knowledge (vii–viii).

As a consequence of those debates, literature and science were completely distanced from one another in the twentieth century. In order to explore the complexity of the problem in Conrad's time, I will focus on two literary genres that are often considered to be more veridical than others. The first is realistic fiction, whose very name declares its commitment to truth telling. The second is tragedy, a form of drama that is thought to mediate so-called 'tragic knowledge' which is itself held to yield insights into unique realms of truth. In order to relate Conrad's fiction to these two august categories inherited from both philosophy and literary theory, I will begin with the complicated story of how arguments about realism resulted in fundamental changes to the late-nineteenth-century novel. In the case of tragedy, its increasingly dispersed possibilities were expressed in new and powerful ways in some of the most famous novels of the period. As D. H. Lawrence would observe in 1928 when opening his last and most (in)famous novel: 'Ours is essentially a tragic age, so we refuse to take it tragically' (Lawrence 1960: 47).

Realism and truth

Conrad's choice of a colonial content for his novels coincided with a crisis in the mission of classical realism. In representing colonial situations and non-European characters in his early Malay novels, Conrad largely adhered to what was by then a well-established contract between writers and readers, and employed the available diction and tropes of naturalistic verisimilitude. In *The Nigger of the 'Narcissus', Heart of Darkness* and *Lord Jim*, however, these practices gave way to narrative and stylistic experiments that undermined the assumptions on which such fiction depended. While boldly incorporating the influence of French aestheticism, Conrad took as his subject matter the social and political consequences of European imperialism. As a budding modernist, he put into question older practices of representation while simultaneously moving his fictions into political areas that were extremely sensitive. In the history of the European novel, this double manoeuvre makes his writing not just experimentalist but truly revolutionary.

The crisis of realism was signalled most notably by Flaubert's *Madame Bovary* (1857), whose publication was preceded by litigation about its morality that made it notorious. The legal success of the defence consolidated the assumption among aesthetes on both sides of the Channel that the world of art was so self-referentially autonomous that its products should not be assessed in terms of either their morality or their politics.[2] Somewhat paradoxically, that separation was confused when artists began to affect hostility towards 'bourgeois morality', and paraded the slogan *épater la bourgeoisie* as their touchstone. The tragic contradictions of this aestheticism were played out in England in 1895, when Oscar Wilde was found guilty on charges of sexual immorality, and began his brutal imprisonment just one month after the publication – worlds away, it seems – of Conrad's first novel.

The heterogeneity of Conrad's moment can be expressed as a tension between style and content in some of the prevailing assumptions that governed serious literature at that time. The tension is visible, for instance, in Conrad's ambition to write popular novels while at the same time being recognized in the world of high culture as a 'man of letters'. As a representative writer of the *haute bourgeoisie*, Flaubert regarded the choice of subject matter as virtually irrelevant. But to Conrad, it was fundamental. By choosing colonial settings for his work, he made it impossible to maintain a comfortable distance between aesthetics and politics.

It is a truism of literary history that the paramount embodiment of realism in the modern period was the novel, which appeared in Europe during the early stages of modern capitalist development and the beginnings of bourgeois hegemony, and developed within that broader historical process. From different perspectives, both Ian Watt and Georg Lukács presented versions of this dual process (Watt 1957; Lukács 1972). But it was Fredric Jameson who first defined it as involving a cultural 'mission':

Indeed, as any number of "definitions" of realism assert . . . that processing operation variously called narrative mimesis or realistic representation has as its historic function the systematic undermining and demystification, the secular "decoding," of those preexisting inherited traditional or sacred narrative paradigms which are its initial givens. In this sense, the novel plays a significant role in what can be called a properly bourgeois cultural revolution – that immense process of transformation whereby populations whose life habits were formed by other, now archaic, modes of production are effectively reprogrammed for life and work in the new world of market capitalism. The "objective" function of the novel is thereby also implied: to its subjective and critical, analytic, corrosive mission must now be added the task of producing as though for the first time that very life world, that very "referent" . . . of which this new narrative discourse will then claim to be the "realistic" reflection.

(Jameson 1981: 152)

Furthermore, Benedict Anderson has argued that the formation of modern nation states depended on the rise of print media, which enabled previously discrete populations to begin identifying themselves with the new and 'affiliative' unit of 'the nation'. This resulted in what he calls an 'imagined community' increasingly remote from the 'real-life' experiences of formerly organic or otherwise traditional societies (B. Anderson 1983). Jameson analyses in materialist terms the social function of the novel as both the dominant literary genre of the new age and a principal exploiter of the new media. In the historical process of bedding down the new social order, he argues, the novel served two functions. One was revolutionary: in 'tearing down the old', it rewrote the inherited traditions and forms. Its conservative function was to present the new order as though things had always been so, and thus normalize it as natural and inevitable. Jameson's broad view of the novel does not imply that literature and art either simply reflect or are structurally homologous with 'real history'. From its very beginnings, the modern novel was aware of embarrassing slippages between words and things, and practised a sleight-of-hand that exploited endless opportunities for irony, self-reflection and creative play. In short, while closely paralleling social developments that affected its potentialities, the novel also revealed a high degree of autonomy.

The importance of Jane Austen in that history cannot be over-estimated. Although she was committed to representing accurately those small communities she knew so well, her realism does not (as critics have often complained) merely reflect such narrow worlds. Partly a rewriting of traditional genres such as romance and fairy-tales, it is also a corrosive critique of the obsolete class values of a displaced aristocracy, as evinced by Sir Walter Elliot in *Persuasion* and the grotesque Mr Collins in *Pride and Prejudice*. Here, Austen is more than a shrewd observer of social foibles. Actively engaged in delineating radical changes to class formations, she envisages new and appropriate codes of living for the rapidly expanding middle classes. In catching the very moment of social change, her dynamic realism gives her work a critical and exploratory edge no longer available to her successors and imitators. The novelists who preceded her belonged to that more adventurous – even heroic – moment of the bourgeoisie which produced militant realism. Austen, on the other hand, relates tangentially to a moment of social consolidation just before Britain attained global hegemony. Within the English tradition, she represents the high point of classical realism.

From the middle of the nineteenth century, a rising generation of novelists began to acknowledge that realistic portrayals of the social world of their middle-class readers were likely to result in the atrophy diagnosed in 1866 by the young Henry James, when reviewing Anthony Trollope's latest offering, *The Belton Estate*:

> [I]t is filled out as Mr. Trollope alone knows how to fill out the primitive meagreness of his dramatic skeletons. The three persons whom we have mentioned are each a character in a way, and their sayings and doings, their comings and goings, are registered to the letter and timed to the minute. They write a number of letters, which are duly transcribed; they make frequent railway journeys by the down-train to London; they have cups of tea in their bedrooms; and they do, in short, in the novel very much as the reader is doing out of it.
>
> (James 1963: 11)

What the young James found so boring in Trollope's novels was later captured precisely by Roland Barthes when complaining that realism tended to produce 'plane projections of a curved and organic world' (Barthes 1968: 29). James' parody of realism's decline into an undifferentiated harmony of text and reader, literary representation and social referent, makes Trollope's method seem like a version of Emile Zola's 'scientifically' accurate naturalism without the science. Zola thought that fiction could aspire to truth by grounding itself on meticulously researched and accurately recorded details of phenomena in the material world. He and his late-nineteenth-century followers thus believed that realism would achieve its mission by staying close to the positivistic science that would finally validate it.

Like James, Conrad served his literary apprenticeship with the French masters, and was aware that Flaubert's break with classical realism opened up new possibilities for the novel. But James' precocious mid-century review of Trollope reminds us that Conrad was by no means the first novelist to destabilize the narrative point of view encountered in life-reflecting realist fiction. His own pre-modernist experimentalism does not distinguish his work from that of other writers with similar interests at the end of the nineteenth century. Conrad differs from his contemporaries by combining two kinds of crisis: one aesthetic (the problem of novelistic form) and the other world-historical (the problem of representing alien peoples and places at such moments). In this respect he anticipates something that would become a twentieth-century obsession, namely the politics of representation. By contrast, the serious novelists of eighteenth- and nineteenth-century Europe had focused mainly on the reorganization of metropolitan social life under the new economic order.

James' tribute to Conrad (quoted in the previous chapter) recognizes that the younger novelist is still working within the received framework of realism. Somewhat surprisingly, its stress on knowledge and totality of vision anticipates two of the abiding terms in twentieth-century Marxist debates about realism. The principal philosopher to make 'totality' the ultimate criterion of realism's knowledge was the Hungarian Georg Lukács, who regarded Flaubert's *oeuvre* as a crucial turning point. Working in post-revolutionary Eastern Europe between the wars and when high modernism was in vogue, Lukács heroically and anachronistically championed older forms of 'great realism' produced by nineteenth-century novelists such as Balzac and Tolstoy. In terms of both historical chronologies and aesthetic preferences, Lukács' work unexpectedly parallels that of F. R. Leavis.

For Lukács, realism is a kind of textual engine which, by transcending the personal and ideologically limiting beliefs of individual authors, produces insight into the 'essential forces' driving society at any given time. As a revolutionary, he could thus defend writers such as Tolstoy or Dostoyevsky, who were regarded by the Party as political reactionaries, on the grounds of their truth-content. Although both had been limited by the social class they belonged to and their hopelessly inadequate proposals for the future, Lukács followed Lenin in claiming that they had nevertheless understood better than any of their contemporaries the forces shaping post-feudal Russia in the nineteenth century. That claim depends, of course, on a particular understanding of the future from the perspective of the 1917 October Revolution. The rigidity of Lukács' interpretative structure is starkly visible when viewed from outside the party consensus that determined his priorities. It is also discernible when the truth-content of classical Russian realism is assessed from the standpoint of either the Stalinist purges in the 1930s or the equally resonant dates of 1956, 1968 or 1989. The use of such historical or political measuring sticks can either be unstated (as in English bourgeois society during the eighteenth and nineteenth centuries) or doctrinaire (as in Stalinist Russia between the wars). Whenever they are refused or cease to command consensus, the authority of realism is eroded, together with the political foundation it had depended upon. The dislocations that then take place do so in a climate of threat and opportunity. Although they may produce a liberating moment of creative upsurge, they are characteristically attended by a hermeneutic *mise-en-abîme*.

Leavis was ambivalent on the question of literary modernism as opposed to realism. In poetry, he championed modernism, praising the 'new poetic' of Pound and Eliot decades before it became fashionable in academic circles. His 'great tradition' of the English novel, on the other hand, was restricted to Austen, George Eliot, James, Conrad and Lawrence, more for their maintenance of a particular kind of moral inquiry than because of their high realism. Consistent with this evaluation was his late and appreciative essay on Leo Tolstoy (Leavis 1967: 9–32) and his arbitrary dismissal of James Joyce (Leavis 1948: 25–6). On the question of modernism in fiction, therefore, Leavis concurs with Lukács, a literary historian who was ideologically his polar opposite. It is remarkable if not ironic that the privileging of high realism over modernism by the virulently anti-Marxist author of *The Great Tradition* should have such affinities with the map of European realism drawn by the Hungarian Marxist, because their ideological agendas as critics differed greatly. Leavis valued realism on account of its 'concreteness' and because it enriches a humanist discourse dedicated to the exploration of moral truth. The truth that concerns Lukács, on the other hand, is the power of literature to read history in terms of current political realities.

I shall discuss in the next chapter how the intervention of Leavis furthered Conrad's reputation. As for Lukács, both the limitations and the trenchancy of his hermeneutic manner are revealed in his brief analysis of Conrad's realism:

> With Joseph Conrad, matters are more complex. Conrad was firmly opposed to socialism . . . Yet in his best writings a strange phenomenon is observable: his faith in capitalism is such that the narrative does not even touch on its social implications. Conrad's heroes are confronted with exclusively personal, moral conflicts, in which their individual strength or weakness is revealed . . . This gives Conrad's work its finished, self-sufficient quality, but it also prevents him from presenting the totality of life . . . Thus Conrad's 'reasonable question', though excluding the most important social problems of his time, makes possible that 'triumph of realism' we find in him.
>
> (Lukács 1963: 71)

These judgements repeat questionable assumptions because Conrad's beliefs turn out on closer inspection to be even 'more complex' than Lukács allows. His simplifications may have resulted from the selection of Conrad's works he was familiar with: for example, his short summary fits *Typhoon* more closely than the novels I will be privileging. But even in the case of *Typhoon*, Lukács' conclusion that Conrad presents 'exclusively personal, moral conflicts' in novels characterized by their 'finished, self-sufficient quality' is hard to sustain in the face of a more open and 'presuppositionless' reading.[3] Lukács was a critic and philosopher whose judgements once carried great authority, and not only in Communist or Marxist circles. What strikes one most when reading him now, however, is the hermetically sealed nature of those circles. What he 'finds' in Conrad (or Tolstoy, Dostoyevsky and other great bourgeois writers) is produced largely by the grand narrative of social history he brings to the reading process within which every writer is to be placed.[4]

In the 1930s, one of Lukács' more penetrating judgements put him in considerable personal danger when he championed Tolstoy and Dostoyevsky against Zolaesque naturalism, which at that time was officially approved, especially in its arid Soviet manifestation as socialist realism. One of Lukács' great strengths was his capacity to relate literature to the dynamics of history. Another was his openness about literary style and form, which he thought were matters for writers themselves to decide. Faced with the challenges of Brecht, his aesthetic appears rigid and prescriptive: Brecht himself maliciously satirized the supposedly Lukácsian injunction that everyone should aspire to write like Tolstoy.[5] But Lukács firmly resisted the two-dimensional prescriptiveness of Zola, whose progressive politics must have greatly appealed to him. He also championed the very un-Tolstoyan poetics of the pre-modernist Dostoyevsky, whose social diagnosis he saw as foreshadowing that representative twentieth-century condition, anomie. Such instances reveal the full power of a Central European intellectual tradition that is eminently relevant to the analysis of Conrad.

At first glance, Roland Barthes' corrosive analysis of the limitations of realism seems to marginalize historical and political questions in favour of punctilious arguments about such matters as points of grammar.[6] Far from trivializing the political, however, Barthes goes to the very heart of the Flaubertian break by uncovering a hidden politics in the different practices of past-tense reportage. His richly poetic analysis of how French realism treats its raw material makes much of the fact that its narratives privilege the preterite, a literary past-definite tense whose function is to limit the scope of the tellable while at the same time propagating a 'plausible lie':

[W]hen, within the narration, the preterite is replaced by less ornamental forms, fresher, more full-blooded and nearer to speech . . . Literature becomes the receptacle of existence in all its density and no longer its meaning alone . . . We now understand what is profitable and what is intolerable in the preterite as used in the Novel: it is a lie made manifest, it delineates an area of plausibility which reveals the possible in the very act of unmasking it as false . . . it involves giving to the imaginary the formal guarantee of the real, but while preserving in the sign the ambiguity of a double object, at once believable and false.

(Barthes 1968: 32–3)

Far from representing reality truthfully, realism drastically restricts it while at the same time propagating the deception that its own representation is an account of how things 'really' are. Barthes' revelation that its verisimilitude depends on a set of literary conventions no less arbitrary than any other threatens the reassuring contract that enables realism to maintain its centrality.

Tragedy and the novel

In modernity, of course, the principal vehicle of realism (or realist representation) is the novel, which is frequently seen as the end of genre rather than merely another instance of it. Jameson calls it a 'processing operation': gathering up and transforming other genres, the novel produces its own representations of modern secular society, using whatever media and addressing whatever audiences it can find. This explains the persistent and ghostly presence in the new form of older texts, which thereby acquire the ideological aura of its 'sources'. Likewise, tragedy, to which Aristotle in his *Poetics* assigned a generic purity that differentiated it clearly from comedy and epic, has become so dispersed since the Renaissance that there is no consensus on what constitutes even its fundamental specificity. In raising the possibility that both tragedy and 'the tragic' are relevant to Conrad, however, I want to return strategically to the meaning tragedy had for the Athenians, whose cultural history expresses with deceptive clarity the exact relationship between tragedy and philosophy.[7] My purpose in doing so is to suggest that Conrad's novels functioned rather like the Athenian tragedies at a comparable moment of discursive crisis.

In this respect my Foucaultian attempt to rethink literary history is strengthened by Timothy J. Reiss' *Tragedy and Truth* (1980), which defines Greek tragedy by neither its internal properties nor its content but by the function it performed in the cultural life of Athens.[8] To simplify his complex analysis, Reiss argues that Athenian tragedy originated in the fifth century BCE precisely in response to a gathering sense of epistemic crisis. It manifested not only a failure of faith in traditional discourses for establishing knowledge and truth but also the excitement generated by those new forms of inquiry that were debated daily in the Athenian agora. This crisis was no doubt related to the revolutionary invention of democracy. But instead of producing yet another account of tragedy in terms of the political and social history of Athens, Reiss focuses on the social function it performed at the level of discourse. In spite of its foreboding and disaster-ridden content, Reiss argues, the historical function of tragedy was to contain the crisis, because tragedy is above all 'the discourse that grasps and encloses a certain "absence of significance"' (Reiss 1980: 3). This sustained and exhaustive act of enclosure – the *progressive* function performed by tragedy at Athens – helped to create a space for new discourses to emerge. The appearance of a new and Socratic discourse of truth was enabled solely by tragedy's capacity to contain the feeling that access to truth was impossible. After a period of struggle, the Socratic tradition of scientific and philosophical inquiry triumphed towards the end of the fifth century. The achievements of Plato and Aristotle superseded earlier Greek sciences, and would be claimed eventually as the origin of our modernity. To regard tragedy as thus enabling an early paradigm shift is to provide a more progressive account of its social function than Friedrich Nietzsche gives in his own narrative of the sudden disappearance of tragedy with the emergence of Socratic rationalism.[9] According to Nietzsche, tragedy and rationalism were simply incompatible. Under the sway of Socrates the young Plato not only forsook his ambition to be a tragedian, but even came to regard that profession as hostile to truth. Nietzsche treats this as a story of loss, because he thinks that tragic knowledge is more profound and comprehensive than the merely ratiocinative kind that displaced it. Reiss accepts this disjunction, but differs from Nietzsche by positing a dynamic relationship between tragedy and philosophy at the moment of epistemological change.

No such line is clearly discernible in the discursive history of the past century, let alone the previous two or three hundred years. Nevertheless, when investigating the affinities between Conrad's novels and tragedy, it is helpful to maintain the distinction Reiss makes between tragedy (the literary/dramatic genre performed at the Festival of Dionysus in Athens) and that later but different development known as 'the tragic' (which labels a particular knowledge). In approaching Conrad this way, I will not be dealing with the supposedly Schopenhauerian origins of his pessimistic philosophy. Nor will I seize on the spectacular downfalls of Lord Jim or Nostromo, those 'Freudian acts' that Jameson regards merely as 'arabesques which seal these two narrative discourses, rather than as genuine symptoms' (Jameson 1981: 209).

Reiss begins with an uncompromising quotation from Henri Gouhier: 'The tragic is a dimension of real existence. Tragedy belongs to literature and to theatre, the tragic belongs to life' (Reiss 1980: 1). He argues that our distinction between literature and 'life' (the external reality it refers to) post-dates the moment of Athenian tragedy, and is 'at least partly the result of a development in the discourse of tragedy' (ibid.). That subsequent 'analytico-referential discourse', as Reiss calls it, is fundamental to our modernity, but had not yet been established when Athenian tragedy first appeared. Recognition of that development prevents us from reading those tragedies in terms incommensurate with their nature. For whereas all discourses of knowledge assume a capacity to communicate meaning, the tragedies themselves represent a world which has lost all access to meaning and truth. By starting here we can avoid thematizing Conrad's relationship to tragedy, and seeking evidence of it in terms of tragic intimations in the content of his novels or his self-conscious echoes of Greek or Shakespearean tragedy, which abound also in the fiction of George Eliot and Thomas Hardy. Instead, we can clarify the affinity between Conrad's fictions and tragedy by situating them within a discursive field at a moment of crisis and profound cultural change.

As Reiss recognizes, post-Athenian tragedies have always been imitative to some extent. Aware of their illustrious antecedents, they have been so conscious of the possible meanings and outcomes of their narratives as to blur Reiss' distinction between 'tragedy' and 'the tragic'. Realism's omnivorous tendency to assimilate earlier genres likewise affects the development of tragedy and the tragic in late-nineteenth-century novels. In George Eliot's *Middlemarch*, for example, the downward career of the middle-class Lydgate conveys such a tragic sense of waste and loss to society as to raise the possibility that this novel is a bourgeois tragedy. The argument for this is that Lydgate's story represents a generic mutation designed to produce in its readers feelings just as painful as those aroused by the powerful narratives of Othello or Oedipus, regardless of the fact that Lydgate is neither heroic nor a military man. Are the stories of Eliot's Lydgate, James' Isabel Archer, and Hardy's Tess or Jude examples of what Lawrence calls 'pure tragedy' or do they operate (in Eliot's phrase) 'below the level of tragedy'?[10] This question reveals the need to broaden our definition of tragedy so that it can incorporate the life experiences of modern people whose culture is not determined by the historical co-ordinates of fifth-century BCE Athens. Because the careers of Kurtz, Jim, Decoud and Heyst resemble the downfall-narratives of Oedipus and Antigone, they can be used to demonstrate the influence of classical tragedy on Conrad. By emphasizing literary continuities, however, such lines of inquiry fail to address the fundamental historical question raised by Reiss: why does tragedy appear 'at certain moments of seemingly abrupt epistemic change', and 'at two such "moments" especially: the fifth century in Athens and the sixteenth and seventeenth centuries in Europe?' (ibid.: 2).

In the nineteenth century the only texts to achieve the literary acclaim accorded to ancient Greek tragedy were Leo Tolstoy's great realist classics, *War and Peace* and *Anna Karenina*. They were intensely debated in twentieth-century Soviet circles. The central question was this: do the insights of Tolstoy's novels outweigh his limitations as a Christian landowner of the Russian aristocracy? In these debates, that is, questions of knowledge and truth were to determine whether Tolstoy was acceptable to the Party in times of rapid social change. The truth at stake here, however, differs from the religious truth on which nineteenth-century controversies about him focused and which were instigated by Tolstoy's own controversial decision to give up writing novels and to search instead for the real truth of Christian teaching. While never resiling from his recantation of *Anna Karenina* as an immoral book he regretted writing, he sometimes relented in the case of *War and Peace*. 'Without false modesty', he confided in his old age to Maxim Gorky, 'it is like the *Iliad*' (Gorky 1919: 57). Modest or not, the comparison draws attention to the fact that the history of Tolstoy's Russia was quite unlike that of the rest of Europe. Its epic struggle to drive Napoleon's armies from Moscow provided material for a modern heroic narrative comparable to the legendary wars of the ancient Hellenic world. More significantly for my present purposes, nineteenth-century Russia almost replicates the conditions for tragedy that Reiss identifies in Athens. Its mid-century moment of crisis was commonly experienced as a 'world turned upside down', since by emancipating serfs it moved abruptly from the protracted feudalism of old Russia into the modern world. If the epic sweep and poetry of *War and Peace* conjure up the heroic world of the *Iliad*, then the later and post-emancipation *Anna Karenina* is more like a Greek tragedy, at least in that half of the novel dominated by Anna.

Anna Karenina can certainly be described as a tragic novel, and not because Tolstoy self-consciously modelled it on the narrative forms of classical Greek tragedy. Unlike English writers such as George Eliot, he did not splice into his novel meditations on the nature of tragedy. By confronting in the story of Anna an impasse so absolute that no interpretation could resolve it, he entered a terrain already occupied by Sophocles and Shakespeare. The inevitability of her death, however, evinces a human drama that has no beyond – an intolerable prospect for Tolstoy as a fundamentalist Christian. His refusal to go on writing novels is almost a sign that he had indeed produced a tragedy, even though Anna's story is counter-balanced by the more hopeful narrative of Levin. Imagining Anna's disturbing situation did not drive him to go beyond the epistemological impasse it produced. Instead, it provoked a frenzied revision of the Scriptures, which led him to found a new Christian religion of his own. In *Anna Karenina*, Tolstoy momentarily articulated the impossibility of naming truth.

Novels that focus on a central tale of woe may be related just as obliquely as tragedy to the history of knowledge, and play a similar role in negotiating a moment of discursive crisis. Conrad's novels in particular can be illuminated by focusing on how they function as cultural forms at specific moments, and in relation to radical discursive change. From that perspective, George Eliot comes closest to classical tragedy in her final novel, *Daniel Deronda*, which goes beyond *Middlemarch* in its open-ended exploration of the unclassifiable Gwendolen Harleth. In creating Gwendolen's character, Eliot drew directly on the diction of contemporary psychology, and even anticipated Freud's discovery of the unconscious. When Conrad left the safe ground of realism, he began writing from somewhere not unlike the tragic space identified by Reiss and evoked in one of Samuel Johnson's remarks on John Dryden: 'He delighted to tread upon the brink of meaning, where light and darkness begin to mingle, to approach the precipice of absurdity, and hover over the abyss of unideal vacancy' (quoted in Reiss 1980: 3). 'Delight' is not the first word that springs to mind when thinking about *Heart of Darkness*. But the idea of treading a fine line between meaning and non-meaning, light and darkness, paradoxically illuminates that problematic text, and enables us to understand both the nature of its power and the evanescent character of its politics.

3 Conrad in England

F. R. Leavis and the distortions of close reading

Geoffrey Galt Harpham has described F. R. Leavis' *The Great Tradition* (1948) as 'the single most influential text in the history of Conrad criticism' (Harpham 1996: ix). Given that Harpham's Conrad diverges sharply from Leavis', his judgement should be taken seriously. It was Leavis' mid-century book that secured Conrad's place on the English syllabus for the next half century. In Conrad's later years, some of his greatest admirers had noted that his reputation was waning: in the era of high modernism, he was beginning to seem a tad old-fashioned. Leavis changed all that, even though his judgements on particular novels attracted as much disagreement as support. Yet Leavis' reading of Conrad also minimized consideration of those themes that are currently regarded as the principal source of his power and appeal: namely, the politics of imperialism and the ideological uses of racial difference. The exclusion of such questions from discussions of literary value shows the power of Leavis' influence. My aim in revisiting the heyday of Leavisism (from the 1930s to the 1950s) is to define the terms on which Conrad's novels achieved 'canonical' status.

The constrictions Leavis placed on his reading of Conrad's work in order to establish its essential 'Englishness' illuminate not only the nature of reading and writing but also the paradoxical subjectivities of both Leavis and Conrad. By insisting both on Conrad's Englishness and on the centrality of moral concerns in his work – in short on his conformity to Leavis' own ego ideal – Leavis protests too much, and possibly overlooks significant elements in himself. Neither his own experience nor the way in which others saw him establishes Leavis as an Englishman of the mainstream. Ian MacKillop, whose fine biography of Leavis (MacKillop 1995) avoids the hagiographic temptations of reminiscences by other former colleagues and students of Leavis, offers us more of a tragic narrative than a celebration of a fulfilling life's work.[1] As in the case of Conrad's own intriguing fictions, the power of Leavis' analysis often resides not in its overt insistences but in those seemingly involuntary exposures that are also self-exposures.

In 1968, Perry Anderson published a sober and much-read essay entitled 'Components of the National Culture' (P. Anderson 1968: 3–57). In attempting among other things to specify the significance of the work initiated by F. R. Leavis and his wife Q. D. Leavis, it inaugurated an ongoing critique of the place of 'English' in both the academy and the wider culture.[2] Anderson concurred with the Leavises that, in the middle decades of the century, native English intellectual culture needed to be rejuvenated. He pointed to the salutary influence on many disciplines of European *émigrés*, such as Wittgenstein, Malinowski, Popper, Gombrich and Klein. The welcome given to intellectual outsiders as an antidote to British insularity had begun in the latter part of the nineteenth century. 'An epoch of expansion seems to be opening up in this country', wrote Matthew Arnold in 1864: 'the ideas of Europe steal gradually and amicably in, and mingle, though in infinitesimally small quantities at a time, with our own notions' (Arnold 1906: 19).

English was in many ways an exception to this tendency. Anderson argued that, by establishing their journal *Scrutiny* in the field of literary studies, the Leavises successfully occupied a vacant space in the national culture. It was vacant because England, unlike Europe and the United States, had failed to develop a discipline such as sociology for analysing society as a totality. University 'English' was to England what sociology was to Germany. Both the ethical inclusiveness of the Leavisian project and its anti-establishment aggression earned from British Marxists a respect that was rarely reciprocated. At the same time, Leavisism helped to shift English studies away from a narrow conception of the literary towards a critique of 'life-values' and society at large. The growth of British cultural studies, which is now resurgent in many parts of the Anglophone academy, can also be traced back through Raymond Williams to elements in the Leavises' programme.[3] Much more, then, would have to be said about Leavis in a full and just appraisal of his achievement. By focusing here on the insularity of his project, I hope to illustrate how literary reputations were created and promulgated in the middle years of the twentieth century.

Leavis made his claim to 'centrality' in the name of specifically English values and traditions. In the inter-war years, when new social classes were being formed and the literate public was broadening, the ownership of cultural authority came to be contested. In the new discipline of English championed by Leavis, pedagogical rigour enabled its proponents to discriminate not only great works from the mediocre but also – thanks to the pioneering work of Q. D. Leavis on pulp fiction (Q. D. Leavis 1932) – literature from popular culture. Leavis argued that literary judgements are irreducibly moral judgements. By melding the moral with the aesthetic, he effectively diluted its content. As a result, 'vulgar' became for Leavis as damning a label as 'evil', strange as that may seem.

The acid test for *Scrutiny*'s claims was the novel, a hybrid form whose roots lie deep in popular culture. Nowhere is this clearer than in Leavis' ambivalent attitude to Charles Dickens, a venerated literary figure who was quintessentially English but also popular and 'vulgar'.[4] Dickens' novels obliged Leavis to refine his conception of the 'moral'. The idea of 'Englishness' likewise became seriously contestable, since its jingoistic potential had to be overlooked. With missionary intensity, Leavis asserted that the values identified by *Scrutiny* were not only transparently true but also normative. But his complicated idealism masked the gloomy knowledge that *Scrutiny*'s values were neither locally nor globally consensual. While different from the values of earlier cultural elites, they were and would remain the property of a closed and increasingly embattled inner circle.

The same ideological fault-line runs throughout British liberalism. It is visible earlier in the work of John Stuart Mill, whose Enlightenment dream of liberty founded on principles of rational justice was applicable only to societies which had already attained a high level of cultural development. The dream excluded, for example, India, from which Mill derived the income that gave him the leisure to write his serious work of philosophy.[5] This contradiction lay at the heart of proverbially Victorian hypocrisy. Victorian morality was two-faced partly because it thought that the mother country was totally removed from the empire that helped to sustain it. In *Bleak House* (1853), Dickens' strained jokes at the expense of that atrocious failure of a mother, Mrs Jellyby, turn on how her philanthropic activity on behalf of ridiculously named tribes on the banks of the Niger cause her to neglect her own family. The expanding empire is reduced here to a trope with which to frame principles of conduct in England. At the same time, however, Dickens' cross-cultural and imperialist allusion performs the deeper ideological work of consolidating those binary oppositions on which the idea of empire depended.[6]

Nowhere is the ambivalence of Leavis' enterprise revealed more starkly than in his attempt to turn the foreigner Conrad into a cornerstone of 'the great tradition' of the English novel. His 1948 book with that famous title was in fact inaugurated in the late 1930s by his *Scrutiny* articles on Conrad, whose novels constituted an overdetermined instance of the need for discrimination. Conrad was a pan-European *émigré* whose dominant subject-matter was imperialism, and whose characters included Englishmen who rubbed shoulders with 'primitive' peoples. Moreover, both the residual elements of popular fiction in Conrad's work and his modernist departures from realistic representation were at odds with Leavis' aesthetic criteria for the novel.

A major effect of the strategies Leavis employed in order to domesticate Conrad's fiction was to repress the narrative of imperialism altogether. His first move was to attack the widely admired *Heart of Darkness*. Following its appropriation by T. S. Eliot, this novel had been read as providing rich mythically and metaphorically charged images for the hollowness or evil of twentieth-century life.[7] Its concern with imperialism was regarded as incidental. Leavis' 'necessary correction' did not involve drawing attention to the novel's intervention in the question of European imperialism. Instead, he simply pointed out that Conrad's excellence resides in the 'concrete' details of his novels and not in their vitiated metaphysics.

Leavis' understanding of realism entailed the voiding of history. He raised no question about whether European realism could be practised in colonial settings by simply applying realist concreteness to new scenarios. At the same time, he forestalled any awareness that colonial encounters might damage the continuities and imagined purity of European or English traditions. His persuasive attempt to downgrade Conrad's most influential work of fiction reveals blind spots which now appear more intriguing than his main line of argument. We might speculate, for example, as to why Leavis had so little patience with Marlow's failure to resolve his confused awareness of the mismatch between the brutal realities of history and the justifying 'idea' that would redeem imperialism from the guilt of its crimes. Was it because Leavis had to resolve comparable problems in his own life? Certainly, whenever he contemplated his own troubled history at Cambridge – where he both 'belonged' and did not and where his own version of a civilizing mission came to be hated – Leavis talked of 'his Cambridge' almost as a Platonic idea, quite different from the real one.[8]

Like the rest of Conrad, *Heart of Darkness* was read for almost forty years in ways that masked its political content as a critique of imperialism. This misreading is not solely the fault of an apolitical interpretative tradition. While Conrad's naturalization led to the denaturing or overlooking of what was alien in him, his desire to be adopted made him complicit in the Englishing of Conrad. Conrad's life and writings, however, are not rooted in any national formation. They are seen more accurately as a long and sometimes painful negotiation of that representative twentieth-century experience, deracination. French readers responded to this Conrad more readily. In a memorial note for *La Nouvelle Revue Française* on the occasion of Conrad's death, André Gide called him the 'perfect example of a man uprooted' (*ce parfait déraciné qu'il était*).[9] Conrad's restless career was marked partly by his desire to compensate for loss, and partly by his determined attempts to establish new roots. Violent swings of feeling and erratic unsettledness accompanied this process. His chronically divided condition is revealed both in his life and in his fictions. Attempts to paper over those divisions misrepresent his case.[10] As everyone recognizes, doubles, dark other sides of the surface personality, misrecognitions and elisions permeate Conrad's fictions. Incidents that seem trivial by the standards of what Raymond Williams calls 'knowable communities' can be painfully significant when they expose sensitive sore spots in outsiders and foreigners (Williams 1973: 165–81).

The year 1910 is often represented as a watershed in Conrad's life and writing. It began with a drastic collapse in his health. Whatever the deeper sources of his 'complete break-down' (Karl 1979: 680),[11] he was undoubtedly anguished by the labour of writing those two tortured European classics, *The Secret Agent* and *Under Western Eyes*. His nervous breakdown on completing the latter laid him low for months and brought him close to death. His gradual recovery and return to writing seem to have been stimulated by an unexpected visit from his old friends, the Hopes, whom he had first met in 'the East', that part of the world which impressed the young Conrad so deeply. Warmth certainly characterizes his recollection, in the final pages of 'Youth', of his first encounter with Eastern culture. No doubt modulated by the wine its older narrator Marlow drinks to lubricate his lengthy tale, Marlow's description is a touchstone of Conrad's attitude to non-Europe:

> We drag at the oars with aching arms, and suddenly a puff of wind, a puff faint and tepid and laden with strange odours of blossoms, of aromatic wood, comes out of the still night – the first sigh of the East on my face. That I can never forget. It was impalpable and enslaving, like a charm, like a whispered promise of mysterious delight . . .
>
> [T]hen I saw the men of the East – they were looking at me. The whole length of the jetty was full of people. I saw bronze, yellow faces, the black eyes, the glitter, the colour of an Eastern crowd. And all these beings stared without a murmur, without a sigh, without a movement . . .
>
> (37, 40)

Charged with sensuous desire, this passage embodies a major component of the orientalist division of East from West – it links Conrad's early writings with the still potent Romantic conception of the exotic East, which was celebrated by Conrad's French and British contemporaries: Paul Gauguin, Pierre Loti and Robert Louis Stevenson. Such writing, which involves an act of remembering, emanates from an earlier and more 'innocent' time in Conrad's writing life, before the 'epistemological break' that resulted in *Lord Jim* and *Heart of Darkness*. Like *The Shadow-Line*, 'Youth' describes a rite of passage and an experience of heightened awareness. More importantly, it tells the tale of a quest that took the young Conrad *away from* the bosom of the British Empire. Enchanted by 'the East', he encountered the Enchanted East. Significantly, the charm of the East which captivates Marlow is broken by an 'outlandish' voice speaking in English. It is a moment of imaginary synthesis.

The long-expected collapse of Conrad's health was triggered by a violent argument with his forbearing literary agent, J. B. Pinker. At the height of this altercation, Pinker enraged Conrad by accusing him of 'not speaking English', a charge that rankled with Conrad long after his recovery. According to his wife Jessie, while he was ill he experienced delirium and paranoia. He would then chatter in Polish, and appeared to be reliving episodes from his childhood. He may even have been speaking Polish to Pinker without realizing it, and have mistaken Pinker's remark for an offensive comment on his heavy accent when speaking English.

Conrad's 'strong accent' remained a sign of his irreducible foreignness and was noted by most people who knew him during his English years. In her memorial tribute on the occasion of his death in August 1924, Virginia Woolf wrote:

> Suddenly, without giving us time to arrange our thoughts or prepare our phrases, our guest has left us; and his withdrawal without farewell or ceremony is in keeping with his mysterious arrival, long years ago, to take up his lodging in this country. For there was always an air of mystery about him. It was partly his Polish birth, partly his memorable appearance, partly his preference for living in the depths of the country, out of ear-shot of gossips, beyond reach of hostesses, so that for news of him one had to depend upon the evidence of simple visitors with a habit of ringing door-bells who reported of their unknown host that he had the most perfect manners, the brightest eyes, and spoke English with a strong foreign accent.
>
> (Woolf 1948: 282)[12]

Seeing that those vocal markers of foreignness are elided in Conrad's otherwise autobiographical portrayals of young British captains, it would have been easy for Leavis to forget that Conrad was not an Englishman. His late essay on *The Shadow-Line* begins by rehearsing a familiar Leavisian theme. Conrad's engagement with English – which Leavis regarded as the essence of Englishness – involved a 'self-committal . . . as inevitable as if he had been born to the language' (Leavis 1967: 93). He concludes another late essay on 'The Secret Sharer' by imagining how its hero's judgement is related to our broader understanding of Conrad the novelist. 'There is no neat or determinate answer', he writes, 'though there is a potent suggestion as to the kind of complex answer a Conway boy who is also an intellectual novelist will have proposed to himself as given by the experience of life' (ibid.: 120). But Conrad was not a 'Conway boy'. He neither looked like one nor talked like one. In his own suggestive metaphor, his relationship to the English language was a matter of 'adoption' (*A Personal Record* v). It was not he who adopted the language, he adds, but the language that adopted him. Virginia Woolf's observation, however, that he became 'our guest', meant that he was never quite 'one of us'.

Misrecognition and *The Shadow-Line*

Leavis wanted to displace the image of Conrad as primarily a novelist of the sea, the tropics, or the merchant marine service. Conrad would have supported that worthy aim. Such crudely categorizing labels ignore the complexity of what Jameson has felicitously called 'the peculiar heterogeneity of the moment of Conrad' (Jameson 1981: 280). Conrad was as conscious of that heterogeneity as he was of his difference from other writers about exotic places. Leavis, however, pursued the narrower project of constructing a Conrad imbued with traditional English values. He read *The Shadow-Line* primarily in terms of moral growth, the celebration of tradition, and (more obliquely) its sterling Englishness. Leavis understood morality to be a more radical and searching activity than mere adherence to a code. In both *The Shadow-Line* and 'The Secret Sharer', he defines the highest kind of moral act as one that allows for – and might even demand – the refusal not only of official moral codes but even of the most sacrosanct values of the community. In this Leavis comes surprisingly close to the severe and radical ethics of Immanuel Kant (Kant 1993: 32–3).

Nor is Leavis' reading of *The Shadow-Line* simply wrong. The motto which precedes the tale – 'Worthy of my undying regard' – applies not to the ship which was the captain's first command but to 'the men of that ship's company' (Author's Note vii). A story of bonding, it held a special place in the author's affections. The book was part of Conrad's personal war effort. His son was perilously engaged in the Great War as an officer, and took part in the Battle of the Somme. The novel which Conrad wrote for those times seems to have taken him back to his own passage from youth through the shadow-line of experience to the command of a ship destined to confront a supreme crisis.[13] The novel to which Leavis responds with such feeling is an intense narrative about an ordeal so stressful that dreams crumble and doubts about human capability are sharpened.

Conrad worked hard to establish clear and unambiguous meanings for those 'few simple notions' with which he said he liked to work. In *The Shadow-Line*, for instance, the strongly positive narrative depicts the young captain's rite of passage from early manhood to maturity, crowned by the acknowledgement of a wise father figure, Captain Giles. Yet this is darkened and deepened by a repressed alternative narrative, which is not the supernaturalism falsely detected by early readers who took the insights of Mr Burns far too much to heart. Nor is it related to the marginalized life of the indigenous Malays and Kalashes of Southeast Asia, who are merely figures in the background in this tale of the merchant marine service. Neither the relationships on board the ship (which in fact are described rather sketchily) nor the exacting circumstances that contaminate the glamour of first command generate the momentum of this tale, which progresses through those oscillations of elation and shame that constitute the captain's subjectivity.

Read with a certain adjustment of attention, the tale now moves at a measured pace, slowly unfolding consciousness rather than events.[14] In its often hypnotic unhurriedness, episodes and scenes such as the becalmed ship are frozen for contemplation. The effect, at times dreamy and remote, is intensified by the way external impressions become locked into the mind of the young captain. This other narrative, which shadows the celebration of a successfully negotiated rite of passage, discloses a story of misapprehension and loneliness, parallax errors and estrangement. When the young man who had mysteriously 'chucked his berth' (and found himself adrift in an Eastern port) enters his cabin for the first time as captain, he is represented both to himself and to Conrad's readers in the form of an image of otherness. Beyond self-conscious awareness, he is caught in a state outside his body, his gaze held by his own reflection:

> Deep within the tarnished ormulu frame, in the hot half-light sifted through the awning, I saw my own face propped between my hands. And I stared back at myself with the perfect detachment of distance, rather with curiosity than with any other feeling . . .
>
> It struck me that this quietly staring man whom I was watching, both as if he were myself and somebody else, was not exactly a lonely figure. He had his place in a line of men whom he did not know, of whom he had never heard . . .
>
> Suddenly I perceived that there was another man in the saloon, standing a little on one side and looking intently at me. The chief mate. His long, red moustache determined the character of his physiognomy, which struck me as pugnacious in (strange to say) a ghastly sort of way.
>
> (53)

In an adult repetition and reversal of the Lacanian mirror-stage, he apprehends his own self-image as a thing detached.[15] When reality intrudes in the form of a crew member, the young captain's everyday unitary self is immediately reconstituted, although in what is now a simulacrum of selfhood. At one level, the captain's experience is solipsistic, in so far as the fullness of being he experiences has little to do with the world outside his own consciousness. His experience is sensuous and psychological, even 'existential', but not at all moral. Such breaks in the narrative flow undermine the gesture made in the opening pages of Conrad's tale to establish its universality as a moral fable. Furthermore, the persistent solitariness of the hero of the story – from the loneliness of his time in port to the proverbial loneliness of command – reveals that *The Shadow-Line* is a study of individual isolation rather than a celebration of the bonding power of work. And when it turns out that the captain's immediate predecessor in the venerable tradition of the service was deranged, an embarrassing break is revealed in the chain of tradition.

Several markers of estrangement dog the narrative. They suggest that the gratitude recalled by the older narrator derives from a memory not of moral triumph but of a brief period of elation when he was welcomed into a group. Those early machinations in the Eastern port, which are misunderstood by the young man and rationalized by the knowing Captain Giles, describe the everyday paranoia of a racial outsider. The truth masked in this tale of personal experience is that what purports to be an essentially English and male experience was lived not by a 'Conway boy' but by a foreigner, who was doubly displaced in being always outside the expatriate collective of Englishmen 'out there'. It was more difficult for the young Conrad to join that inner circle which made up the bonds of the sea and empire (and thus become 'one of us') than he lets on in this moving story. Conrad was so out of place in each of his national identities that he chose to mask an element of his personal experience in composing this novella. Neither a Polish nor an English Conrad will ever quite fit.[16]

Part of Conrad wanted no doubt to belong, especially at a time when patriotism had to be unquestionable. Yet his behaviour and writings during the war years are unusually hard to label. Mismatches appear between his public and private attitudes: his sentiments vary, depending partly on his interlocutor and more particularly on whether he was speaking in an English or a Polish context. One notable English instance was provoked by the execution of (Sir) Roger Casement for treason on account of his alleged anti-British activities in the abortive Dublin Easter Rebellion of 1916.[17] A companion of Conrad in the Congo, Casement had subsequently renewed their acquaintance. No acrimony is discernible in their apparently mutual respect. When Casement was sentenced to death, Conrad was asked to intervene on his behalf. Recalling the stance he then took on the issue, in a conversation some years later, he states with chilling finality: 'Casement did not hesitate to accept honours, decorations and distinctions from the English Government while surreptitiously arranging various affairs that he was embroiled in. In short: he was plotting against those who trusted him' (Najder 1983: 415). Conrad's views on imperialism did not extend to the Irish situation, which he saw as quite different from Poland's long-cherished desire for national independence. In short, he took a British view of Ireland. Another reason may have been that in war time, with his son about to go to the Somme and he a man of European and not English descent, he was reluctant to be involved publicly in such a controversial case. But if certain blind spots in his attitude to British imperialism partly explain his questionable reluctance to help save Casement, his position on that affair does not therefore evince an unequivocally pro-British attitude. Conrad frequently refused to accept honours from Britain, such as a knighthood offered by the Prime Minister Ramsey MacDonald. In doing so, he remained unbound by those obligations of loyalty he felt were owed by Casement.

That Leavis would have difficulty in accepting a non-English Conrad might have been predicted from his famous critique of A. C. Bradley's reading of *Othello*. It is the savagery of the attack – not just on Bradley's criticism, but on Othello's character – that is so memorable. Self-dramatizing, self-regarding and self-indulgent, Othello emerges from Leavis' analysis as an emotional cripple, drastically under-developed. Apart from a muffled comment that 'the cult of T. E. Lawrence has some relevance here' (Leavis 1962: 152), Leavis never mentions the fact that Othello is a non-European, a black no less. A kind of Renaissance forebear of Conrad, Othello too was a traveller in strange places who brought even stranger tales back to Europe. He enchanted his European hosts when he took up residence among them. Unlike Conrad, however, Othello originated in the world outside Europe, and was unable to hide his black face as readily as Conrad could mask his strong foreign accent behind a written text. The black man in Shakespeare's play is represented as the object of superstition and myth: sexually and culturally acceptable within limits, he is useful for certain purposes. Othello has himself internalized this myth. When requesting permission to take his lovely young wife with him to the wars, he stresses to his Venetian masters that this has nothing to do with sexual desire ('appetite'). Interrupted and deferred, conjured up in Iago's imagination and gossiped about in the raciest terms, the Moor's first penetration of the fair Desdemona (II, iii) is kept tantalizingly just beyond the audience's gaze, while the forestage is occupied by rioting, drunken Venetians, most of whom have expressed their desire for Desdemona. Academic criticism did not confront the interface between race and sexuality in *Othello* until the 1980s, when Shakespearean studies responded to the pressure of postcolonial recognitions, and explored aspects of the plays that hitherto had been politely overlooked.[18]

While Leavis felt obliged to stress [Conrad's] foreignness – that he was a 'Pole whose first other language was French' (Leavis 1948: 17) – he fails to examine the significance of that foreignness. Instead, he simply asserts that by choosing to write fiction in English Conrad became 'inevitab[ly]' and 'unquestionably a constitutive part of the tradition, belonging in the full sense' (ibid.: 18). Although, as Francis Mulhern has argued, ethnocentrism was fundamental to the 'governing values of Leavisian discourse', it only rarely issued in racially prejudiced utterances (Mulhern 1990: 250–64). It is discernible nevertheless in patterns of elision, and in Leavis' habit of homogenizing texts whose narrative performances are palpably or even deliberately unstable into enactments of unequivocal and sustained moral awareness.[19] Previously favoured novels such as *Lord Jim* and the other Marlow narratives are dismissed as 'flawed' on account of their staged and vulnerable insistence on the redemptive code of British honour. They are not read as embodying critiques of the ideology of imperialism. Leavis' account of Conrad's interrogation of values is untouched by the fact that Britain continued to maintain a vast overseas empire despite the growing clamour for independence in the 1920s and 1930s.

A sign that Leavis' time was passing was his outburst in the 1960s against the novelist C. P. Snow for proposing that there were two cultures in Britain and not just one (Leavis 1962a). In treating science as a culture, Snow fell far short of addressing the cultural diversity of post-war Britain. But his mere suggestion of cultural plurality was enough to elicit a thundering rejoinder from Leavis. After all, Conradian narrative had been not only appropriated but drastically reduced by the determined monoculturalism of the *Scrutiny* group. The execution of that process in a university that had fostered cultural relativism by housing the Cambridge School of Anthropology was certainly ironic. Q. D. Leavis herself had published an appreciation of one of its founding fathers, A. C. Haddon (Q. D. Leavis 1943: 1–7). Significantly, she emphasized Haddon's academic struggles against entrenched institutional inertia more than his struggle to turn recalcitrant fieldwork data into knowledge of South Sea Island communities. Her enthusiasm for both Haddon's anthropology and a traditionally English way of life is a small instance of the ruse that prevented Western knowledge of the Orient from impinging too closely on the basic assumptions of European civilization.

Although Leavis' championship of Conrad had its limitations, Harpham is right to stress its efficacy in establishing Conrad's reputation. Later, when questions were being asked (particularly in England and Commonwealth countries) about the canon of literary classics, Leavis' Conrad became a site of productive disputation. Whether Conrad himself would have approved of an emphasis being placed on either the solidarity of community or the bond of work under the sign of an august tradition is of course unknowable. But Leavis' warm regard for *The Shadow-Line* is interestingly symptomatic. For what his celebration of the novel leaves out (or represses) is the experience of isolation, of not belonging. This was a feature of Leavis' own life in his beloved Cambridge. Native to the place in which he was always regarded as an unwelcome guest, Leavis in his later years would claim that

> Cambridge . . . figured for us civilization's anti-Marxist recognition of its own nature and needs – recognition of that, the essential, which Marxian wisdom discredited, and the external and material drive of civilization threatened, undoctrinally, to eliminate. It was our strength to be, in our consciousness of our effort, and actually, in the paradoxical and ironical way I have to record, representatives of that Cambridge. We *were*, in fact, that Cambridge; we felt it, and had more and more reason to feel it, and the confidence and courage came from that.
>
> (Leavis 1963: 'A Retrospect'. No page numbers)

The grandiosity of this claim is matched only by Leavis' strange identification with a Platonic Idea of Cambridge, which is related to but radically other than the real Cambridge of class privilege and enormous cultural power. The charged embarrassment of his tortured articulation of that impossible claim provides a glimpse of the tragedy of Leavis' own bleak, yet successful life's work, and his unadmitted pain in achieving it. In other words, Leavis' (mis)reading of *The Shadow-Line* is most interesting at the point where it ignores its controlling directives and registers momentarily an unconscious response to deeper and unspoken elements in the novel. Paradoxically, such a reading also signals the need to go beyond Leavisian habits of analysis.

Remembrance of things past: the old organic society

If a comparatively straightforward story such as *The Shadow-Line* contains traces of its author's characteristically bifocal vision, how could a reader as acute as Leavis represent Conrad as relatively unproblematic? The Conradian texts frequently register the imperfect fit between language and its referents, that is, the 'reality' it refers to, or seeks to 'express'. The contract made by classical realism with its readers depends upon the assumption (or illusion) that words can represent things beyond themselves in a relatively unproblematic way. In stressing the importance of concrete detail in the writing of the best novelists, Leavis appeals indirectly to that contract. This helps to explain why Leavis praised *The*

Shadow-Line but condemned *Heart of Darkness* for being deeply imbued with the linguistic anxieties of modernist poetics.

Leavis was ambivalent on the subject of literary modernism, especially in relation to the novel. The question of language also touched on the different problematic of how to represent the past. Francis Mulhern's analysis of Leavis' attitude to history is again suggestive. 'In this cultural zone', he writes,

> nearly all seasons are bad ones. The imagined time of Leavisian criticism . . . is that of impending loss . . . The meaning of modern history, for Leavis, was the dissolution of 'community' . . . Where once there had been an 'organic' community, there were now two mutually opposed and unequal realities: 'civilization', the world of means and quantities, which drove forward according to the autonomous logic of industrial production, and 'culture', the world of qualities and ends, the memory of a 'human norm' that could never again find general social acceptance . . . This is the past not as history but as 'tradition' . . . Tradition, as Leavis himself noted, is akin to memory . . . [Its] function is to defend identity against the threat of heterogeneity, discontinuity and contradiction.
>
> (Mulhern 1990: 252–3)

For writers, the process of remembering is governed by and articulates their relationship with the past. Leavis' 'tough' moral stance eschewed nostalgic reminiscence and proscribed day-dream longings for the return of past values. That toughness was possibly one source of his lack of interest in *Lord Jim*, whose point of departure is Jim's adolescence, which was dominated by his fantasy longings. But the ever-encroaching threats of modernity gradually transformed Leavis' toughness into the characteristically bitter despair of his writing. He discovered signs of resistance to that despair in certain approved modern writers: Conrad, Lawrence and T. S. Eliot. Admired for their modernist experimentations, they also exhibit a strain of cultural pessimism that happened to coincide with Leavis' own vision of history. In their different ways, and at different stages of their life, all four men lived through the trauma of the Great War. The younger three – Lawrence, Eliot and Leavis – emerged from the debacle to contribute to a powerfully ideological position on the relation of past to present. They believed that the industrialized present, now scarred by the dehumanizing devastations of the Great War, threatened all that was strong and healthy in pre-industrial ways of life. The past invoked by Lawrence in the first half of *The Rainbow* (1915) materializes as the immemorial village and farm life of the English countryside. Eliot's mythical past corresponds either to that fullness of life evoked in *Four Quartets* (1935–42) and still possible in the early Tudor period in England or (elsewhere) to the medieval Christianity epitomized by Dante. Leavis' ideal past was not unlike his 'real' Cambridge, but was even more mythic. It was embodied most explicitly in the notion he developed during the 1920s and 1930s of the 'old organic community'.[20] The nostalgic concept of the 'old organic community', however, does not illuminate Conrad's world-view, even though he scorned aspects of modernity.

One way of grasping this important difference is to recall another contemporary of Conrad whose work is relevant to discussions of modern memory – Marcel Proust. Like his comic counterpart, Jorge Luis Borges' fictional 'Funes the Memorious', the name of Proust is virtually synonymous with the act of remembering.[21] A striking marker of the distance between Leavis and Conrad on this question of memory is Leavis' distaste and Conrad's thoughtful enthusiasm for Proust, the great modern poet of remembrance. The older Conrad's reading, Najder tells us, was for a time

> apparently confined to Proust, who had died on 18 November 1922. In December Conrad wrote a fine note, praising the Frenchman's "veiled greatness," consisting of masterly analysis carried to the point where it becomes creative. Jean-Aubry believed that Conrad, next to José Ortega y Gasset, had been the first writer to have fully appreciated Proust . . .
>
> (Najder 1983: 472)

When Proust died, his English translator, C. K. Scott Moncrieff, wrote to ask Conrad to contribute to a commemorative volume, that was published eventually in 1923. Conrad's reply, as edited for that publication, contains the following judgement:

> I admire him . . . for disclosing a past like nobody else's, for enlarging, as it were, the general experience of mankind by bringing to it something that has not been recorded before. However, all that is not of much importance. The important thing is that whereas before we had analysis allied to creative art, great in poetic conception, in observation, or in style, his is a creative art absolutely based on analysis . . . I don't think there has ever been in the whole of literature such an example of the power of analysis and I feel pretty safe in saying that there will never be another.
>
> (Conrad 1986: 103)

This contrasts starkly with Leavis' characteristic *ennui* on the subject of Proust: 'I don't know that I wouldn't sooner read through again *Clarissa* than *A la recherche du temps perdu*', he commented after remarking that the sheer length of *Clarissa* made such a task prohibitive (Leavis 1948: 4).

Most of Conrad's creative work involved acts of both remembering and analysis. It is therefore not surprising that he responded so readily to that dual operation in Proust's masterpiece, and that he was interested in how process impacted on the art of writing. Even in his earliest works – the 'Malay' novels and most of what he wrote in the 1890s, where his style comes closest to the prevailing realist practices of exotic fiction – Conrad consciously wrestled with the task of converting 'real-life' memories into fiction. Whether representing colonial adventurers from Europe or the domestic life of native villagers in Borneo, Conrad's prose goes evenhandedly about its work of describing some of his earliest experiences of 'the East'. This apprentice period ended with the break that produced *Heart of Darkness*. That too involved an act of memory. But now the personal, emotional and political dimensions of the case elicited a different kind of writing:

> "Youth" is a feat of memory. It is a record of experience; but that experience, in its facts, in its inwardness and in its outward colouring, begins and ends in myself. "Heart of Darkness" is experience, too; but it is experience pushed a little (and only very little) beyond the actual facts of the case for the perfectly legitimate, I believe, purpose of bringing it home to the minds and bosoms of the readers. There it was no longer a matter of sincere colouring. It was like another art altogether. That sombre theme had to be given a sinister resonance, a tonality of its own, a continued vibration that, I hoped, would hang in the air and dwell on the ear after the last note had been struck.
>
> (Author's Note vii)

In Conrad's emphatic phrase, *Heart of Darkness* is 'another art altogether' from those acts of colourful remembering that generated his earliest fictions. It was made possible by his discovery of the power of analysis that he identified in Proust. In order to write *Heart of Darkness* Conrad had simultaneously to occupy the place both of the 'understanding' analyst and of the 'remembering' analysand of those traumatic experiences before which, as he recorded elsewhere, he was a 'perfect animal' (Kimbrough 1988: 195). His response to Proust offers insights into that creative leap which transformed Conrad from a writer of merely exotic tales into the analyst of Europe's empires. These he interrogated through deliberate acts of personal memory that provided him with his subject matter. Unlike Proust, however, Conrad did not make the process of remembering the principal subject of his writing. He thus clearly differentiated his own work from that of the younger writer he understood so precisely and esteemed so highly.

Sometimes Conrad's fictions do indeed include sentimental responses to older times, especially in his tales of the sea. Yet even these tend to be localized rather than coming from a generalized position. In *The Nigger of the 'Narcissus'*, for instance, Old Singleton hankers after the days before steamships replaced the great sailing ships, but he remains marginal to the main narrative. Likewise, in the opening pages of *The Shadow-Line*, the young captain-to-be ruefully regrets that same change: it is important that, for his first command, the ship which he comes to possess as *his* own is a sailing ship. Its beauty accentuates the element of libidinal enchantment and fantasy of the experience. As if to show how desire originates in long-forgotten experiences, the story commits itself to a process of emotional reminiscence. The resonant opening pages link the specifics of memory to a rite of passage, and present what follows as the displaced narrative of a sexual coming-of-age. Significantly, the overlapping recollections of a transition from youth to manhood in the male world of work – expressed in terms both romantic and sexual – were shadowed by a different and more personal recognition: his fathering of a son who now faced the likelihood of death. The effectiveness of *The Shadow-Line* derives largely from the Proustian respect both for the plenitude of remembered actualities and for the analytical processing that directs and shapes their representation.

4 Conrad and Marxism

Theoretical politics: from Williams to Eagleton

The years in which the foreigner Conrad was transformed into an English man of letters began in the 'Marxizing thirties', as Leavis would call them, and continued into the decade dominated by the Second World War. After a brief but tantalizing flirtation with Marxism, in the1930s *Scrutiny* waged a successful academic war against the English version of it. One effect of this victory was to keep political questions out of literary studies for a generation. As Raymond Williams lucidly remarks when discussing *Scrutiny*'s narrative of 'the destruction of an organic society by industrialism and by mass civilization':

> In the 1930s this kind of diagnosis overlapped, or seemed to overlap, with other radical interpretations, and especially, perhaps, with the Marxist interpretation of the effects of capitalism. Yet almost at once there was a fundamental hostility between these two groups: a critical engagement between *Scrutiny* and the English Marxists, which we can have little doubt, looking back, *Scrutiny* won. But why was this so? That the *Scrutiny* critics were much closer to literature, were not just fitting it in, rather hastily, to a theory conceived from other kinds, mainly economic kinds, of evidence? I believe this was so, but the real reason was more fundamental. Marxism, as then commonly understood, was weak in just the decisive area where practical criticism was strong: in its capacity to give precise and detailed and reasonably adequate accounts of actual consciousness: not just a scheme or a generalization but actual works, full of rich and significant and specific experience.
>
> (Williams 1980: 18–19)

The most striking manifestations of *Scrutiny*'s great Pyrrhic victory were clearly interlocked. First, a radically re-formed canon of the best 'English' authors and texts. And second, a pedagogy for reading them with a moral emphasis which, Williams argues, depended upon a peculiarly English combination of blindness and insight. The semantic plurality of Conrad's texts was a casualty of this process which, by repressing both their critique of imperialism and their negotiation of social worlds beyond those of Europe, failed to recognize the impact of such momentous changes on the very idea of a unitary human subject.

The English Novel from Dickens to Lawrence (1970) is Williams' revisionist reading of Leavis' Great Tradition. In addition to appraising the buried historical and political contexts of novels, it opens a space for working-class experience. Its more ambitious successor, *The Country and the City* (1973), questions the universality of those civilized values that Leavis assigns to the English literary tradition by demonstrating their derivation from a disproportionately narrow social world. After exposing the ahistorical fiction of 'the old organic society' and revaluing the country house tradition in English poetry, Williams turns to some of those new writers just emerging from former British colonies whose works were early instances of the phenomenon that in 1989 would be labelled 'the empire writes back'.[1] Williams thus enabled the later project of transforming specifically literary studies into a politically oriented cultural studies. Nevertheless, like other radical English critics of that time, he showed remarkably little interest in Conrad and the politics of imperialism.

Debates about Conrad's politics were immanent in the earliest (private) responses to his work, and always a possibility during those 'Marxizing thirties'. But they did not eventuate until the politicizing decades of the 1960s and 1970s, and when they did they were fought on the contiguous grounds of imperialism and racism. A younger generation experienced the 1960s as a time when pressing issues of the day called for clear-cut political choices and affiliations. Stirred by such major world events as various Cold War crises and the wars of national liberation, the young demanded radical change rather than the nuancing and even-handedness that result in hesitation. Famously, university campuses in Western countries became sites of protest over grievances that ranged from the American war in Vietnam to the English Literature syllabus. To be political was to belong to the Left: anti-imperialism was *de rigueur*. Inevitably, Conrad would be caught eventually in the crossfire.

In British literary and academic circles, a sign of the times was a temporary rift between Raymond Williams and some of his prominent protégés, most notably Terry Eagleton, who was himself a product of 'Cambridge English', although not of its Leavisite wing.[2] Williams was no armchair radical. Yet his endemic intellectual caution – manifest in his chronic hesitations over committing himself to Marxism – tested the patience of that new generation of politicized intellectuals which Williams had been influential in forming. Around this time Eagleton, who was responsive to continental influences, launched an attack on his former mentor, which at one point focused on a remark of Williams' about the Romanian Marxist, Lucien Goldmann:

> Writing of his admiration for the work of Lucien Goldmann, [Williams] comments revealingly: 'The fact that I learned simultaneously that [Goldmann's work] had been denounced as heretical, that it was a return to Left Hegelianism, left-bourgeois idealism, and so on, did not, I am afraid, detain me. If you're not in a church you're not worried about heresies: the only real interest is actual theory and practice'. One can almost see the approving marginal tick of the relieved liberal reader.
>
> (Eagleton 1975: 32–3)

Eagleton's acerbic attack on what he considers to be a disturbing reticence in Williams came at the height of Althusserian influence on Marxist theory in England. By the mid-1980s, however, Eagleton was acknowledging the deep soundness of Williams' stance:

> Williams' work has prefigured and pre-empted the development of parallel left positions by, so to speak, apparently standing still. When structuralism and semiotics were most in fashion, Williams abided by concern with the 'non-discursive' only to see the erstwhile devotees of structuralism rejoining him in their discovery of Volosinov and Foucault. While other materialist thinkers, including myself, diverted into structuralist Marxism, Williams sustained his historicist humanism only to find such theoreticians returning under changed political conditions to examine that case less cavalierly, if not to endorse it uncritically.
>
> (Eagleton 1984: 109)

In retrospect, Eagleton's re-examination of Williams does not depart significantly from his earlier assessment. He merely replaces his charge of 'left Leavisism' with the then more respectable 'historical humanism', although nowadays the change appears more rhetorical than substantive.[3] Eagleton's 'recantation' is largely a matter of tone and gesture. But it restores the image of Williams as a man who holds steadfastly to the true path, an elder statesman who patiently keeps alive an all but lost tradition. The anguish of this transient rift between an eminent academic and his most famous student, however, is less important than the fact that this episode marked a major shift in the discourse of literary studies in Britain, effected by its embrace of continental critical theory.

Throughout his writing career, Williams appealed to 'real history' as the indispensable antidote to historical myths. It was an unusually candid position to maintain in poststructuralist times, when his younger admirers – Eagleton in England, Jameson and Said in the United States – never risked invoking an unproblematic 'real' in the way in which Williams does. The authenticity-effect in his writing derives from his familiarizing strategy of regularly incorporating parts of his own story into that greater historical narrative which it was his life's work to construct. Of the central thesis of *The Country and the City*, he remarks:

> [I]t is as well to say at the outset that this has been for me a personal issue, for as long as I can remember. It happened that in a predominantly urban and industrial Britain I was born in a remote village, in a very old settled countryside, on the border between England and Wales . . . Before I had read any descriptions and interpretations of the changes and variations of settlements and ways of life, I saw them on the ground, and working, in unforgettable clarity.
>
> (Williams 1973: 2)

Despite the 'Welshness' that derives from his border-country affiliations, Williams' emphasis on both personal disclosure and belongingness reveals his strong affinities with English writers such as Hardy, whom he effectively championed against academic patronage, and Lawrence, whom he helped to rescue from Leavisian hagiography. In opposing ruling-class appropriations he affirms a different kind of Englishness from Leavis', and is proudly conscious of being a part of both the history and literary history he surveys. Unabashed about confiding his connections with communal struggle, he identifies with the aspirational tradition of working-class males in ways that empower him to write persuasively and in a distinctive voice. Just as his style is grounded in personal experience, his theory and practice of interpretation depend upon his conviction – maintained against the grain of what became academic orthodoxy – that the real is unproblematical. As evidence of genuine political commitment, such a stance would soon appear at best an obsolete possibility. By the mid-1970s, when political criticism in Britain began coming to terms somewhat anxiously with French poststructuralism, it no longer seemed viable.

In addition to sharing with Leavis the work of refreshing English liberalism, Williams was also a pivotal facilitator in the British reception of continental and Marxist critical theory. He seized on the most vulnerable moment of Leavis' radical transformation of Cambridge English, when its triumphant redefinition of the canon coincided with its dwindling influence. While appropriating both the Leavisite canon and the critical rigour that sustained it, Williams exposed not only its elitism but its original sin against history in propagating the myth of a pre-industrial organic society. Williams substituted for that myth – which in the post-war period resulted in affiliations with reactionary politics that betrayed *Scrutiny*'s early radicalism – a specific and 'real' history of industrial capitalism. In half-a-dozen pages Jane Austen is politely dislodged from her uncomfortable pedestal as foundress of the Great Tradition, and joins William Cobbett and Gilbert White as one of 'Three Around Farnham'. With her novels now incorporated into the narrative of history, Austen acquires significance masked by Leavis' emphasis on literary values separable from historical contingencies.

Despite Williams' disclaimers, *The Country and the City* evinces a revisionist Marxist reading of literary history. Stripped of nineteenth-century triumphalism, and marked by the more sombre stress that Lukács and Jameson put on the discouraging story of reification, Williams' affiliations are clearly with the pessimistic and sceptical branch of the Marxist tradition:

> Capitalism has in this sense always been an ambiguous process: increasing real wealth but distributing it unevenly; enabling larger populations to grow and survive, but within them seeing men only as producers and consumers, with no substantial claim on society except in these abstract capacities.
>
> (ibid.: 82)

Theoretically more sophisticated than Williams, and less troubled by uncertainties in their relationship with Marxism, cultural and literary critics such as Jameson, Said and Eagleton constitute a development Williams pointed to, namely a politically engaged criticism which would successfully negotiate an increasingly evident defect in its inherited practices: Eurocentrism. Williams not only fought for the inclusion of what is valuable in local and even idiosyncratic strands of English radicalism, but also, and to a lesser extent, anticipated developments initiated in countries outside Britain.[4]

The greatest threat to Williams' humanism came from the French Marxist philosopher, Louis Althusser, who questioned the efficacy of human agency. Althusserian structuralism makes literature dependent on ideology, with which it remains unavoidably complicit even when critiquing it. It imperilled both Williams' 'real history' and the cultural tradition he reclaimed for himself, and negated the dignity and efficacy of human struggle. Eagleton's most Althusserian book, *Criticism and Ideology* (1975), locates his oppositional critiques of great writers firmly within a dominant ideological field. Even if they reject ideology, he contends, their refusal of it does not enable their writings to transcend the determinants of their historical moment. Milton and Bunyan 'do not in fact "belong" to "Restoration ideology" at all', Eagleton argues. 'It is equally true, however, that their modes of ideological disinheritance from their contemporary historical moment are determined, in the last instance, by the nature of that moment itself' (Eagleton 1975: 59). When re-reading the writers selected by Leavis and Williams to represent their respective traditions, Eagleton sometimes appears to be describing the historical failure of British bourgeois ideology to resolve its own internal contradictions. At other times he seems to point, like Althusser, to literature's endemic inability to occupy a place outside the 'lived experience' which is inscribed ideologically in the language that nurtures it. The hermeneutic and theoretical activity which constitutes *Criticism and Ideology* is distinctly Althusserian: since art is not Marxian science, it does not aspire to be knowledge, but gives us something else instead. As Althusser puts it:

> What art makes us *see*, and therefore gives to us in the form of '*seeing*', '*perceiving*' and '*feeling*' (which is not the form of *knowing*), is the *ideology* from which it is born, in which it bathes, from which it detaches itself as art, and to which it *alludes*.
>
> (Althusser 1971: 222)

This now classic Althusserian formulation surprisingly echoes Conrad's description of his own aim as a writer of fiction: 'by the power of the written word, to make you hear, to make you feel – [and] before all, to make you *see*' (*The Nigger of the 'Narcissus'* x). Conrad also agrees with Althusser that, although a text can be used for political purposes, it can never know what they are: since *écriture* may produce meanings and enable effects that are completely independent of language, it cannot be responsible for them. Politically and epistemologically, the role of literature is merely ancillary. Even criticism, once regarded as wholly dependent on literature, might come to seem a more effective medium, as A. P. Foulkes argued apropos Eagleton's own writing:

> Eagleton seems to be denying fiction the same degree of detachment from a culturally determined position that was being claimed by contemporary writers of non-fiction. If *The Heart of Darkness* [*sic*] reinforces imperialist assumptions 'to the precise degree' that it questions them . . . then fiction is a weak substitute for such critical works as J. A. Hobson's The Psychology of Jingoism.
>
> (Foulkes 1983: 40)

In his compact diagnosis of this political problem, Eagleton presents some persuasive suggestions about Conrad and imperialism. Nevertheless, they remain locked tightly into an Althusserian grid: all of

Conrad's novels are read in terms of their ideological contradictions and the demands of the 'moment'. To this extent, his 'counter-revolutionary' European novels seem no different from his fiction of imperialism. A contradictory ideological field is shown to determine the limits of Conrad's critique of European imperialism. In his fiction this results in a distancing operation which, by exposing the contradictions without being able to see beyond them, fails to constitute the kind of knowledge that only Marxian 'science' can produce. Thus framed within an Althusserian version of the literary, Conrad is shown to be cognitively limited and politically impotent. Eagleton subsequently changed his mind about many things, especially 'ideology' (Eagleton 1991). But he never modified his evaluation of Conrad.

Marxism and imperialism

Having noted the historical constraints that determined Eagleton's own position in the 1970s, I must now examine a fault line in Marxism's inherited attitude to imperialism, which eventually undermined the 1960s assumption that imperialism is a matter of pre-determined political choices.

In the modern European sense, 'imperialism' describes both a historical process and an abstract concept or category of understanding. It synthesizes various histories and practices that developed over several hundred years, and resulted in Europe's global domination by 'the penetration and spread of the capitalist system into non-capitalist or primitive capitalist areas of the world' (Warren 1980: 3). But in naming both the 'system' and the event, the word also refers to imperialism's self-knowledge, as it were.[5] Most analysts agree that this dual definition finally emerged between 1880 and 1914, that is, during Conrad's working lifetime. The moral and political associations of European imperialism changed radically in the twentieth century, and especially within Marxism, where its connotations became extremely negative.[6] In the mid-nineteenth century, however, the founding fathers of Marxism had accepted a basically Hegelian theory of history, which regarded Europe's imperialist expansion as essentially progressive, and therefore a necessary stage in humanity's self-realization.

In the journalistic articles he wrote in 1853 on British India, Karl Marx evaluated the effects of economic imperialism. More clearly than any contemporary European, he understood that it involved the irreversible destruction of traditional ways of life in other parts of the world. Split between heart and head, his perceptions vacillate between local pain and historical necessity:

These small stereotype forms of social organism have been to the greater part dissolved, and are disappearing, not so much through the brutal interference of the British tax-gatherer and the British soldier, as to the working of English steam and English free trade. Those family-communities were based on domestic industry, in that peculiar combination of hand-weaving, hand-spinning, and hand-tilling agriculture which gave them self-supporting power. English interference having placed the spinner in Lancashire and the weaver in Bengal, or sweeping away both Hindu spinner and weaver, dissolved these small, semi-barbarian, semi-civilized communities by blowing up their economical basis, and thus produced the greatest, and, to speak the truth, the only *social* revolution ever heard of in Asia.

Now, sickening as it must be to human feeling to witness those myriads of industrious patriarchal and inoffensive social organizations disorganized and dissolved into their units, thrown into a sea of woes, and their individual members losing at the same time their ancient form of civilization and their hereditary means of subsistence, we must not forget that these idyllic village communities, inoffensive though they may appear, had always been the solid foundation of Oriental despotism, that they restrained the human mind within the smallest possible compass, making it the unresisting tool of superstition, enslaving it beneath traditional rules, depriving it of all grandeur and historical energies.

(Marx 1973: 305–6)

After scathingly enumerating those manifestations of Oriental 'backwardness' that called for such harsh remedies, Marx ruefully concludes:

England, it is true, in causing a social revolution in Hindustan was actuated only by the vilest interests, and was stupid in her manner of enforcing them. But that is not the question. The question is, can mankind fulfil its destiny without a fundamental revolution in the social state of Asia? If not, whatever may have been the crimes of England she was the unconscious tool of history in bringing about that revolution.

(ibid.: 306–7)

Although this observation has been subjected to a great deal of mainly negative criticism in postcolonial studies, it has never been effectively refuted.[7] Its 'plain speaking' is deceptively elusive on account of that dual temporal perspective which enables Marx to set the tragedy of the immediate moment against an as yet untheorized *longue durée*. The 'truth' of the chronicled events of history, it appears, is now to be measured in terms of those massive shifts in modes of production which take place in something akin to geological time.

Marx never developed a theory of imperialism *per se*. Instead, he interpreted it as merely one aspect of international capitalism. In British colonial activities in India (and presumably elsewhere) he saw the operation of an impersonal system that transcended personal attitudes and impulses. Given that Marx's intellectual heritage originated in the German Enlightenment, his ethical position here might even be described as Kantian. The highest ethical choice, Kant had argued, is not dependent on those emotionally grounded or affective considerations that he called 'pathological'.[8] On the contrary, one does one's duty because it is right, and regardless of the good or ill it might enable (Kant 1993: 32–3). As Marx puts it, England's motives 'in causing a social revolution in Hindustan' are 'not the question'. Although his remarkably 'split' response pits morality against political 'science', it is clear that questions inherent in Marx's analysis remain unanswered to this day. A case in point that I will be examining shortly is Chinua Achebe's mixed feelings when commemorating the communal village life of his grandparents' generation in Nigeria at the very moment of its devastation by European intervention, and the link between this episode and his blunt allegation that Conrad was racist.

Marx's powerful though confused commentary on this matter became openly contentious in Conrad's time, and has continued to be debated. The dominant questions it raises include: the hegemony of Enlightenment values when determining how history should be written; the assumption that European modernity is the destiny of the whole world; the rhetorical authority – even in so informed and corrosively oppositional a thinker as Marx – of Orientalist assumptions and tropes; and a tragic split – almost at the originary moment of the Marxist tradition – between fact and value, progress and compassion. Marx supposedly broke with the Hegelianism of his earlier thinking. Yet whenever he contemplated the relationship between Europe and that 'semi-barbarian, semi-civilized' and 'under-developed' world beyond it, the oppositional terms in which he did so were Hegelian in their asymmetry (Hegel 1956). It is now clear that Marx's treatment of the 'India question' was informed by that faith in the doctrine that ends justify means which came to disfigure much that was done under the banner of Marxism in the twentieth century. His analysis rests on the assumption that a Eurocentric world-view could suddenly be internationalized. The 'sickening' spectacle of a triumphant imperialism, motivated only by the 'vilest interests', did not compel him to reconsider those assumptions. Indeed, his final position on imperialism might even be taken as an affirmative response to the question posed by Marlow's quest in *Heart of Darkness*: can the brutality of the colonizing process be justified by a redeeming 'idea at the back of it'? (51). The nineteenth-century faith in progress that supports Marx's justification of imperialism is considered part of the problem in *Heart of Darkness*. But a more noticeable difference between the two writers is the leitmotif of despair in all of Conrad's colonial novels, right through to *Victory*. The idealism of one moment lurches into the tragic and ironic vision of the next, and with the same dramatic abruptness with which democratic hope in the century of Athenian glory shifted from its zenith to its nadir.

Those flawed origins of the Marxian critique need to be remembered by anybody who tries to define the grounds for a political judgement of Conrad's assessment of imperialism. In the decades leading up to the Great War, both liberals and Marxists felt the need for a far more searching analysis of imperialism and its ideological orchestration. It was answered creatively by *Heart of Darkness* and discursively by the oppositional writings of liberals including J. A. Hobson and Marxists such as Rosa Luxemburg, Rudolf Hilferding and Vladimir Lenin. The latter group broke radically with those founding fathers and their critique often forms the implicit standard against which more recent Marxist critics have judged Conrad. Those who reconsidered the repressed origins of Marx's critique of imperialism have strongly contested the story that it is unequivocally evil and destructive. Against the progressive and secular doctrines of the Enlightenment, its hostility even appeared marked by an older colonial and ultimately pre-colonial polemics. The upshot is that in the uncertainties of the post-Cold War world, political readings of Conrad can no longer be grounded in an assumed knowledge and consensual evaluation of imperialism. This situation, however, presents an opportunity to renegotiate (via Conrad) those unresolved problems in both Marx's analysis of the colonialist subjugation of India and his strained belief in what he thought was best for the subcontinent. This will involve re-examining Marlow's quest for the 'justifying idea' behind imperial conquest, then developing from it a political analysis of Conrad's colonial novels that questions received ideas not only about imperialism and Marxism but also about capitalism.

'Unimitable' Jameson[9]

After escaping the Althusserian straitjacket in the 1970s, Conrad re-emerged in Anglo-American Marxist criticism as a pivotal test case for Fredric Jameson in *The Political Unconscious* (1981). This remains a challenging book. In the prevailing academic climate of the time, however, most of the debates that it engendered ignored Jameson's own recommendation by focusing on his critical theory.[10] 'I would . . . be content', he had written, to have the theoretical sections of this book judged and tested against its interpretive practice. But this very antithesis marks out the double standard and the formal dilemma of all cultural study today, from which *The Political Unconscious* is scarcely exempt: an uneasy struggle for priority between models and history, between theoretical speculation and textual analysis . . .

(Jameson 1981: 13)

Jameson's lengthy discussion of *Lord Jim* in this book remains the most comprehensive political reading yet attempted of any Conrad novel. Far from being merely an illustration of his method – one site of 'the struggle for priority between models and history, between theoretical speculation and textual analysis' – it is the place where Jameson actually resolves that 'uneasy struggle' (ibid.). His Conrad chapter does much more than 'practise theory'. It unveils a new discursive technique, which foregrounds and questions its own modes of operation while meditating at the same time on history, praxis and textuality.

'Meditation' may seem an oddly passive term to use of Jameson, whose erudite work is characterized by the restless and ratiocinative rigour manifest in his penchant for system building. By defamiliarizing Jameson's book I aim to draw attention to its contrary tendencies. Sometimes discernible only as rhetoric and style, they resist assimilation to 'vulgar' and otherwise rigid forms of Marxism. Jameson was Europeanized as a undergraduate student of French and German literature, which exposed him to continental theory more directly than would have been the case if he had studied English. Seeing that he modelled himself academically on European polymaths such as Erich Auerbach and Herbert Marcuse, Jameson has always been hard to categorize in terms of specifically American institutional affiliations.[11] That background gave him the credentials to identify with the *soixante-huitards*, and accounts for his easy-going attitude (reminiscent of the Sixties) towards received structures of knowledge and criteria of proof. *The Political Unconscious* is the perfect instance of 'high Jameson', because it is a work which is neither pure philosophy nor literary criticism, but something else (and perhaps because it is both). Like other path-breaking thinkers of that era, such as Lacan or Derrida (who are interlocutory influences on his own habits of thought), Jameson thinks it is wise to remain open to the possibility that criteria of proof may lie outside even the broadest of those epistemological categories that we inherit. All three challenge the reasonableness of academic discourse by pushing it to the limits so that new kinds of knowledge can emerge. By doing so they threaten the consensus on which the academy depends, and which it needs in order to justify itself to the public.[12] Perhaps Jameson's most extraordinary achievement has been to command respect from an academy he has systematically campaigned against.

Jameson's impeccable pedigree as a high-culture academic was complemented by his Sixties-style openness to popular culture, which he wanted to bring into an academy inclined to define popular culture as 'low-brow'. That conjunction of opposites makes much less surprising his responses to certain theoretical departures from received versions of Marxist literary theory. His development of Raymond Williams' division of culture into dominant, residual and emergent discourses exemplifies how he appropriates other people's models (Williams 1980: 40–2). Jameson seizes on the dynamic possibilities of Williams' model, which flexibly incorporates residual traditions, the governing consensus of the moment, and that potential for change which is always immanent in the unresolved tensions of the present, and sometimes actually present in the activities of marginal or minority movements. Williams' model appeals to Jameson because it combines flexible inclusiveness with a powerful and totalizing structure. The following passage exemplifies how he both used and developed it:

> [The] categories of periodization employed in such readings – troublesome indeed if we take them as exercises in linear diachrony where they seem to generate the usual unanswerable questions about the chronological establishment of this or that "break," this or that "emergence" – are meaningful only on condition we understand that they draw on a linear fiction or diachronic construct solely for the purpose of constructing a synchronic model of coexistence, nonsynchronous development, temporal overlay, the simultaneous presence within a concrete textual structure of what Raymond Williams calls "residual" and "emergent" or anticipatory discourses.
>
> (ibid.: 218)[13]

This brief metacommentary, which simultaneously employs and moves beyond Williams' categories for analysing a period (or in my terms, 'moment') is symptomatic of Jameson's methodology throughout *The Political Unconscious*. His book oscillates continuously between synchrony and diachrony, structure and text, vision and history. Dialectical to a fault, and unembarrassed by its unfashionably Hegelian heritage, it allows no single 'slope' of the analysis (as Jameson calls it) to remain isolated from its other.

Consequently, before evaluating Jameson's interpretative practices, I want to examine some aspects of the theory (or rather system) that structures the hermeneutic model that his reading of *Lord Jim* demonstrates. From one 'slope', *The Political Unconscious* presents an unashamedly Marxist attempt to describe the state of literary theory circa

1980 while foreshadowing the elements of a new political mapping of literary and cultural history. In this respect, one of its most liberating and confronting attributes is the slightly manic and subversive wit displayed in the erudite catholicity of its sources. Its opening sentence – which begins with a thundering call to arms that, Brahms-like, soon dissipates into a modest, self-conscious rumble – almost epitomizes the book as a whole: 'Always historicize! This slogan – the one absolute and we may even say "transhistorical" imperative of all dialectical thought – will unsurprisingly turn out to be the moral of *The Political Unconscious* as well' (ibid.: 9). This initial sally both avows and apparently distances itself from a commonly held view of Marxism by self-consciously paying less attention to its 'message' than to its own intricate and inconclusive methods and strategies. Then as the book unfolds, Jameson's closest intellectual allegiance is not to the most famous Marxist theoretician of the day, Louis Althusser, with whom he contests the central issue of interpretation. Instead, it is to a Jesuit philosopher, Paul Ricoeur, and Hans-Georg Gadamer, a disciple of Martin Heidegger, some of whose work was affiliated with fascism. Ricoeur enabled Jameson to recognize that his own hermeneutics is rooted in the medieval Christian system of biblical exegesis. And from Gadamer he acquired not only his intense commitment to hermeneutic openness but also specific concepts – such as the 'horizon of meaning' that determines every interpretative act – which would become strategically central to his argument in *The Political Unconscious*.[14] These instances of intellectual respect are nothing if not liberatory and anti-sectarian. Their ambivalence is at one with Jameson's productive hankering after 'contradiction' in his political literary criticism. This is manifest in his decision to focus on two writers – Joseph Conrad and Wyndham Lewis – whose personal politics he will openly say are at best conservative and at worst counter-revolutionary. This apparent complication is one that Jameson shares – as he does in other matters – with Georg Lukács.

Whenever Jameson borrows insights from Gadamer or Ricoeur, he does so with the proviso that their apolitical methodologies will need to be completed by re-enclosure within a horizon whose parameters are Marxism and History. This most basic strategy of the Jamesonian system derives ultimately from Hegel. Its ambition is to include all that has been known and expressed in the narrative totality of Spirit, *Geist*, that force which drives humans to achieve both completion and greatness, and whose workings are discernible in every manifestation of human culture. But, as Terry Eagleton has demonstrated, Jameson's Hegel had already been rewritten by the Marxist tradition. Marx himself famously turned German Idealist philosophy on its head when he obviated the need for talk about *Geist* by emphasizing human labour instead, thus rendering its dialectics materialist. But more explicitly influential was that 'great chapter on German Idealism in *History and Class Consciousness*' by Lukács, whose 'breathtakingly audacious gesture there, rewriting as he does the whole of that philosophical history in terms of the commodity', was arguably for Jameson 'a moment of revelation, an intellectual apocalypse one can never go back beyond' (Eagleton 1986: 71).

There is no more appreciative analysis of the already somewhat *passé* Lukács than the one in Jameson's earlier book, *Marxism and Form* (1971). Eagleton discovers in its paradoxical title not only the secret of Jameson's self-presentation as a literary stylist but the surety that he will avoid the dangers of 'vulgar' Marxism by neither prioritizing content over form nor privileging political considerations over everything loosely classifiable as 'aesthetic'. Under Lukács' direction, Jameson steers clear of triumphalist emphases on the Revolution, the Party and the ultimate victory of the proletariat. Instead, he undertakes the exacting task of analysing those contradictions of capitalism which are yet to be played out as the inexorable processes of commodification continue to reify human relationships. In terms of the intellectual structure that governs his own re-writings of cultural traditions and contemporary societies, Jameson's Hegel/Lukács lineage locks him into a powerful and Eurocentric tradition that fortifies him against commonly accepted ethical, metaphysical and aesthetic assumptions. Such is the 'preternatural consistency' of Jameson's work that he would regard it as otiose to revise or update a single sentence in even his earliest writings. It is nicely caught in Eagleton's image of Jameson undergoing something like a religious conversion that left in its wake the consistency of commitment known only to converts.

Jameson derives from Lukács the other powerful pole of his negative critique: the future-gazing aim 'to wrest a realm of Freedom from a realm of Necessity' (ibid.: 19).[15] I have already noted one instance of this Utopian strain in Lukács: his insight that the counter-revolutionary novels of Tolstoy and Dostoyevsky display a deep understanding of the forces that drive History, despite the fact that their particular 'answers' to questions of historical options are misdirected. That interpretative structure, he observed in 1924, typifies the analytical power of the great realists, and underlies the genius of Lenin and Marx:

> *The actuality of the revolution: this is the core of Lenin's thought* and the decisive link with Marx. For historical materialism as the conceptual expression of the proletariat's struggle for liberation could only be conceived and formulated theoretically when revolution was already on the historical agenda as a practical reality; when, in the misery of the proletariat, in Marx's words, was to be seen not only the misery itself but also the revolutionary element 'which will bring down the old order'.
>
> (Lukács 1970: 11)

The great revolutionary analysts of history are able to descry the essence through mere phenomena, and achieve a totality of vision that comes into view only when 'the actuality of the revolution' is felt. The tragic writers who precede such culminating moments – Tolstoy for Lukács, Conrad for Jameson – grasp the social forces that determine it.

Just as the capitalist world order (or, in a different register, 'mode of production') is constantly undergoing internal changes, so too the moment of great realism must pass, and not necessarily with the triumph of the revolution. Both Lukács and Jameson describe the course of the novel as running into a watershed at such moments of change. For Lukács, it is the dead letter of naturalism and socialist realism; for Jameson, the process that drives into the unconscious the high degree of political awareness that Conrad attained in *Nostromo*. That Jameson has a more flexible system than Lukács' is evident in his treatment of those representative novelists he pays most attention to. Jameson's 'new' canon – selected more to demonstrate his thesis of the trajectory of nineteenth-century realism than on purely aesthetic grounds – might be read as a refashioning of the Lukácsian one: his choice of Balzac, Gissing and Conrad is simply a variation on Lukács' narrative of great realism, with Lukács' moment of crisis (1848) deferred to a later date and manifested throughout Conrad's career. As Jameson notes elsewhere, realism is different from other literary genres because it makes a 'claim to cognitive as well as aesthetic status' (Adorno *et al.* 1977: 198). His project is to go beyond Lukács by accepting the demands of this particular totality. 'In practice', he observes, 'an over-emphasis on its cognitive function often leads to a naive denial of the necessarily fictive character of artistic discourse, or even to iconoclastic calls for the "end of art" in the name of political militancy' (ibid.). In the same context, Jameson praises the 'adeptness with which [Lukács] walks this particular tightrope' between the truth-value of realism and its aesthetic quality as fiction. By the time he wrote *The Political Unconscious*, however, Jameson had abandoned his funambulistic metaphor and saw himself rather as engaged 'within a Homeric battlefield' whose complexity goes beyond Lukács (Jameson 1981: 13).

Jameson departs crucially from Lukács in analysing the aesthetic power of the great novelists, and (more importantly) diagnosing it as something more significant than a pleasurable additive to textual meaning.[16] That recognition is consistent with Jameson's valorization of style in his own writing. Although a recent commentator has strangely denied that Jameson's writing is marked by its style, Terry Eagleton is surely closer to the mark in regarding Jameson's writerliness as fundamental to his meaning.[17] The characteristically complex nuances of Jameson's style can be felt as soon as he begins to define the 'heterogeneity' of the Conradian moment:

Nothing is more alien to the windless closure of high naturalism than the works of Joseph Conrad. Perhaps for that very reason, even after eighty years, his place is still unstable, undecidable, and his work unclassifiable, spilling out of high literature into light reading and romance, reclaiming great areas of diversion and distraction by the most demanding practice of style and *écriture* alike, floating uncertainly somewhere in between Proust and Robert Louis Stevenson.

(Jameson 1981: 206)

This relaxed introduction simultaneously delivers a compressed announcement of themes and problems to be elaborated in the next hundred or so pages. It connects heterogeneous elements in Conrad's *oeuvre* with the question of his place in literary history and the challenges that his case presents to both politics and theory. Its nautical metaphor is no mere affectation, since it opens the commentary to the world's great waterways and the fictions they have inspired. More than mere settings for Conrad's own tales, they evoke that geopolitical space of work and empire that constitutes the object of Jameson's gaze. Although Conrad's peculiar generic choices make his writings difficult to classify, they too derive from personal maritime experience at the moment of high imperialism, and create complexities that can be grasped only 'by the most demanding practice of style and *écriture* alike' (ibid.). Jameson's phrase diagnoses Conrad's will-to-style as a product of that heterogeneity. It could also stand as a fair description of Jameson's own writing.

5   Conrad in the postcolonial world

Remembering Sartre

A few months after Egypt's President Nasser had precipitated what
Europeans call 'the Suez crisis' by nationalizing the canal, Jean-Paul
Sartre was asked to contribute an Introduction to Albert Memmi's now
classic text of the anti-colonial movement, *The Colonizer and the Colonized*
(1957). He began by quoting a remark typical of North American racist
discourse: 'Only the Southerner is competent to discuss slavery, because
he alone knows the Negro . . . ' (Memmi 1965: xxi). Sartre went on to
recommend Memmi to all those who are intimidated by this 'criminal line
of reasoning', which lies at the heart of colonial racism. Its powerful yet
specious claim is to speak with the authority of authentic experience.

Although an anti-colonial activist, Sartre did not feature prominently
in the developing discourse of postcolonialism, not even as an influence
or precursor. The politicizing of literary criticism had hardly begun in
the Anglophone academy of the 1950s, when Sartre was the most famous
French philosopher alive. Like the Paris he inhabited, he became the
rallying point for an anti-colonial movement well informed by political
theory and committed to direct action. It is therefore arguable that
Sartre's championing of Albert Memmi, Frantz Fanon and others –
together with his personal commitment to anti-colonial struggles in
Algeria and elsewhere – is an underestimated component of the
academic discourse we now call postcolonialism. Because his theoretical
analysis of the colonial 'system' was inseparable from involvement in
political action, its aims differed significantly from those that characterize
the kind of postcolonial studies which grew and flourished in times of
more muted politics.[1]

Sartre's interventions not only contributed to the demise of French
colonialism but also inaugurated the need to tell its story differently.
Ironically, however, those historical opportunities were marked by an
instant forgetting, because the inequities of the colonial era embarrassed
both the emergent new nations and other countries involved in the
processes of decolonization. From opposite sides of the divide,

colonialists and the anti-colonialists were buttressed by the divisive and essentialist categories that defined them. But those binarisms that structured the colonial world were instantly erased when the victories of National Liberation triumphantly superseded them. Leela Gandhi nicely catches the amnesiac moment between the ending of one order and the birth of a new discourse of knowledge that would claim intellectual ownership of the whole process:

> [P]ostcolonialism can be seen as a theoretical resistance to the mystifying amnesia of the colonial aftermath. It is a disciplinary project devoted to the academic task of revisiting, remembering and, crucially, interrogating the colonial past. The process of returning to the colonial scene discloses a relationship of reciprocal antagonism and desire between coloniser and colonised.
>
> (Gandhi 1998: 4)

Gandhi's book remembers and extends the Sartrean legacy. Her brief and challenging definition self-consciously repeats the Manichean terms that shape Memmi and Fanon's analyses of colonialism. In accepting that colonial relationships could be positively as well as negatively reciprocal, she refines Sartre's powerful insight that '[a] relentless reciprocity binds the colonizer to the colonized – his product and his fate' (Memmi 1965: xxviii). She also undercuts two widespread assumptions in postcolonial studies. First, that the politics of postcolonialism is more important than that of any other area of academic study, because by concerning itself with 'real' struggle and oppression it has a powerful impact on realms outside the academy. Second, that postcolonialism automatically guarantees a political commitment to the cause of repudiating colonialism's injustices. By stressing reciprocity, however, and asking how far the colonized accommodated the colonizer, Gandhi invites us to supplement the well-documented antagonisms that marked colonial relationships by investigating the mutual desires they concealed.[2]

Memmi demonstrates unequivocally the colonial system's power to neutralize 'middle' positions. Equally clear about the psychological complexities that develop in such structures, he refuses to explain them simply in terms of opposition and repression:

> How could the colonizer look after his workers while periodically gunning down a crowd of the colonized? . . . How could [the colonized] hate the colonizers and yet admire them so passionately? (I too felt this admiration in spite of myself.)
>
> (ibid.: x)

These are not rhetorical but real questions that demand urgent answers. Fanon, who was a psychiatrist, goes even further in acknowledging the colonized's psycho-sexual desire for the colonizer. His psychoanalytic approach – which anticipates later developments in postcolonial theory – meets Sartre's humanistic Marxism half way. Basically, Sartre urged France to be true to its highest (revolutionary) ideals by allowing the colonized Algerians to enjoy the same benefits as mainland French citizens. From a different angle, however, his generous and challenging position on this matter might be criticized for advocating cultural assimilation. This is a vivid instance of the ideological limitations enforced by the Algerian 'moment': Sartre's well-intentioned advocacy brought him into conflict even with Fanon. From our perspective, it seems that only subsequent experience could break the impasse created by these theoretical and political contradictions. At that time, the notion of an erotics of colonialism was just as unacceptable to anti-colonialists as it had been to the colonizers. Fanon clearly reveals the distortions produced by an antagonistic model that rigidly demarcated one party from the other, and in doing so induced a postcolonial forgetting. The more that memory misrepresented colonial realities, the harder it became to admit – however tentatively – that relations between colonizer and colonized had always been more complex than is assumed by those who model them in oppositional terms.

Sartre, Memmi and Fanon agreed, however, that only a violent revolution would bring down the colonial system. Violence in the cause of national liberation would reciprocate the original violence of colonization. Both physical and epistemic, it would involve language as much as suffering and death. What motivated their movement and generated the quasi-universal ideology of libertarianism in the 1960s was the hope for a new humanism that would be far more inclusive than a by then discredited liberalism. For instead of liberating humanity, liberal humanism had in fact effaced arguments for revolutionary change. African revolutionaries accepted (however guardedly) both Sartre's support for their anti-colonial struggle and the philosophical idealism he represented, even though its imaginary solution was Hegelian and thus yet another European narrative. At that time, however, Sartre thought it offered the only way out of the impasse of colonial subjection. Even Memmi's Jewishness was affected by colonization, since in colonial Algeria it put him in the impossible position of being neither colonizer nor colonized. As Sartre puts it:

> [C]aught between the racist usurpation of the colonizers and the building of a future nation by the colonized, where the author "suspects he will have no place," he attempts to live his particularity by transcending it in the direction of the universal. The

transcendence is not towards Man, who does not yet exist, but towards a rigorous reason enforcing its claims on everyone.

(ibid.: xxii)

The position Sartre describes here differs from the one occupied by Memmi's doomed 'colonizer who refuses' – whether from inclination or principle – to be identified with colonialism's racist inequities. Memmi thinks that this worthy aspiration cannot be achieved in colonial conditions, since no colonizer can identify with the colonized 'natives'. A perfect example of Memmi's 'colonizer who refuses' is Cyril Fielding, a character in E. M. Forster's *A Passage to India* (1924). Fielding wants to identify with Indians by seeking their friendship. But as long as the colonial structure is in place, this is not a matter of individual choice, because he can never abdicate the colonial privilege which the system bestowed on him the moment he entered India. The only effective course of action for a 'colonizer who refuses', Memmi argues, is to return home. Memmi's own position, on the other hand, seems to have enabled a kind of political agency rather like that advocated subsequently by Homi Bhabha, which involves occupying the subversive role of 'mimicry' or turning colonial 'hybridity' into a principle for action (Bhabha 1994: *passim*).

Anti-colonial struggles escalated throughout the post-war period. The principal focus of attention in the 1960s was the military intervention of the United States in Vietnam, which starkly exposed the fissures created by European imperialism. Both the dichotomous structure of global power and the Eurocentric bias of liberal humanism were constantly attacked. Previously avoided links between politics and theory, and analysis and action, began to be explored. Political resolutions of these divisions would remain incomplete at best, and new forms of disillusionment were to follow the victories of National Liberation. But many problems raised in that now distant time would remain matters of contention. Like Sartre's calls to arms, the 'Sixties' is still invoked as a moment when an engaged criticism, a political practice informed by theory, and a vision of the Revolution incarnate inspired a younger generation to desire the impossible. Its most utopian goal was to terminate the global hegemony of Europe and North America. While the postcolonized and the postcolonizers were working to establish new kinds of relationships, those processes were replicated in the academy as a theoretical discourse of new knowledge. In a remarkably short time, postcolonialism was born, named and assimilated into the global university curriculum.

Sartre showed how left-wing European intellectuals could collaborate with colonial resistance movements in a united front to end colonialism. The link they forged, however, was hardly a perfect fit. The Sartre/Fanon relationship was in part a real-life version of Fielding's failed friendship with Aziz in *A Passage to India* as well as being prototypical of other frictions between allies in the long aftermath of the defeats of colonialism. One point of contention was their different evaluations of the *négritude* movement. Sartre regarded it as just a transient stage in the progress of European humanism. But Fanon could never think of it as merely a 'term in the dialectic':

> I felt that I had been robbed of my last chance. I said to my friends, "The generation of the younger black poets has just suffered a blow that can never be forgiven." Help had been sought from a friend of the colored peoples, and that friend had found no better response than to point out the relativity of what they were doing.
>
> (Fanon 1967: 133)

The gap that separated Western from colonial intellectuals and revolutionaries reappeared in 1975, when the Nigerian novelist Chinua Achebe challenged the reputation of Joseph Conrad. On that occasion the separate spheres of academic literary criticism and real-world racial inequalities collided embarrassingly. In the solemn context of a public lecture, Achebe upset his American hosts by denouncing Conrad as a racist.[3]

Another manifestation of this fault line between potential comrades appeared in 1992, this time in an argument between two left-wing literary theorists, Fredric Jameson and the South Asian academic, Aijaz Ahmad. More in sorrow than in anger, Ahmad challenged the Eurocentric assumptions of Jameson's 1986 intervention in debates about the nature and status of 'Third-World' literature (Jameson 2000: 315–39; Ahmad 1992: 95–122). Jameson had written his influential essay in response to the much-acclaimed work emanating from what was then called the 'Third World'. The significance of such writing, he argues, is commensurate with its inclusion of a dominant narrative of nationalist development. Ahmad objected to Jameson presuming to comment on a heterogeneous body of Third-World writing without knowing much about it. He challenged not only the prescriptiveness of Jameson's evaluative criteria but also his unquestioned assumption that the culture of non-Europe must always and forever be assessed in terms dictated by the West. Ahmad's position in this important essay resembles that of the Subaltern Studies group of Indian historians, whose project is to rewrite Indian history as something other than an episode in the grand narrative of Eurocentric and particularly British nationalism. Ahmad's critique of Jameson's essay could equally apply to the final chapter of *The Country and the City* (1973), where Raymond Williams welcomes writings from the postcolonial world – known in those days as 'Commonwealth Literature' or 'New Writing in English' – as the latest episode in the timeless dialectics of English social and literary history. Although Williams' inclusiveness is well intended, it reinforces the idea that postcolonial literary developments are important principally as subsets of Western cultural history.[4]

In 1987, Benita Parry attempted to counter such criticism by speaking specifically from a 'metropolitan' position. Her hegemonic critique of colonial discourse-analysis was directed mainly against Third-World intellectuals with a First-World education. The deconstructionist practices of poststructuralists such as Gayatri Spivak and Homi Bhabha, she argued, lack the political clout of earlier anti-colonialist polemics (Parry 1983: 27–58). Parry has sustained her own polemic right down to the present time, despite being accused of harbouring a conservative desire for authentic and uncontaminated native voices (Spivak 1989). She may be equally nostalgic, however, for the political clarity and authority that was available to a Fanon in the 1960s, but had then been lost in the subtleties of postcolonial theory. Yet more is involved in such shifts than changing academic fashions.

Such disputes are provoked by the fact that postcolonialism and poststructuralism are not exactly commensurable with one another. For whereas postcolonial theory developed out of the violent divisions produced by Europe's intrusion into non-Europe, poststructuralists have worked to erase the binary thinking that structured colonialism in the first place. These Manichean and divisive terms constantly frustrate attempts to establish a new and inclusive world order. Incursions that began in early modern Europe created a dividing line that reappears with every attempt to re-write their history. Postcolonialism heralds the voices of formerly colonized people, which have greatly enlarged and complicated the language of representation. The assembly of those diverse voices reveals among other things the appalling restrictiveness of colonial epistemology. Whatever his shortcomings, Sartre's recognition of this fact is a measure of his greatness.[5]

Theorizing racism

I wish to return for a moment to what Sartre calls a 'criminal line of reasoning', which attempts to silence those who question racism by disqualifying them from speaking about life in conditions that they themselves have not experienced. As a contemporary Australian academic who is comfortable with Sartre's repudiation of the racist's put-down, I occasionally get into an argument about the Australian 'black question'.[6] Sometimes it is with people from what Melbourners like myself jocularly refer to as 'the deep North', who see themselves as speaking with authority because they have to live daily with the 'problem'. I am easily effaced by the voice of authentic experience, even when it comes from someone who has merely visited those remote places. Postcolonialism has succeeded in getting the question of race put on to the curriculum alongside imperialism. But in doing so it has highlighted several problems that are still unresolved. One raises the question of authenticity: who is entitled to name the racist? A second concerns the so-called 'speaking position' from which authentic knowledge can be voiced – the authorial subjectivity of postcolonial critics, ethnographers, film-makers and writers of fictions.

Claims to authentic knowledge nowadays challenge political criticism by exposing the underlying presuppositions in automatic answers to the question of who is to name the racist. This is not simply a matter of nominating the one who is without sin in this regard. Wearing a badge that proclaims 'I'm no racist' might well signify (in its Manichean assertion of difference) 'I am the real racist'.[7] Embarrassed by this revelation we turn to poststructuralism, which theorizes the relation between subjectivity and its speaking position. Yet sometimes this process appears to be no more than the voicing of an older self-consciousness in a new terminology. That recognition has uncovered new sensitivities. How can one declare any speaking position appropriate without instantly being accused of political correctness? If that dilemma cannot be resolved, attempts at formulating a new political criticism will never get beyond mere relativity.

To substantiate one of Gayatri Spivak's main arguments in her disagreement with Benita Parry, in a gesture of mimicry I too will introduce myself and declare an interest[8]:

> I am an eighth-generation Australian, or more precisely (in current local parlance), an 'Anglo-Celtic Australian'. In my case this hybrid label is reasonably accurate. But it cannot relate me to the oldest type of Australianness (which some call authentic) without repressing a great deal in Australian cultural history. My oldest known forbear was an Irishman transported to Botany Bay as a convict in 1803 and the dominant strain in my genealogy is Irish Catholic.[9] In the 1940s, when mainstream Australia was Protestant in name but already becoming secular, the large Catholic minority was aggressively separatist. We attended our own schools to be taught the religion by nuns, wore distinguishing uniforms, practised medieval religious ceremonies conducted in Latin, ate fish in place of meat on Fridays and were dissuaded from getting too close to 'non-Catholics'. For one religious ceremony, at the age of six I was dressed in a white silk blouse and pantaloons with a silk purse full of rose petals around my neck. I had to kiss these before floating them in the path of a processing statue of the Virgin Mary as I walked slowly backwards

down the church aisle. Inside the church this was fine; but having to walk a mile to get there along a public highway dressed in this fashion made me feel distinctly different. We often expressed our difference as a strong but ambivalent anti-Englishness; less rationally, in our sense of being at once embattled and spiritually superior. Our family seemed to thrive on unquestioning loyalty to a forever losing Labor Party, which nevertheless had its own heroes, Prime Ministers past and gone. The non-Catholic religious services we were forbidden to attend included civil services such as Anzac Day, which we could observe only from a distance because they were taboo. One effect of this is that Kipling's 'Recessional' (1897) is not ingrained in my memory:

> God of our fathers, known of old,
> Lord of our far-flung battle-line,
> Beneath whose awful Hand we hold
> Dominion over palm and pine –
> Lord God of Hosts, be with us yet,
> Lest we forget – lest we forget!
> (Kipling 1964: 76)

Does this anecdote obliquely illuminate my later interest in Conrad, the Vietnam War and postcolonialism? I suspect it might. But it will not help to define my 'speaking position' in the sense in which literary theorists use the term. Perhaps it is a question of collective rather than personal experiences, which might explain why the term 'postcolonial studies' refers to significantly different formations in Britain, Singapore, New Zealand, Africa, the United States – and elsewhere. The same process fragments an ideal Conrad into materially different British, Polish, French and African 'Conrads'. Although each component in such clusters is shaped by a collective and distinctively national experience, none of them is entirely homogeneous. To Terry Eagleton, for instance, 'postcolonial' probably connotes Irish rather than Indian or Australian history.[10] These diversities suggest that current postcolonial theory has set itself an impossible task in attempting to specify the appropriate subject positioning for a postcolonial cultural critic. Until it stops assuming that the terms 'imperialism' and 'racism' refer only to 'Western imperialism' and 'white racism', the ground on which older oppositions rest will become increasingly contested. In the colonial period, the strong oppositions between colonizer and colonized, centre and periphery, European and native generated the astringent and passionate clarity of Fanon, Memmi and Sartre. It is important to ask how far those older experiences have been superseded.

Yet doesn't the great title of Fanon's book, *Black Skin, White Masks*, imply some notion of violated authenticity? The answer may depend on whether we take it to be an oxymoron or a chiasmus. It can of course be read as both. Its binary terms remind us that, like class and gender, race is a category fissured by differences and contrasts. Racial categories are meaningless in isolation, because their markers of difference always serve the function of identification. The drawing of borders encourages operations at interfaces, which result in a dangerous confusion of attractions and refusals. Poststructuralism has taught us that, although the opposition of 'black' and 'white' has powerful consequences, it is merely one of those cultural constructs that William Blake – alert to their duplicitousness – called 'mind-forged manacles'. But isn't Fanon's title also partly essentialist, in so far as skin cannot be put on like a mask, but is something natural whose colour links us profoundly to 'our own people'? What skin and masks have in common, however, is that both mark the interface between self and world. Moreover, they share with language this spatial positioning at the border. All three come together in live theatrical performance, an art form that uniquely mediates paradoxes of representation and presence, the real and the imaginary, surface and depth.

Skin and masks both identify and hide. In performances of Greek tragedy, audiences identified with the hero represented by the mask rather than the nondescript Athenian actor whose face it concealed. Conversely, the mask worn by a terrorist conceals the dangerous face beneath. But skin too can mask as well as identify. In the Eurocentric world, skin-colour is always culturally loaded and may be a strong element in the formation of subjectivities whose identity it masks. Racism is as vulnerably reliant as colonial authority on a frustrated desire to make skin-colour signify identity. Its political and ideological function was to sustain the social cohesiveness of the colonizers. These are the people invoked in *Lord Jim* when Marlow calls its hero 'one of us'. Marlow's insistence on this point reveals anxieties comparable to those engendered by the dizzying dislocations in Fanon's title: black/white, skin/masks; white skin/black masks. The sense of alienation produced by colonialism originated partly in the way in which knowledge was linked to such clumsy and deceptive 'positioning'. In the colonial world, 'white masks' might indicate the hapless plight of 'natives' condemned never to know their rulers. The reverse corollary of that lack is represented by Adela Quested's sad 'quest' in *A Passage to India* to encounter the 'real India'.

During the 1980s, race came to be treated, like gender, as a literary-political problem and best approached by deconstructing the binary thought-processes that had generated traditional views on such matters. Critiques of those ideological formations were produced by people most disadvantaged by them, namely women and increasing numbers of writers and intellectuals in Europe's former colonies. In response to the ever-changing conditions in the 'Third World', postcolonial theory obliged an academy habituated to taxonomical clarity to radically restructure its cultural categories and evaluative systems. How long can we go on thinking of Salman Rushdie or Chinua Achebe as Third-World writers, now that they constitute a multicultural cadre of First-World intellectuals? In their successful careers as international hybrids, have they created a World Literature, completely beyond such old and oppressive oppositions? Who is included in the 'we' who ask such questions? And what is the status in all this of Western self-consciousness? Does Gayatri Spivak's urgent question – 'Can the subaltern speak?' – entail as its corollary, 'Should Western postcolonialists stop speaking'? That possibility is so unimaginable that the question has never been asked seriously by such people.

Some of these questions are embedded in the so-called 'debate' between Fredric Jameson and Aijaz Ahmad.[11] It is arguable that Ahmad misunderstood what Jameson was trying to achieve, in what Jameson himself calls a 'sweeping hypothesis' about 'Third-World literature' (Jameson 2000: 319). When Ahmad complains that Jameson's sketchy analysis denigrates that literature he seems to echo Fanon's protest about Sartre's stance on *négritude*. In replying to Ahmad, Jameson tries to correct that false impression by explaining that his value-judgement was intended to have the opposite effect:

> [I]t seemed important to me to stress the *loss* of certain literary functions and intellectual commitments in the contemporary *American* scene. It seemed useful to dramatize that loss by showing the constitutive presence of those things . . . in other parts of the world.
>
> (Jameson 2000: 315 [my emphases])

That said, another question remains. Are the protocols of argument and proof sanctioned by the Western academy capable of adjudicating in the matter raised by Ahmad? The debate took place under the aegis of international academic standards. Or is his disagreement with Jameson an instance of what Jean-François Lyotard calls a *différend*, that is, a difference incapable of being settled in any one court?

> As distinguished from a litigation, a differend [*différend*] would be a case of conflict, between (at least) two parties, that cannot be equitably resolved for lack of a rule of judgment applicable to both arguments. One side's legitimacy does not imply the other's lack of legitimacy. However, applying a single rule of judgment to both in

order to settle their differend as though it were merely a litigation would wrong (at least) one of them . . .

(Lyotard 1988: xi)

I think it would overstate the case to describe the 'difference' between Jameson and Ahmad as a Lyotardian *différend*, because – like comparable differences between Conrad and Achebe, or Sartre and Fanon – it does not replicate the deeper one between colonizer and colonized. Neither does it approximate the differences between Western-inspired systems of law and indigenous or customary law. Nevertheless, even though such well-aired disputes are likely to be resolved by appealing to Western standards of argument and evidence, the unanswered question is why they are so potent in generating new terms for defining what is at stake on these occasions. Like many of the problems confronted by postcolonialism, racism is imperfectly understood when examined solely through the prism of generally accepted 'rationality'.

Edward Said's modest idea of 'travelling theory' (Said 1983: 226) enables us to address this problem while avoiding the abyss of the *différend*. Primarily concerned with questions of temporal and spatial location, Said's proposal is designed to broaden the notion of a 'speaking position'. By asking 'whether a theory in one historical period and national culture becomes altogether different for another period or situation' (ibid.), Said conflates the Enlightenment ideal of universal and rationally based truth with the contingencies which determine its political function or efficacy. He does not argue that contexts efface the value of a theory 'in itself'. Instead, like Žižek he thinks that the meaning of a text is not immanent in it as an imagined truth but determined by an 'interpretative tradition'. Such an approach does not completely relativize meaning. By encouraging us to read 'against the grain' of the text, it offers alternatives to simply reversing the terms of debate while leaving untouched the binarism that structures it.

In this respect, Jameson was right to point out to Ahmad that the target of his polemical essay is the North American curriculum and its canon. He does not exclude the Third World and popular culture from that curriculum in order to defend the existing canon against contamination. On the contrary, he aims to situate the canonical texts of an older tradition within a richer curriculum, in order to question the politics of canonicity. Students in the United States would thus broaden their literary knowledge by recognizing the cultures of societies other than their own. Given the magnitude of American self-centredness, this is indeed a political intervention. Such a strategy might have a chance of breaking down those value-systems that are buttressed ideologically by the existing canon in the form of cultural capital. But it does not imply that Third-World writers will never make it to the big league, nor does it prescribe what they should be writing about.

Not until the 1980s did the Western academy intensify its interest in the question of racism by investigating its dispersed and sporadic history. There had been no entry for either 'race' or 'racism' in the first edition of Raymond Williams' influential *Keywords* (1976) although a subsequent revised and expanded version included under 'racial' a comprehensive genealogy of terms denoting race (Williams 1983). Noting that the scientific study of race and the ideological practices of racism had been imbricated in one another historically, Williams expresses regret that 'legitimate inquiry' into racial differences had been compromised by defenders of racial superiority. In doing so, he appears locked into older discursive assumptions. Unlike the contributors to Goldberg's *Anatomy of Racism* (1990), Williams continues to believe that an objective and non-exclusive inquiry into the subject of racial difference is possible. Rejecting the widespread presumption that racism is inherently irrational, *Anatomy of Racism* demonstrates that at different stages the study of race has assumed the mantle of scientific theory, philosophical rationality and morality. This revisionist etiology completely displaced those older taxonomies of race and racism that produced what Williams describes as important work. A watershed moment in this history was Hans Jurgen Eysenck and Arthur R. Jensen's work on intelligence differentials between the races, which, while aiming to be both scientific and objective, was deemed so offensive as to create a minor public scandal (Eysenck 1971). Their project probably foundered as much by drifting unwittingly beyond the limits of an older scientific paradigm as by failing to examine its Eurocentric assumptions – although, of course, such a neat separation is difficult to maintain.

Whereas class and gender were analysed with a view to eliminating bias from these social categories, earlier attempts at theorizing race notoriously supported racist rather than anti-racist practices. Attention shifted away from what genetics and psychology had regarded as the irreducible 'fact' of racial difference when a burgeoning cultural studies became the academic locus of inquiries into this topic. In its early stages, this hotly contested domain incorporated linguistics, literary theory, revisionist anthropology and French philosophy. Racism came to be seen not as a thing-in-itself but as a dense network of ideological practices, whose long history is discernible in linguistic usages as well as in gender and class relations. The study of it thus raises previously unencountered problems of representation and interpretation. Neither a discreet nor a discrete field of inquiry, in proclaiming a political agenda of liberation and emancipation it consorts freely with feminism, colonial discourse-analysis and (a little nervously) some forms of Marxism. It aims to track down and expose racism, although not in the name of an older liberalism, whose morality and truth have been shown to be so disablingly compromised that it is part of the problem and not the solution. Nor is it committed to either Eurocentric Marxism or Third-World nationalism. Its affinities are with writers like Fanon, but a Fanon as re-presented (in the aftermath of Derrida, Foucault and Lacan) by Homi Bhabha. In turn it has given postcolonial studies a more urgent and complex political project than simply revisiting and reassessing the old colonial world.

In order to establish a genealogy for the subject and make its archive more accessible, a number of earlier anti-racist publications were re-issued in the 1980s. Written by social scientists, they included the anthropologist Ruth Benedict's *Race and Racism* [1942], the psychiatrist Frantz Fanon's *Black Skin, White Masks* [1952, but not translated into English until 1967] and the Freudian Joel Kovel's *White Racism* [1970] (Benedict 1983; Fanon 1986; Kovel 1984). The writing of these books had involved moving away from a particular disciplinary training and into a new discursive space that not even the most tolerant form of liberalism had imagined. Goldberg's *Anatomy of Racism* includes selections from works by this earlier generation of writers, who perceived that a non-scientistic yet rigorous discourse was needed in order to confront racism adequately. Extracts from Fanon, Barthes, Julia Kristeva and Etienne Balibar testify to the power of the French connection. The new academic gurus of postcolonial studies are identified as Edward Said, Homi Bhabha, Anthony Appiah and Henry Louis Gates, Jr. This group attests to the importance of non-European and 'hybrid' life-experiences in the constitution of the new discipline.

Whether white or black, postcolonial critics must learn how to avoid the traditionally bland tone and comfortable closure of academic discourse, because the colonial and postcolonial texts they analyse deal with human happiness and misery on a global scale. Postcolonial critics who believe that no text is ever innocent or transparent cannot lay claim (as an older generation of academics did) to value-neutral objectivity. Some even include such claims in the process of analysis. Both leftist academics who had felt disenfranchised since the 1970s and a new generation of students disenchanted with politics thought that the world-historical importance of postcolonialism's subject-matter would automatically guarantee them political seriousness. That mood was consolidated after the world-wide defeat of 'the Left' in the closing decades of the twentieth century. Just as in the case of academic feminism, an emergent discourse of postcolonialism in the academy developed a terminology that appeared arcane and a set of manoeuvres remote from such questions as world poverty. Did this mean that realpolitik had been trivialized into 'academic politics', and that while the immiseration of the greater postcolonial world was continuing unchecked the only struggles taking place were over syllabuses, appointments and promotions? Such self-doubt might yet prove fatal to postcolonialism's ambitions.[12]

This leaves a couple of blunt questions unanswered. Was Conrad a racist or not? And is it possible to read his famous literary fiction 'otherwise', that is, from the perspective of the margins? The discursive space in which to answer these questions was lost as soon as Achebe made his accusation (which, if true, would make nonsense of the term 'postcolonial Conrad'). The sudden shift from long-cherished liberal assumptions to a radical questioning of the bases of liberalism itself generated uncertainties about the most appropriate discourse for such an interrogation. From its beginnings, postcolonialism was implicated in this broader development.

Conrad and niggers

The liberal view of Conrad is that he was not a racist because he never engaged with racist discourse. Very early in his writing career he presented himself as conscientiously anti-racist, and sympathetic to the plight of subjugated peoples. This was a moderately controversial stance to take at that time, and somewhat 'oppositional'. He may have impressed his liberal readership as the right kind of 'annexer' of new territories for British fiction. But even though the language of liberal tolerance eventually proved inadequate for registering either Conrad's most potent vision of the world or a radical anti-racism, his early statements on these matters indicate that he was not a racist.

From the start, Conrad saw that his writing mission was discontinuous with settled English social life, and involved speaking for ('representing') non-Europeans. The full implications of that recognition, however, remained to be negotiated. His first exercise in literary criticism was an Author's Note intended for publication as a Foreword to *Almayer's Folly*. Conrad begins by taking up the question of the exotic in the novel which he had subtitled *A Story of an Eastern River*:

> I am informed that in criticizing that literature which preys on strange people and prowls in far-off countries, under the shade of palms, in the unsheltered glare of sunbeaten beaches, amongst honest cannibals and the more sophisticated pioneers of our glorious virtues, a lady – distinguished in the world of letters – summed up her disapproval of it by saying that the tales it produced were "decivilized". And in that sentence not only the tales but, I apprehend, the strange people and the far-off countries also, are finally condemned in a verdict of contemptuous dislike.
>
> A woman's judgement: intuitive, clever, expressed with felicitous charm – infallible. A judgement that has nothing to do with justice.

The critic and the judge seems to think that in those distant lands all joy is a yell and a war dance, all pathos is a howl and a ghastly grin of filed teeth, and that the solution of all problems is found in the barrel of a revolver or on the point of an assegai. And yet it is not so. But the erring magistrate may plead in excuse the misleading nature of the evidence.

(Almayer's Folly vii)

These terse sentiments could be invoked to defend Conrad against even more sophisticated charges of racism. They help to explain, for example, why he gave his narrator Marlow in *Heart of Darkness* traces of racist diction. Yet the first edition of *Almayer's Folly* had to take its chances without them, since that 'Author's Note' was not published until the Uniform Edition of 1923.

I will overlook for the moment the fact that Conrad resorts here (and indeed elsewhere) to chivalrous sexism as a polemical strategy. Aware that he is opening up a controversial field for serious literature, his tone is both anxious and excited. He recognized from the start that his writing would have to be in some respects ethnographic, and that his readers could not be relied upon to accept that mission automatically. He saw this problem as inherent in British prejudices about the non-European world. In writing with muted anger on behalf of unrepresented and misrepresented strange peoples, he anticipates the diagnostic polemics that their descendants would produce in the late twentieth century itself. The racism Conrad identifies in his 'Author's Note' could not be dealt with adequately by the liberalism he expresses. Yet the fact that he explicitly addresses the question of racial prejudice at the outset of his public career shows why his novels would inevitably become test cases in postcolonial analyses of European racism.

Achebe's attack on Conrad opened up a range of interrelated problems. The jury is still out on whether 'we' are now better placed to judge whether Achebe's accusations are justified, although the academic consensus is probably that they are not. Equally contestable is whether 'we' now agree that three hundred years of Shakespearean criticism elided the fact that, far from merely dramatizing 'motiveless malignity', *Othello* is an early exposé of European racism, and specifically its fearful fascination with what nineteenth-century racists came to call 'miscegenation'.[13] If we accept Homi Bhabha's view that to refuse to be fully inscribed within the discourse of the colonizer is one kind of political resistance available to the colonized, should we then privilege textual hybridity and celebrate – after all that has been said and done in their name – the messy novels of Salman Rushdie?

Achebe's tendentious attack was embarrassing partly because it was so surprising. He exposed a problem ignored in even the most politicized analyses of his novels, and did so in a manner that violated the codes of academic civility at a moment when Western academics were unprepared to deal with such transgressions. This is why initially the main participants in the ensuing debate were Third-World intellectuals. A further source of embarrassment was that this cogent and passionate accusation – which sounded like the authentic voice of protest – came from a highly respected and internationally acclaimed African writer. It certainly found its mark: Conrad's caricatures of blacks in *Heart of Darkness* included Achebe's own grandparents.

This was, however, a fleeting moment. The wind of change that empowered Achebe's criticism also stimulated other developments in academic discourse, such as the poststructuralist analyses of language that quickly superseded his trenchant logic. But if Achebe's blunt challenge came to seem unsophisticated in terms of contemporary academic agendas, it presented First-World intellectuals with some still unresolved problems. Can an academy entrenched in the traditions of Western modernity correct Achebe's passionate misreading of *Heart of Darkness* without further reinforcing the hegemony of Western discourse? The same can be said of the view that Sartre's analysis of the political limits of the *négritude* movement was more right than wrong. And something similar can be said of Ahmad's altercation with Jameson: Ahmad makes a reasonable point about Jameson while badly misreading him, and does so because he and Jameson operate in different contexts. The correction of 'error' in many such cases is made in the name of another dominant influence on postcolonial theory, poststructuralism, which regards textual meaning as radically unstable and incapable of being constrained by either historical context or authorial intentions.[14]

Achebe's 'error', then, was to misread *Heart of Darkness* as a stable embodiment of Conrad's political beliefs and attitude towards blacks. *Heart of Darkness* is a text too slippery to be pinned down in this way. It presents through its narrator a series of inconclusive and ironic meditations that neither encourage the need for political action nor merely represent a quietist awareness of the philosophical absurd. What has such a text to do with political change? Not until much later in his life did Conrad describe what went on in the Belgian Congo as 'the vilest scramble for loot that ever disfigured the history of human conscience' (*Last Essays* 17). The political edge of this remark is arguably sharper than Marlow's criticisms in *Heart of Darkness*. But they all sound moderate in comparison with the voices of African anti-colonialists such as Memmi or Fanon, or Achebe himself. In evoking both the early colonial period of *Heart of Darkness* and the contemporary world of neo-colonial Africa, Achebe's own powerful novels straddle the proud but fraught emergence of national liberation.

Achebe charges Conrad with dehumanizing Africans in *Heart of Darkness* by denying them the presence and individuality accorded to European characters in the novel. This happens because they are both under-represented and misrepresented. Anyone tracing Conrad's development as a novelist, however, is likely to think that Conrad's refusal to represent African life fully and directly is precisely what gives *Heart of Darkness* its sophistication, authenticity and power in comparison with the earlier novels. The book admired by literary historians for challenging the old colonial novel's implicit claim to omniscience is read by Achebe as a reductive account by a European of the African world of his own grandparents. Conrad's text contains, but is not contained by, Marlow's limited and prejudice-ridden liberalism. Marlow embodies the liberal-humanist ideology that underpinned European imperialism at the end of the nineteenth century: the civilizing mission, the work ethic, and the superiority of civilized man. In confronting European readers with the inherent contradictions of that ideology, *Heart of Darkness* appears to signal its doom. To that extent, it can be read as a book that takes apart colonialism without being able to imagine what lies beyond it. Only Kurtz is permitted to peer into the limitless darkness of that zone.

This is not to say that Achebe is therefore simply wrong. Unavoidably enmeshed in the wider politics of its afterlife, the text's consistent refusal to fully represent or even name its non-Europeans leaves it open to the charge of treating Africans as less than human.[15] Conrad presents the Congo as a late instance of colonialist intervention, and does not speculate about life in Africa prior to this 'fantastic invasion'. His story evokes a moment of disruption at a fairly advanced stage of European colonial expansionism. Framed by the benighted past of Europe's involvement with Africa and an unimaginable future, its narrative meditates on horrors past, present and to come. Resituated within the ideological context that Conrad shared with contemporary readers, some of the examples Achebe finds offensive yield quite different meanings. The slipperiness and instability of Conrad's text thus becomes available for a different kind of politics.

Marlow's attitudes certainly mimic European prejudice. 'To look at him', he remarks of the native African who was his fireman, 'was as edifying as seeing a dog in a parody of breeches and a feather hat walking on his hind legs. A few months of training had done for that really fine chap' (97). Marlow's racism is hardly negated by his patronizing sympathy. Yet this Marlow, who is more engaged with processes of historical change than with individual entities, directs both his anger and contempt towards the disruptive system that denatures Europeans and Africans alike. And like the Africans, most of the European characters in the tale are also left unnamed, and portrayed as general types.

If Marlow's narrative in *Heart of Darkness* could be said to embody a 'message', then it would be that Africans and Europeans should each stay in their own place: the blacks belong in the 'jungle', while Europeans have advanced beyond that state. At the same time, his ambivalence threatens the ideology of progress on which the European presence in Africa depends for its moral justification. If some sort of Darwinian evolution is implied, the human species is hardly advanced by the activities of the Europeans, whose brutal use of native Africans is challenged not on moral grounds but in terms of wanton stupidity.

Since the essential superiority of white over black is never questioned at such moments, Achebe rightly regards them as instances of racial slighting. But the truth they attest to is merely Marlovian. Shortly after the 'native' attack on the boat, Marlow's sanity and moral sense receive a profound shock with the death of his black helmsman. The disturbed and even schizophrenic writing of this episode privileges Marlow's experience of the event, while at the same time undermining the code of civility to which he clings. Marlow's horror at the death of his helmsman becomes confused with his panicked concern to change his shoes, now uncomfortably clogged with blood. Symbols of civil order (shoes, neatness) appear incongruously in Marlow's mind in his disjunctive moment of bonding with a black man he has unconsciously become close to. At this point of disruptive intensity, the dying African's inarticulateness is transformed into a mute indictment of Europe:

> We two whites stood over him, and his lustrous and inquiring glance enveloped us both. I declare it looked as though he would presently put to us some question in an understandable language; but he died without uttering a sound, without moving a limb, without twitching a muscle. Only in the very last moment, as though in response to some sign we could not see, to some whisper we could not hear, he frowned heavily, and that frown gave to his black death-mask an inconceivably sombre, brooding and menacing expression.
>
> (112–13)

Such moments of stillness in the narrative are at the heart of Conrad's story. They are at least as significant as the narrative climaxes that follow: the encounter with Kurtz, his death, and the (anti-)climactic (non-)disclosure of Marlow's meeting with Kurtz' Intended. The scene of the helmsman's death is dislodged from those ideological formations that frame the narrative quest. It provides a fleeting glimpse of something that Marlow might call 'unmistakably real'. In Lacanian terms, the scene offers an evanescent glimpse of the (unrepresentable) Real.[16]

Achebe's intervention does not allow for the possibility that both black and white can be winners and losers. His own truth-telling ironically benefited Conrad, in so far as it made the reading of Conrad's fiction a far more exciting activity than it had been previously. When he shocked an academic audience with his views in 1975, Achebe ruptured the order of things, just as Conrad himself had done at the turn of the century by publishing *Heart of Darkness*. In the then pervasive New Critical practice of 'English' in the United States, negative depictions of blacks were passed over without comment. Achebe's attack effectively called for equality of representation, which could be achieved only by deconstructing the mind-set that sanctioned the current system of race relations. Instead of being banished from the curriculum (a recommendation implicit in Achebe's critique), Conrad's place was reaffirmed, although with new terms of reference. The close attention given consequently to all of Conrad's writings in turn encouraged readers to deconstruct the binary structures of racist discourse.

Hybridity and mimicry are among the strategies used by Achebe in his own novels about the early European trespass into Africa, *Things Fall Apart* (1958) and *Arrow of God* (1964). Written in English, and laced with Ibo words, they do not profess to represent wholly authentic African experiences. Like Conrad's novels, they participate in an ethnographic project, and have problems with it even though their author is an 'African'. In representing the master narrative of European imperialism, Achebe reverses the relative importance of its chief players. To enter into that other story, Anglophone readers must engage with a text clogged with untranslated Ibo words and untranslatable concepts, practices and assumptions. They find themselves confronted with the contradictions and cruelties of a traditional village life, presented with an anthropological impassiveness never salved by 'sympathy', even though the invading Europeans are shown to be both grotesquely ignorant and lethally effective.

Achebe's mode of presentation is not as different from Conrad's as the virulence of his subsequent attack on his predecessor might lead one to expect.[17] His revisionist evocation of the historical period Conrad wrote about might even be read as a creative dialogue with *Heart of Darkness*. The dialogical strategy of *Arrow of God* is evident in both its use of pastiche and its overt acknowledgement of Conradian ancestry, especially in the chapters that present the life of the British District Officer:

> He would wonder what unspeakable rites went on in the forest at night, or was it the heart-beat of the African darkness? Then one night he was terrified when it suddenly occurred to him that no matter where he lay awake at night in Nigeria the beating of the drums came with the same constancy and from the same elusive distance. Could it be that the throbbing came from his own heat-

stricken brain? He attempted to smile it off but the skin on his face felt too tight. This dear old land of waking nightmares!

(Achebe 1958: 29–30)

Achebe's colonial novels, which negotiate his personal genealogy from the pre-modern and communal life of the Ibo, see and know things that Conrad did not. The fact that Achebe wrote in his own language (English), and with a subjectivity deeply inscribed by the West, precludes the possibility of regarding his voice as authentically native. Like Conrad, Achebe chose to write in English, a choice that enabled both of them to reach a particular readership. When he attacks Conrad, he admits that he does so from his privileged position as an inhabitant of both African and Western cultures, which gives him undeniable advantages. This claim conjures up momentarily the fantasy of Teiresian knowledge. The more sober observation to make, however, is that neither *Arrow of God* nor *Heart of Darkness* can avoid becoming implicated in what Gayatri Spivak calls the constant re-coding of the culture of the West, despite their roles in building modern African traditions. And as Achebe reminds us, that endeavour now takes place in the postcolonial moment, when the discredited imperial past is firmly inscribed in the quest for a global modernity.

Shakespeare's Iago didn't have to explain to his audience why he 'hated the Moor': they knew by simply looking. Like the strange interface of race and sexuality in Othello's unconscionable passion for Desdemona, the disturbing silence of Conrad's dying helmsman points towards that new kind of understanding which we now belatedly approach.

Part II

The great novels of imperialism

6 *Heart of Darkness*
History, politics, myth and tragedy

Above politics?

When the first instalment of *Heart of Darkness* appeared in *Blackwood's Magazine* in 1899, Conrad seemed delighted that his good friend, R. B. Cunninghame Graham, not only liked it but read it as anti-imperialist. This can be used as a corrective to the view that Conrad was deeply conservative, because Graham was a fervid socialist and devotee of Marx, an active anti-imperialist and a founding member of the Scottish Labour Party. 'I am simply in seventh heaven', Conrad wrote back to his friend, 'to find you like the "H. of D." so far. You bless me indeed.' But he added a cautionary proviso:

> Mind you don't curse me by and bye for the very same thing. There are two more instalments in which the idea is so wrapped up in secondary notions that You – even You! – may miss it. And also You must remember that I don't start with an abstract notion. I start with definite images and as their rendering is true some little effect is produced. So far the note struck chimes in with your convictions – mais après? There is an après. But I think that if you look a little into the episodes you will find in them the right intention, though I fear nothing that is practically effective.
>
> (*Letters* 2: 157–8)

This much-read letter reinforces the truism that Conrad's politics are hard to pin down. Even if we take it at face value, all we can say with certainty is that the author of *Heart of Darkness* was comfortable with the idea that his novel might be thought anti-imperialist. As usual when writing to famous or respected friends, Conrad's tone to Graham is characteristically both modest and deceptive. For after agreeing with Graham that his novel is broadly anti-imperialist, Conrad then refuses to share a political platform with him to oppose the British war against the Boers in South Africa. Leaving aside for the moment the question of his complex loyalties to Britain, Conrad is evidently sceptical about political convictions in general and idealistic causes above all.

In alerting Graham to the fact that the complete text of *Heart of Darkness* will contain some 'secondary notions' which he fears will disappoint his political friend, Conrad may be referring to its 'metaphysical' interests, which T. S. Eliot and others thought of as 'beyond' politics. Or he may have in mind other kinds of apolitical tendencies, which were more important to him than Graham's 'practically effective' politics. For in the rest of this very long letter he explains to Graham the exact nature of his own political convictions. Moreover, in choosing to write this part of it in French, he seems to indicate that his political position can be defined precisely only by means of French categories and understandings (Hay 1963: 17–28). The future author of *The Secret Agent* describes himself politically as an *anarchiste*. In the English context, however, Conrad's non-committal proviso makes him appear at least equivocal if not conservative about political commitment. I have already noted how much Conrad's apolitical stance appealed to his mid-twentieth-century supporter, F. R. Leavis, whose preferred novelists tended to keep aloof from 'real' politics. Conrad's response to Graham indicates how readily he could be installed, with whatever distortions and misunderstandings, into an 'essentially' English (i.e. conservative) tradition.

Leavis' attempt to downgrade the widely admired *Heart of Darkness* had two lasting effects. First, it confirmed E. M. Forster's misgivings about the 'central obscurity' in Conrad's writing, which Leavis thought was vitiated by 'adjectival insistence', as exemplified in the repetition of words such as 'inscrutable', 'inconceivable', 'unspeakable' and so on. Conrad's failure to 'realize' the nature of a 'horror' he can only gesture towards is said to be at odds with his 'best' writing, which is marked by 'concrete' details (Leavis 1948: 173, 177). Even the powerful title of *Heart of Darkness* draws attention to this alleged flaw, and manifests the same weakness. Leavis' persuasive line of attack continued to frustrate defenders of *Heart of Darkness*, whether they read it for its metaphysical meditations or as a critique of imperialism. The other immediate and durable effect of Leavis' criticism was to confirm and perpetuate an apolitical habit of reading the twentieth century's most famous literary condemnation of European imperialism.

Before reconsidering the controversial heart of Leavis' case against the novel, we should remember just how responsive he could be to those elements in Conrad that he considered 'concrete' or 'fully realized':

> By means of this art of vivid essential record, in terms of things seen and incidents experienced by a main agent in the narrative, and particular contacts and exchanges with other human agents, the

overwhelming sinister and fantastic 'atmosphere' is engendered. Ordinary greed, stupidity and moral squalor are made to look like behaviour in a lunatic asylum against the vast and oppressive mystery of the surroundings, rendered potently in terms of sensation. This mean lunacy, which we are made to feel as at the same time normal and insane, is brought out by contrast with the fantastically secure innocence of the young harlequin-costumed Russian.

(ibid.: 176–7)

Whatever the shortcomings of Leavis' final judgement of *Heart of Darkness*, they clearly do not derive from his failure to appreciate Conrad's text. This fine example of the old art of practical criticism demonstrates how a rigorous attention to textual subtleties can result in a sense of 'inwardness' with authorial meanings. Leavis' most compelling insight in this passage is that *Heart of Darkness* is preoccupied with something other than 'normal' greed. Furthermore, its juxtaposition of conflicting elements creates a paradoxical world at once 'normal and insane'. But instead of exploring the nature of that ethically and psychically split world, Leavis veers off on his own polemical agenda, which is to reveal that the novel fails to live up to its own best moments by abandoning the 'concrete' for something vaguely metaphysical, and straining unsuccessfully after 'atmosphere'. In the era of postcolonial critique, however, that world which was at once 'normal and insane' came to be identified as the colonial condition, incomparably evoked by *Heart of Darkness*.

In the 1970s, Terry Eagleton accepted Leavis' argument that *Heart of Darkness* is marred by its 'empty adjectival insistence', but developed it very differently by foregrounding political questions, and in particular those concerning the politics of 'the text'. He presented *Heart of Darkness* as a classic instance of the incapacity of any literary text to transcend the ideological determinants of its own historical moment. 'The message of *Heart of Darkness*', he warned a new and politically aware generation that was beginning to read Conrad's novel as a radical rejection of imperialism, 'is that Western civilisation is at base as barbarous as African society – a viewpoint which disturbs imperialist assumptions to the precise degree that it reinforces them' (Eagleton 1975: 135). More damningly, Eagleton contends that this limitation enmeshed Conrad in the same ideological contradictions that his text exposes. His analysis thus endorses Chinua Achebe's view that Conrad's representation of African people reinforces (albeit at a more sophisticated level) the racist disfigurements of imperialist propaganda.

Because Eagleton's insights into this matter have been so highly influential, they form a suitable point from which to investigate the political efficacy of *Heart of Darkness*, which Conrad first took up in his letter to Graham. In one of the few books to address *in toto* the question of Conrad and imperialism, Benita Parry argues that Conrad's 'duplicity' and propensity for paradoxes amount to political fence sitting. She describes Conrad's writing as a 'contrapuntal discourse where the authentic rendering of imperialism's dominant ideological categories is undercut by illuminations of the misrecognitions and limitations in a form of cognition which saw the world in black and white' (Parry 1983: 2). In addition to reproducing Eagleton's position in her analysis of the politics of Conradian interpretation, Parry also accepts Edward Said's emphasis on race in his critique of orientalist discourse. She goes on to elaborate how, 'competing with exposures of imperialism's manichaeism and tunnel-vision, there are fantasy representations' in *Heart of Darkness* 'of the colonial universe seen across a metaphysical divide which act to endorse racial solidarity, invite the closing of ethnic ranks, and confirm western codes' (ibid.). Parry's postcolonial reading of Conrad raises the question of whether the 'duplicity' Eagleton uncovers in *Heart of Darkness* is best appraised from that perspective. Are the classic texts of Western traditions illuminated or distorted when read from the point of view of those excluded from them? A related question bears more generally on the relation between literature and politics: can the necessities of political action be combined with those refined subtleties of human experience on which art seems to thrive? Is fidelity to the task of reading a text accurately and, by being fully attentive to the complexities of its 'weave', compatible with fidelity to a political cause? Conrad's response to Graham's enthusiasm for *Heart of Darkness* shows him to be well aware of these problems. He might even have agreed with Eagleton's political evaluation of his novels of imperialism.

On the other hand, both Leavis' and Eagleton's readings of *Heart of Darkness* suffer from the exclusions they enforce. Each addresses a truncated version of the text, and includes only those elements that are relevant to his political interests. In order to produce a more comprehensive but still political reading of *Heart of Darkness*, we need to take account not only of Conrad's 'position' on imperialism and his representation of non-European peoples but also of those 'secondary notions' which he regarded as important but which Leavis and Eagleton dismissed as weaknesses. To what do they refer?

The indeterminacy of *Heart of Darkness* begins to look different once we recognize that Conrad staged his vision of the last stages of European imperialism in the dispersed and volatile conditions of tragedy. Like Shakespeare's *King Lear*, *Heart of Darkness* depicts a world doomed to imminent ruin – morally, if not materially. The most famous tragedies commonly resist offering clear-cut ethical and political judgements, which is not to say that they embody universal or trans-historical human truths. Marked by their own historical moments, they are as responsive to historicist analysis as other texts. Their ability to juxtapose past and present in a single compelling vision gives them something in common with Marx's *longue durée* of history. Horrors from the 'nightmare of history' – such as the depredations of colonialism, or the Atlantic slave trade and its aftermath – confront a future nothingness in a zone whose governing condition is a state of radical indeterminacy. In that context, *Heart of Darkness* (1899) articulates Conrad's tragic moment. To establish this conception of its meaning involves seriously reconsidering that supposedly empty 'adjectival insistence' which has worried so many critical readers. *Heart of Darkness* has a pre-eminent place in Conrad's work because it attempts to mediate a moment of awareness about imperial subjugation that in certain respects resembles comparable moments in the creation of famous tragedies. Having negotiated it successfully, Conrad opened the way for a sustained meditation on European imperialism, not only in his own fiction – *Lord Jim* (1900), *Nostromo* (1904) and *Victory* (1915) – but also in the work of scores of other authors throughout the twentieth century.

The politics of deconstruction

A familiar historicizing approach to *Heart of Darkness* is to determine what was the political or ideological field it sought to intervene in, which might include debates about imperialism, liberalism and even democracy. 'Liberal imperialism' is a case in point since it generated anxieties that bear upon Marlow's dilemmas. This strange and self-contradictory term appears to have been coined to mediate the harsh realities of imperialist subjugation that resulted from the mid-nineteenth-century liberal doctrine of free trade. Liberal humanism itself came under threat in the 1880s when Britain, in the face of industrial competition from the United States and Germany, participated in what was commonly called the carve-up of Africa at the Congress of Berlin in 1885 (Lichtheim 1971). The humanitarian ideal of a civilizing mission in Africa was used to conceal the by then shameful origins of Empire in military conquest and the Atlantic slave trade. Its idealistic aspirations underwent a new crisis just when Britain was about to reach its high point of imperialism. The great imperialist debates of the period coincided with the near eclipse of the Liberal Party in the 1890s, and the Boer Wars at the end of the century. Such major events are chronological markers of the discursive field in which *Heart of Darkness* intervened.

As Conrad himself saw, it is difficult to make so ambivalent a text as *Heart of Darkness* serve a precise political purpose. Like Sophocles' equally 'enigmatic' *Oedipus Rex*, it has spawned a bewildering range of readings in an interpretative process that shows no sign of abating. While drawing on the forms and emblems of received cultural myths, it complicates things by becoming itself a powerful modern myth. As such, it attracts plausible but mutually contradictory interpretations. And because its content derives from a contemporary site of the 'new imperialism', the Belgian Congo, it is simultaneously readable in what are generally taken to be the incompatible realms of myth and history.

Roland Barthes, however, throws light on the complexities of that relationship:

> The signifier of myth presents itself in an ambiguous way: it is at the same time meaning and form, full on one side and empty on the other . . . When it becomes form, the meaning leaves its contingency behind; it empties itself, it becomes impoverished, history evaporates, only the letter remains . . . [T]he essential point in all this is that the form does not suppress the meaning, it only impoverishes it, it puts it at a distance, it holds it at one's disposal. One believes that the meaning is going to die, but it is a death with reprieve; the meaning loses its value, but keeps its life, from which the form of the myth will draw its nourishment . . . [W]e can say that the fundamental character of the mythical concept is to be *appropriated*.
>
> (Barthes 1972: 117–19)

Barthes does not conclude that the process of emptying out the 'original' content of a myth renders it powerless. A glancing comparison with Freud's semiological system enables him to make a large claim for myth. In Freud, he writes, 'the parapraxis is a signifier whose thinness is out of proportion to the real meaning which it betrays' (ibid.: 120). Although, like the Freudian dream, myth may include visual images, Barthes defines it as essentially linguistic in nature. This leads him specifically to the Freudian unconscious, and more generally to that discourse of psychoanalysis which was contemporaneous with the twentieth-century trajectory of Conrad's novels. Psychoanalysis promises insights into the meaning of *Heart of Darkness* which are inaccessible to the politics of imperialism as traditionally understood.

The mythic character of *Heart of Darkness* enables it to resist political readings principally because no appropriation of a myth can ever be final. Since no interpretation can therefore remain stable for very long, mythic writings are too evasive for the exigencies of political action (or as Conrad put it, to be 'practically effective'). Myth-critical readings of *Heart of Darkness* barely mention its colonialist content, whereas more recently it has generally been read as a classic statement against imperialism, although occasionally – and somewhat less convincingly – as an outright defence of imperialism.[1] The powerful propaganda of Marlow's initial disgust at the wanton devastation wrought by the European invaders is superseded by his increasing fascination with an 'unspeakable' darkness.

To put it another way, the linear river – which enables the 'fantastic invasion' to take place and the loot to be brought back – is bordered by an untameable 'jungle', whose darkness can be read literally, or metaphorically, or allegorically (76). By revealing that language itself is always duplicitous, *Heart of Darkness* subverts realism's faith in the ability of narrative to express truth. This perception then becomes the novel's meaning, in a move that subordinates the colonial content to those broader philosophical concerns that Conrad called 'secondary notions'. No matter how resolutely we regard Conrad's text as essentially 'about' imperialism, its meanings slip and slide. The sordid purpose of the colonizers' frantic activities might be morally 'dark', just as colonization turns the 'white space' of Marlow's old colonial map into a 'place of darkness'. But because 'dark' is both a metaphor for Africa and a descriptor of African skins, Conrad's text refuses to adjudicate between different ideological appropriations of the white/black binary opposition. And so while at one moment the narrative confidently exposes the naked greed of colonialist exploitation, at another it reflects nervously on the impossibility of using language to communicate truth.

Marlow begins his tale by distinguishing a civilizing colonialism from mere conquest, using these terms to distinguish older formations such as the Roman Empire from the enlightened imperialism of modernity (Fleishman 1967: 79–126). But that opposition – like the one between black and white, or civilized and barbaric – instantly breaks down:

> 'The conquest of the earth, which mostly means the taking it away from those who have a different complexion or slightly flatter noses than ourselves, is not a pretty thing when you look into it too much. What redeems it is the idea only. An idea at the back of it; not a sentimental pretence but an idea; and an unselfish belief in the idea – something you can set up, and bow down before, and offer a sacrifice to . . . '
> He broke off.
>
> (50–1)

In the faltering movement of this passage, Marlow seems on the verge of recognizing that if colonialism were not underpinned by racist assumptions and materialistic desires it would not require redemption in the first place. But his tentative thoughts on this matter gradually turn into a brittle rhetoric before breaking down altogether, perhaps under the haunting recollection of Kurtz' nocturnal practices.

Marlow is not merely a 'vehicle' for the narrative in *Heart of Darkness*, let alone a spokesman for Conrad. He is a fully dramatized character, and as such speaks for himself. As a man of compassion, outrage and insight, he is at once a sympathetic apologist for colonialism and also an exacting critic of it. At the same time, Conrad's text clearly and consistently exposes what Marlow himself feels but only imperfectly understands. The intolerable contradictions of his role can be sourced to the fact that the rhetoric of the civilizing mission persuaded Europe to ratify the abomination of King Leopold's Congo: in that respect, 'all Europe contributed to the making of Kurtz' (117). Marlow subsequently experiences abhorrence when he is confronted by the chain gang; but when the 'reclaimed' native guard in charge of it complicitously gives him a 'large, white, rascally grin', he grimly recognizes that he 'also was a part of the great cause of these high and just proceedings' (65).

Marlow's problem is played out through his spiritual journey to find Kurtz. How is he to separate the redeeming idea 'behind' colonialism from its sordidly economic manifestations? Are they simply two sides of the same coin, each either debased or vindicated by the other? Marlow and Kurtz are not considered by their cynical compatriots who run the Company as redeemers sent to atone for the original sin of colonial trespass. Instead, they are disparaged as late arrivals and members of the 'gang of virtue' (79). Both Marlow and Kurtz are deeply compromised by their colonial experiences and their different encounters with the heart of darkness. By the time they meet it is hard to remember that their reasons for being there include a boyhood fantasy in Marlow's case and a susceptibility to Christian altruism in Kurtz'. The temporal ordering that positions them as 'belated' is linked uneasily to the religious notion of atonement. Despite its universalizing appeal, the myth of atonement evinced here refers to two separate moments of colonial history, in so far as the justification comes after the original invasion. Either way, the effect is to neutralize the triumphalist narrative of imperialism. In *Heart of Darkness*, however, the mythic narrative of a triumphant West begins not with a trespass at all, but in an allegedly innocent age of English exploration and romance that coincided in fact with the rise of capitalism, and extended from Sir Francis Drake to Sir John Franklin (47).

At one level, then, *Heart of Darkness* recounts Marlow's loss of innocence. The story of his failed quest for the redeeming idea is framed within a narrative whose origins and borders are as blurred as his own 'inconclusive' tale (51). Drawn into his Congo adventure by the residual force of a boyhood memory, Marlow comes to repudiate the glamour that motivates the fantastic harlequin. Forced into complicity with Kurtz' final nihilistic utterance, Marlow overcomes his repugnance for lying by protecting both Europe and Kurtz' Intended with a lie. Sadly, and in ways he cannot properly grasp, his liberal hopes and Protestant work ethic are exposed as a mere hotchpotch. Like Albert Memmi's 'colonizer who refuses' (Memmi 1965: 19–44), Marlow becomes increasingly irrelevant to what the Congo is all about. The 'redeeming idea' with which his tale begins turns out to be no more than a 'great and saving illusion' (159).

In assigning a radically anti-imperialist meaning to *Heart of Darkness*, this line of interpretation assumes that Conrad succeeded in critically distancing himself from his narrator. But separating Marlow from Conrad does not completely settle the matter. For a start, 'Conrad' is nowhere present in the text as a counter to Marlow – not even as an 'author-effect'. Just as Kurtz 'kicked himself loose of the earth' (144), *Heart of Darkness* is not grounded in the realist novel. Its complete meaning is not enunciated by the Buddha-like Marlow, nor does it issue from a stable cognitive field enclosed by the framing narrative. Its two distinct narrative strands – the representatively bourgeois gathering on the *Nellie* and the narrative-proper of Marlow's Congo journey – simply meld. The inconclusiveness of one matches the uncomprehending silences of the other. Both 'tales' end with their remaining participants gazing mutely into a metaphysical 'darkness', while the actual darkness engulfing London lies ominously behind them. If *Heart of Darkness* can be said to have a 'deep' meaning, it is simply its profound uncertainty of meaning, which cannot be reached by assuming that a realist narrative contract will serve to interrogate the text. Its semantic uncertainty resides in the treachery of its poetry, which constantly hovers between myth and history, and confronts truth telling with the self-conscious duplicity of its own language.

Conrad starts by evoking a remote past in which Marlow discerns the beginnings of modernity: the age of European exploration and early settlement. His language is subtly equivocal:

> They had sailed from Deptford, from Greenwich, from Erith – the adventurers and the settlers; kings' ships and the ships of men on 'Change; captains, admirals, the dark "interlopers" of the Eastern trade, and the commissioned generals of the East India fleets. Hunters for gold or pursuers of fame, they all had gone out on that stream, bearing the sword, and often the torch, messengers of the might within the land, bearers of a spark from the sacred fire. What greatness had not floated on the ebb of that river into the mystery of an unknown earth! . . . The dreams of men, the seed of commonwealths, the germs of empires.
>
> (47)

Marlow's tale is positioned partly as a response to this introductory passage, which rehearses the familiar progressivism of nineteenth-century historians. Its idealism amalgamates post-Enlightenment humanism, the Darwinian narrative of humanity's triumph over the natural world, and Britain's (if not Europe's) glorious destiny as the noble project of modernity. But even at this stage, Conrad presents the *longue durée* of history in terms that cunningly disturb that pleasant dream. The motley crowd of Europeans swarming across the globe carry swords and torches as emblems of both power (conquest) and light (civilization). But these traditional symbols can function properly only as long as the meanings they embody remain stable. The 'fire' in this untrustworthy passage will be qualified when we encounter the fire that Marlow negotiates on his own river journey. The great Promethean 'advance' of fiery torches was in any case always ambivalent: like swords, torches destroy, and although they benefit mankind they can also become weapons of violence and oppression. Just as the rewards of progress – the 'spark from the sacred fire' – are ambivalent, the 'gigantic tale' of Europe's global destiny also falters in its steady progress. Marlow's peroration on '[t]he dreams of men, the seed of commonwealths, the germs of empires' might appear to celebrate imperial expansion. But as a narrative of desire, this movement from 'dreams' through 'seed' to 'germs' represents Europe's penetration of the dark places of the earth as pathogenic. It not only looks back to some mythic Golden Age but also anticipates those 'midnight revels' in which a latter-day 'emissary of light', Mr Kurtz, indulged.

Such indeterminacies are not just rhetorical flourishes that occasionally blur textual meaning. They constantly thwart Marlow's quest for his justifying idea. It is quite possible that Conrad himself wanted to hold on to an 'idea' that would vindicate colonialism. Like Marlow, he might have enjoyed the privileged luxury of scorning the various versions put forward of that idea. But even if it could be ascertained beyond doubt, the question of what ('finally') this novel means would still remain. All we have is Conrad's text, indeterminacies and all, with a Conrad-like narrator at its centre. This raises the problem of how *Heart of Darkness* works as text.

As Jeremy Hawthorn has argued, other texts incorporated into Conrad's narratives sometimes afford precious hints that help to resolve such problems (Hawthorn 1979: 7–36). Like Conrad, Marlow prefers the no-nonsense 'honest reportage' of Towson's or Towser's *An Inquiry into some Points of Seamanship* (99) to the overblown humanitarian rhetoric of Kurtz' Report. Again, however, the ground slips from beneath Marlow's certainty as he muses on this honest, practical book:

> Within, Towson or Towser was inquiring earnestly into the breaking strain of ships' chains and tackle, and other such matters. Not a very enthralling book; but at the first glance you could see there a singleness of intention, an honest concern for the right way of going to work, which made these humble pages, thought out so many years ago, luminous with another than a professional light. The simple old

sailor, with his talk of chains and purchases, made me forget the jungle and the pilgrims in a delicious sensation of having come upon something unmistakably real.

(99)

Sentimental moments like this eulogy over the simple old sailor's involvement in writing a practical book which had no ideological implications are occasionally still taken to represent Conrad's own deeply held convictions. Even if they do, that is not how they are presented in *Heart of Darkness*. For while Marlow is inviting his listeners to dwell on this anonymous and forgotten author's simplicity of purpose, Conrad's text surreptitiously intrudes an echo from the past that would devastate Marlow's purpose, were he to hear it. For the technical terms of measurement used in *An Inquiry into some Points of Seamanship*, 'chains and purchases', conjure up the repressed horrors of the Atlantic slave trade and the Middle Passage, whose efficiency must have depended upon the work of many an 'honest' sailor. In its deconstructive ability to empty words of histories that it then untowardly restores, *Heart of Darkness* undermines idealism by mocking its own narrator.[2]

What is gained and what is lost when the disturbing nightmares of history are displaced into a blank and unnameable 'horror'? When the vividly 'concrete' details of African slavery dissolve into the emptiness of Kurtz' final vision, it is arguable that real cruelty is thereby masked. But before the question of gains and losses can be answered, it needs to be clarified. One way of doing this is to compare the strategies used in *Heart of Darkness* with those of a novel that shows its readers the everyday realities of a world of unimaginable horror.

Speaking the unspeakable

The English author Bruce Chatwin can certainly be considered one of Conrad's spiritual descendants. Chatwin's career as a late-twentieth-century writer of novels and travel books had some interesting parallels with Conrad's. In his extraordinary novel, *The Viceroy of Ouidah* (1980), Chatwin appears to be attempting what Conrad refuses to do in *Heart of Darkness*: to name the unnameable, and speak the unspeakable. In this respect he avoids Leavisite strictures against Conrad for failing to specify Kurtz' 'unspeakable horrors'. The referent Chatwin substitutes for Conrad's visionary 'horror' is the Atlantic slave trade. In one particular African hell-hole, the trade was prolonged well after abolition officially proscribed it. Chatwin's 'heart of darkness' is located in the West African country of Benin, formerly called Dahomey, which is ominously mentioned in the novel's epigraph as the site of horror:

Beware and take care
Of the Bight of Benin.
Of the one that comes out
There are forty go in
SLAVER'S PROVERB
(Chatwin 1980)

The French steamer that took Conrad to the Congo on the voyage that changed his life left Bordeaux on 10 May 1890. It was named the *Ville de Maceio* after a Brazilian coastal town. The imaginary triangle evoked by these names intersects the Atlantic between Europe, the Americas and Africa. Both the voyage and the boat link Conrad with Chatwin, although with a significant difference. For Chatwin's personal journey was the reverse of Conrad's. An inveterate traveller and writer by trade, Chatwin seems to have travelled in order to divest himself of the Englishness that Conrad voyaged to achieve. The wanderlust of both, however, grew from obscure childhood fantasies. At the age of ten, Conrad/Marlow looked through a shop window at the open pages of an old atlas, and conceived the ambition to go to one of the last undiscovered places on earth, the source of the Congo. Chatwin's first book, *In Patagonia* (1977), records his travels to the most distant place he could imagine, led there partly by the attraction of its extreme remoteness, and partly by his childhood ambition to recover the lost brontosaurus. He had once believed that his household contained a relic of this creature, but it turned out to be merely part of a Giant Sloth (Chatwin 1977: 5). Nevertheless, in the language of *Heart of Darkness*, Chatwin might well have imagined himself as 'travelling in the night of first ages' (*Heart of Darkness* 96).

Conrad's outward voyage took him past Dahomey, which was the heartland of slave trafficking until late in the nineteenth century, and the place where *The Viceroy of Ouidah* was to be set. Chatwin originally conceived of his book as a historical biography of Francisco da Silva, who founded a Brazilian colonial dynasty in Dahomey. The nature of the material and the incomplete state of the archives led Chatwin to write the story as a novel, on the grounds that in the circumstances it would be a better medium for reaching the truth. The question of writing – and in particular of the proper lexicon for recording the alien – is raised on the first page, which describes one of da Silva's numerous descendants on the occasion of a family gathering to commemorate the one hundred and seventeenth anniversary of their great ancestor:

Father Olimpio da Silva had come into town from the Séminaire de Saint-Gall. A white-haired presence in a crimson cassock, he stood on the south steps, surveying his relatives through steel-rimmed spectacles and swivelling his luminous bronze head with the authority of a gun-turret.

Not only a priest but an ethnographer by calling, he had attended the lectures of Bergson and Marcel Mauss at the Sorbonne; had published an intricate volume, *Les Sacrifices humains chez les Fons*, and was unable to begin a sentence without a qualifying adverb: '*statistiquement . . . morphologiquement . . .*'

(Chatwin 1980: 13)

The novel describes in gruesome details the everyday life of the old slave trade, whose disappearance is now mourned by the present day da Silvas since it took place in 'a lost Golden Age when their family was rich, famous and white' (ibid.: 14). From the current entropy of the family in Ouidah the narrative moves back into that golden age. Barely tolerated by the Marxist government, their decadent annual ritual is quaintly out of joint in a world of governmental revolutionary jargon, ethnographic mumbo-jumbo and touristic bric-a-brac:

[T]he ladies took no notice: their attention was drawn to the Python Temple where a European tourist was photographing the *féticheur*. The old man stood on one leg, a blue cloth round his midriff, pulling a face of absolute contempt, with the python's head nuzzling his left nipple and its tail coiled round his umbilical hernia.

(ibid.: 16–17)

As the novel slowly works backwards into the nightmare world of Francisco da Silva, Chatwin adopts a narrative tone of unruffled poise: always detached, and occasionally wry or ironic. The polished surface of the writing suspends moral judgements. Unlike Marlow's narrative, which anxiously projects its readers forward to the focal meeting with Kurtz, Chatwin's moves elaborately but calmly and evenly backwards. After spending his early life in the poverty and degradation of Bahia, a focal point of the slave trade in Brazil, da Silva's personal journey takes him to its African source on the 'Slave Coast'. With British connivance, this forgotten part of the globe has managed to evade the civilizing constraints of abolition. The inhumane horrors are muted in the scientistic detachment with which the sacerdotal da Silva had described them in his orientalist book. They are presented in appalling detail as the business-like actualities of hunting down and marketing human merchandise:

The loading was done in the cool of the evening, when the sea was down – the same scene repeated year after year: the ship, the waves, the black canoe, the black men shorn of their breechclouts, and the slave-brands heating in driftwood fires.

Francisco Manoel preferred to do the branding himself, taking care to dip the red-hot iron in palm-oil to stop it sticking to the flesh.

The chains were struck off at the water's edge, so that, in the event of capsize, one man would not drag the others down. Only occasionally, in a final bid for freedom, would one fling himself to the breakers; if, later, his shark-torn carcass was washed ashore, Taparica would bury it in the dunes, sighing, '*Ignorantes!*'

(ibid.: 77)

The numberless black people sold into slavery – or (less efficiently) wantonly tortured, sacrificed or murdered by the monstrous King of Dahomey – are not the main focus of Chatwin's narrative. Instead, the novel paradoxically becomes a sympathetic study of the King's trading 'viceroy', da Silva, who has a bland commitment to the trade he 'took to . . . as if he had known no other occupation' (ibid.: 75). The novel focuses not only on his personal frustrations and extreme sufferings but also on his tender affections and touching loyalties.

Like Conrad, Chatwin also breaks or ignores the grid that separates colonizer from colonized, and models their relationships exclusively in terms of European exploitation versus non-European victimization. By eschewing the languages of compassion and moral outrage, and speaking the unspeakable, Chatwin's text enters that void in Conrad's novel which encases Kurtz, and whose all-devouring maw would engulf the world. Both the nihilism of Marlow's decision or 'choice' for Kurtz and the postmodernism of Chatwinesque style are disavowals that make the quest for transcendental truth or justification seem 'hollow'. As many readers have observed, the horror of Marlow's search is revealed neither in his anti-climactic meeting with Kurtz at the end-point of his journey nor in his self-incriminating and even more bathetic lie to the Intended. Instead, it is 'encountered' in the form of failed encounters at various stages along the way: in the grove of death, for instance, when the hand of a starving black closes slowly over the biscuit Marlow gives him, or at the moment when his black helmsman dies. It may even have gone unremarked when the outward-bound French ship Marlow was on steamed past the coast of Dahomey.

The problem of setting the terms for a new political reading of *Heart of Darkness* is of course not resolved simply by comparing Conrad with Chatwin, whose horrifying vision is merely one of many attempts to specify those horrors of colonialism that Conrad does not name. If revealing 'concrete images' might have distinct advantages over 'empty' adjectives, such a comparison would support Leavis' objections to Conrad's style. The fact remains, however, that the 'horror' Kurtz sees is not the vicious enslavement of blacks any more than it is the specific and different European horror of 'miscegenation', the future so-called 'quagmire' of Vietnam, or even a prophetic vision of AIDS.[3] It is both less and more than the contents of such narratives. The unanswered challenge posed by *Heart of Darkness* is not to decide exactly what Conrad is referring to in the phrase, 'The horror! The horror!' (149) but to determine how the deconstructive activity of the text generates potent and polysemic images. Conrad told Graham that he liked to work with 'definite images'. One such image juxtaposes the civilized efficiencies of the Central Station, exemplified by the manager, the 'papier-mâché Mephistopheles' (81), with the grove of death; another is the groans of the 'nigger' being beaten for his 'responsibility' for the fire (76). Since both images show how the moral basis of colonial authority has collapsed, the binary terms that structure its language are here turned against the colonizers. The Kenyan novelist, Ngugi Wa Thiong'o, points to another unforgettable image in the novel: the skulls on poles facing Kurtz' house. No African writer, he said, 'had created so ironic, apt, and powerful an image' of the moral failure of European colonization (Kimbrough 1988: 285). Ngugi is well aware of both the political limits of Western self-recognition and its rarity. Conrad's success in *Heart of Darkness* was to infiltrate the idea of failure into an ideological frame that allowed no space for it.

The Lacanian Thing

The image of the skulls on poles works in complex and uncontainable ways, and embodies meanings that provoke political and ethical questions. Minimally, it exposes a violent and sadistic underside of the civilizing mission. Its macabre suggestions of veneration reveal a spiritual sickness that is systemic. A complementary and equally symbolic image is that of the emaciated Kurtz, desperately crawling through the 'jungle' towards the lights and drum-beats of whatever black ritual is going on beyond the colonial compound (140–5). The linear structure of *Heart of Darkness* draws both Marlow and Conrad's readers ever closer to Kurtz, tracks him exactly to the point where he had been, and to where he desires to return. We, however, are not permitted to see what is both literally and metaphysically beyond the colonial outpost, so that this climactic episode in the events of Kurtz' life becomes an anti-climactic moment in the narrative of them. It certainly disappoints the readerly expectations satisfied by traditional conventions such as tragic catharsis or realist closure. But if the question of this emptiness is raised in a different discursive domain from that of literary theory – which belongs to what Lacan calls the 'discourse of the university' – Conrad's 'adjectival insistence' takes on other meanings.[4] By relocating the text in this way, we also get an opportunity to answer a question raised implicitly and explicitly in the 1990s, namely, what can a Lacanian reading of *Heart of Darkness* tell us about the politics of imperialism?[5]

A Lacanian analysis helps to restore to the narrative elements such as Conrad's 'secondary notions', which politicizing readers excluded as irrelevant. But it must be conducted with Lacan's important caveat in mind:

> If I were not to have taught you anything more than an implacable method for the analysis of signifiers, then it would not have been in vain . . . If it is true that what I teach represents a body of thought, I will not leave behind me any of those handles which will enable you to append a suffix in the form of an '-ism'.
>
> (Lacan 1992: 251)

This cautionary note appears in *The Ethics of Psychoanalysis: Seminar VII* (1959–60), which has only recently attracted the attention of Anglophone literary analysts (Rabaté 2001). The fact that the seminar was prompted by Freud's later writings, which introduce his concept of the 'death drive' and include the suggestively titled *Civilization and its Discontents* (1933), makes it a good place from which to start re-reading *Heart of Darkness*. As one of Lacan's most literary seminars, *The Ethics of Psychoanalysis* draws extensively on canonical literary and philosophical texts from Aristotle to Kant and de Sade, and touches on the courtly-love lyricists, the English 'metaphysical' poets and Shakespeare's *King Lear*. It also develops a challenging theory of tragedy and elaborates a detailed and strikingly original reading of Sophocles' *Antigone*. Lacan argues that psychoanalysis should resist using the 'good' as a test for ethical behaviour. Tragedy and psychoanalysis, he maintains, are deeply implicated in one another, and Sophocles' Antigone has a central position in Lacan's radically different ethics. While using her example to resist those everyday codes that regulate behaviour in civilized society, Lacan insists that the ethics he is proposing is ineluctably binding. Although Lacanian ethics is not designed to be universalist, its injunctions are binding not only for the heroes and heroines of tragedy but also for those who embark – as both analyst and analysand – on the treacherous journey of analysis.[6]

Two elements in Lacan's complex analysis of *Antigone* are immediately suggestive in terms of *Heart of Darkness*. One is his use of the strange Greek concept of *Até*, that state of radical disarray or confusion that leads to destruction and ruin, and is equivalent to a 'break-down'. In Lacan's reading of Sophocles' tragedy, Antigone's *éclat* becomes most potent for the audience when they follow her in her desire to 'go beyond' *Até*, to her death no less. From the moment Antigone embarks on her quest to defy the laws of the city, which are reasonable though unjust, she enters a place which Lacan situates 'between two deaths' (Lacan 1992: 270–83). At the end of his journey up the Congo, Marlow finds Kurtz in a similar state of radical otherness, groping his way towards some place 'beyond *Atê*'. Because Marlow glimpses but does not understand this, he feels bound to Kurtz, and opts for him when given 'a choice of nightmares' (138). He does this even though he can no more accompany Kurtz down that path than Ismene could follow her sister Antigone.

The other element in *The Ethics of Psychoanalysis* that bears on *Heart of Darkness* is Lacan's use of an even more abstruse concept, introduced into psychoanalysis by Freud: *das Ding* ('the Thing'). This term, which has Kantian echoes, designates a psychic or existential realm outside the Symbolic order of language, knowledge and the Law. As such, it is beyond representation, and stubbornly resists definition or even exemplification. Like the evanescent Unconscious, upon which the entire structure of psychoanalysis is built, *das Ding* can be inferred only through its effects. It is the absent cause or 'lost object' of Desire, and occupies the space that both underlies and remains beyond it. Kurtz' mad pursuit of various objects of desire that might fill his own empty space is conducted at the level of lived reality. But in so far as *das Ding* has no existence there, and cannot be represented in the Symbolic order, it is located in Lacan's order of the Real, that is 'in the realm of being, not appearances' (Evans 1996: 159). In his derangement, Kurtz babbles about the various but inadequate objects of his insatiable desire: 'My Intended, my station, my career, my ideas . . . ' (147). Those 'goods' to which he has dedicated his life are here reduced to a chain of empty signifiers, obliterated by his fleeting vision of a final Emptiness: 'The horror! The horror!' (149). Words and phrases dismissed by Leavis as empty gestures – 'impenetrable', 'unspeakable', 'heart of darkness' – can now be read as intimations of a psychic state described equally problematically by the abstruse and neo-Freudian terminology of Lacan.

Yet this still leaves unanswered the question I began with: what can Lacanian analysis tell us about the politics of imperialism? The short answer is that it enriches political analysis by introducing into it the most sophisticated account available of the category of desire.[7] It exposes the disturbing possibility that the drive for colonial expansion is always a project without a rationale, the product of collective impulses that are beyond rational control because they derive from a deeply split structure. The education of colonial desire is essential to propagate and sustain the system. But the energies generated in this process reproduce individual insatiability – the desire for desire – as a structural feature in the institution of colonialism. Lacan's radical re-alignment of ethics shows that the Good, which in colonial conditions justifies conquest in the name of civilization, is situated in a psychic economy hell-bent on overcoming every obstacle to its satisfaction. This insight exposes the factitiousness of all 'justifying ideas'.

Unlike many others of Freud's followers, Lacan took seriously his later preoccupation with the death drive, in a way that illuminates the nature of Kurtz' desire. Although, for example, a morally sanctioned union with his Intended would be a safe and honourable thing, it is seen as deeply opposed to those other objects craved by Kurtz once he had loosened the bonds of European community. At the end of his life Kurtz might have mourned, like Shakespeare's Macbeth, the loss of 'that which should accompany old age,/As honour, love, obedience, troops of friends' (V, iii, 24–6). But once he has embarked on the path of his desire, he has no more chance than Macbeth of reversing its trajectory. Both present us with awkward ethical questions. Desire and the Law, according to Lacan, exist in a state of reciprocity and tension, because the Law not only constrains desire but generates transgressive forms of it that cannot be appeased. Moreover, the Law itself in Lacan can strike back in the 'obscene, ferocious figure of the superego' (Lacan 1977a: 256). In *Heart of Darkness*, this accounts for that cataclysmic guilt, sexual in origin, which finally destroys Kurtz.

How are such intimations communicated and perceived? If Lacan is right and psychic states that lie outside the Symbolic order cannot be represented within it, then they can be glimpsed only through the gaps in language. In Leavis' terms, they can never be 'realized', only evoked. Similarly, Marlow's journey towards Kurtz can be read as the pursuit of a different kind of 'knowledge' from the one institutionalized in universities and exemplified by ethnography's quest for authenticity. Because it is knowledge of the unspecifiable, it resists translation into any other discourses of the known, and may even – like the Lacanian unconscious – lie outside discourse altogether. Lacan's audacious project gives voice to that knowledge which can be accessed only in analysis and is incapable of being transmitted outside of that context. It thus requires a modicum of faith in the validity of truths that can be apperceived but not named:

> When the space of a lapsus no longer carries any meaning (or interpretation), then only is one sure that one is in the unconscious. One knows.
>
> But one has only to be aware of the fact to find oneself outside it. There is no friendship there, in that space that supports this unconscious.
>
> All I can do is tell the truth. No, that isn't so – I have missed it. There is no truth that, in passing through awareness, does not lie.
>
> But one runs after it all the same.
>
> (Lacan 1977: vii)[8]

The desire that produced psychoanalysis coincided with the moment when Conrad was abandoning his conventional earlier fictions to embark on *Heart of Darkness*. It took the form of a quest for a risky kind of knowledge. In giving up his even-handed representations of 'primitive peoples' (the moment of epistemological crisis in *Heart of Darkness*), Conrad accepted the conditions of his own incomplete capacity to know. Recognizing that black Africans might be knowable to Marlow and his audience only through the language of the colonizer, he set himself the task of dramatizing the process of such a transmission. The 'natives' would no longer be 'realized' in the language of their oppressors, but henceforth merely glimpsed fleetingly. Among the powerful intimations of their ontological reality that *Heart of Darkness* gives us is the puzzled 'mute' look on the face of Marlow's black helmsman at the moment of his death, or the untoward intrusion in the 'grove of death' passage of a soft black hand clasping a biscuit.

7   *Lord Jim*
Popular culture and the transmission of the code

The 'Flaubertian break' and popular culture

Fredric Jameson accepted Conrad's view that Flaubert influenced his own writing only in terms of style (Jameson 1981: 212). That judgement, however, needs some qualification, since it implies too sharp a separation between form and content. It also occludes an important aspect of the 'Flaubertian break' with realistic representation, namely that Flaubert treated style as part of the content of his novels. From this point of view, the most significant content of *Madame Bovary* is not those frank accounts of Emma's sexual transgressions which brought the novel instant notoriety, but the aestheticization of her experience of dissatisfaction and tragedy. The literary language used to represent her consciousness thus becomes as important as the state of mind depicted.

Flaubert uses pastiche to show how Emma's daydreams – her most palpable reality – are constructed from the tropes of the romantic literature that fed her convent-school imaginings. The result is not just a stylistic innovation but a new kind of content embodying a new understanding of how subjectivity and desire are formed. Although Flaubert would later profess a lack of interest in the subject matter of his fictions, his exceptional literary self-consciousness did not take him to the extremity of thinking that literature refers to nothing but itself. For one thing, by regarding literature as instrumental in the education of desire, *Madame Bovary* anticipates a major preoccupation of twentieth-century psychoanalysis. Instead of abandoning realism's aspirations to say something true about 'life', Flaubert pioneers a more inclusive and complex psychological realism. That is one reason why Conrad found much more to interest him in Flaubert than technicalities of narrative style.

In order to resituate *Lord Jim* in literary history, Jameson painstakingly sifts through literary texts and interpretative systems in search of the right themes and tools. Unusual among Anglophone critics of Conrad, he is acutely aware that those developments in French realism that influenced him were part of his Europeanness. Jameson begins by analysing the significance of *bovarysme* in Jim's early formation. Like Emma, Jim was susceptible to the enchantments of myth: his adolescent daydreams – derived from 'light literature' or popular adventure fiction written for boys – are as delightfully vague as hers. Yet they have more specific outcomes than Emma's, because their evocations of a lost and heroic mythos persist in Jim's boyish and imaginary adventures. At the moment of high imperialism, they even point to a career:

> He saw himself saving people from sinking ships, cutting away masts in a hurricane, swimming through a surf with a line; or as a lonely castaway, barefooted and half naked, walking on uncovered reefs in search of shell-fish to stave off starvation. He confronted savages on tropical shores, quelled mutinies on the high seas, and in a small boat upon the ocean kept up the hearts of despairing men – always an example of devotion to duty, and as unflinching as a hero in a book.
>
> (6)

I will leave aside for the moment the fact that Conrad grants Jim a 'real-life' version of this dream in the second half of the novel. At this point of the novel, situational clichés mollify the rigours of those real-life experiences that might correspond to Jim's youthful fantasy. Their fantasy quality differs from the 'great cadences of the Flaubertian lyric illusion', in Jameson's resonant phrase (ibid.: 212), because at this moment in history a young man of Jim's modest background could translate his fantasy life into a career at sea. Jim can thus choose to venture out into the world, even though his education seems to deny him any freedom of choice. The ideological field into which Jim is drawn extends from Robinson Crusoe's colonial existence on a desert island with his compliant 'savage' to the most powerful and allegedly benign empire the world has ever known. By combining the tropes of fantasy-inducing light literature with an intense analysis of subject formation, Conrad situated *Lord Jim* somewhat precariously between popular fiction and high art, and at a time when the intervening gap had widened considerably since the days of Charles Dickens.

Terry Eagleton once posed informally a related question about this capacity to cross literary class lines by contrasting the canonical Conrad of English Literature with the 'yo-ho-ho shiver-me-timbers' author admired by a popular readership. 'How does that fit, if at all, into the history of reception?' he went on to ask. 'What are these works which can appeal at once to Leavis and the short-trousered consumers of comic books?' In a different key, this is the same Conrad that Jameson finds 'floating uncertainly somewhere in between Proust and Robert Louis Stevenson' (ibid.: 206). I am not sure that Conrad's novels do appeal nowadays to short-trousered consumers without being translated into more accessible forms of popular culture. The related critical question posed by *Lord Jim* is how its aestheticization of ripping yarns enables them to be included among the forces that drive mainstream history. Jameson thinks that *Lord Jim* challenges political criticism to explain how the ruling values of British imperialism could be analysed so profoundly in an almost anachronistic tale of lost honour. In the first half of this famously split novel, Conrad's recognition that Jim's jump from the stricken *Patna* threatens the imperial code evinces the novel's 'political unconscious' (ibid.: 265).

Jameson does not fully account for Conrad's less convincing narrative of his hero's life in Patusan as Tuan ('Lord') Jim, which also draws on popular fiction, and specifically the 'feminine' genre of love romance. The potentially shocking inclusion of Jim's relationship with Jewel – sexual, extramarital, inter-racial – can easily be overlooked by concentrating on the dominant metropolitan understandings of imperialism, from which (as Marlow comments in *Heart of Darkness*) 'the women' are to be excluded (115). When Jewel fears that Jim will leave her for reasons concerning his original homeland, Conrad touches on the unequal terms of such relationships in colonial conditions. But any challenge which Jim's liaison with Jewel might have presented to British understandings of appropriate sexual behaviour by women is effectively and pleasantly countered by the muffled and tragic quality of the narrative. Jim's encounter with female sexuality was a missed opportunity for Conrad.

H. Rider Haggard's treatment of inter-racial sex in the widely read *King Solomon's Mines* (1885) reminds us of the limits that decorum placed on Victorian discussions of sexuality. A crisis of censorship and disclosure is created in the domains of both race and sexuality when a white explorer, Good, falls in love with the African woman, Foulata. Popular fiction at this time could evidently at least broach (and of course exploit) the subject that jointly tabooed both race and sexuality, and which racial 'science' had recently labelled 'miscegenation'. 'Fortunately' – for that is how the woman herself and the narrator see the matter – Foulata's timely death resolves the difficulty presented by the affair, particularly as both she and Good are sympathetic characters:

> I am bound to say that, looking at the thing from the point of view of an oldish man of the world, I consider her removal was a fortunate occurrence, since, otherwise, complications would have been sure to ensue. The poor creature was no ordinary native girl, but a person of great, I had almost said stately, beauty, and of considerable refinement of mind. But no amount of beauty or refinement could have made an entanglement between Good and herself a desirable

occurrence; for, as she herself put it, 'Can the sun mate with the darkness, or the white with the black?'

(Haggard 1885: 241)

The fact that Foulata has thoroughly absorbed imperialist ideology perhaps accounts for her 'refinement of mind'. She certainly shows greater consideration and better manners in this regard than Kurtz' African mistress in Conrad's *Heart of Darkness*.

Victorian censorship played a significant role in sustaining the notion of Empire by representing 'the code' as something remote from sexuality. In promoting high ideals by enclosing them in pre-pubescent tales written for enthusiastic young men, it repressed the 'problem' of sexual desire for 'native' people by aestheticizing it as an adolescent romance. *Lord Jim* conforms to this standard by combining a truncated analysis of colonial desire with a sanitized version of male psychology.

Nostalgia and the British Empire

Of the four colonial fictions I am discussing at length, *Lord Jim* is the only one whose focus is clearly British. It thus provides the best opportunity for re-examining the question of Conrad's relationship to British imperialism. Politicizing readers of *Heart of Darkness* in the 1960s and 1970s often asked whether its negative critique of imperialism was directed specifically at Belgium (for perversely distorting in the Congo an otherwise worthy ideal) or included Britain as well (Hawkins 1979). Conrad's more oblique approach to the politics of empire in *Lord Jim* presents a similar problem by masking its 'true' meaning with what Jameson calls 'strategies of containment' (Jameson 1981: 210–19, 266–70). One such 'strategy' was to locate the novel in darkest Borneo, instead of the more familiar and bureaucratized imperial centre of India, that vaunted 'jewel in the crown' overseen by the Raj in its heyday. By contrast, the only 'jewel' Jim embraces is his Eurasian mistress, Jewel, who is emblematic of the most precious gift Patusan gave him: a second chance. Conrad may have chosen Borneo simply because he saw a market for tales about it, or because it provided him with 'material' drawn from his own real-life experiences of the Malay Archipelago. Yet neither reason quite settles the matter. The existence at that time of a 'taste' for the kind of fiction Conrad provided is not in itself a neutral fact. It reveals that the social matrix represented by the reading public at least encouraged and perhaps required those strategies of containment displayed in *Lord Jim*.

These complications are multiplied by the effects of cultural changes on our own modes of reading. The survival of the phrase 'jewel in the crown', for example, reminds us that imperial nostalgia did not disappear with the passing of Edwardian England. Knowing that 'the glamour's off' (*Heart of Darkness* 52), Conrad ironically juxtaposes with his own benighted present *Lord Jim*'s turn-of-the-century narrative of former glory, forgotten heroism and the longing for a lost golden age of adventure. That faraway signal of the impending loss of empire would return to Britain in the early 1980s, amplified as nostalgia for past glory and manifest in the bizarre phenomenon known as 'The Falklands War'. On a tiny and obscure remnant of empire off the coast of Argentina, a British Tory government belatedly staged the archaic rhetoric of heroic struggle, in order to consolidate itself in office.[1] That apparent eagerness to recall an imperial past surfaced in a Britain divided between a hard-nosed economics and nostalgia for the glamour of former glories.

The mood of the moment was expressed in gorgeous movies, lavishly illustrated coffee-table books and a rash of new themes for various media. A famous product of colonial Britain, Salman Rushdie, evokes that ambience amusingly and trenchantly when diagnosing it as 'Raj Nostalgia':

> Anyone who has switched on the television set, been to the cinema or entered a bookshop in the last few months will be aware that the British Raj, after three and a half decades in retirement, has been making a sort of comeback. After the big-budget fantasy double-bill of *Gandhi* and *Octopussy* we have had the blackface minstrel-show of *The Far Pavilions* in its TV serial incarnation, and immediately afterwards the overpraised *Jewel in the Crown*. I should also include the alleged 'documentary' about Subhas Chandra Bose, Granada Television's *War of the Springing Tiger*, which, in the finest traditions of journalistic impartiality, described India's second-most-revered independence leader as a 'clown'.
>
> (Rushdie 1991: 87)

Rushdie's caustic reviews of movies such as Richard ('Mahatma Dickie') Attenborough's *Gandhi* (1982) or David Lean's *A Passage to India* (1984) show how the contradictions of the colonial system are reproduced in ways that affect postcolonizer and postcolonized differently. Rushdie responds by combating nostalgic recollection with rigorous critique. For several decades, period costume dramas have sustained the television and cinema industries in Britain, the heritage appeal of whose past is so much in accord with popular and middlebrow taste that it can be marketed globally. Academic and 'serious' writers, however, have responded oppositionally to this cultural desire by politicizing the study of literature, rewriting literary classics and admitting into the canon the disturbing narratives of subjugated and dispossessed peoples.[2] These contradictory uses of the same cultural space recall not only Walter Benjamin's counter-imperialist dictum about the reciprocity between barbarism and civilization (Benjamin 1968: 258) but also Žižek's constant address to the dark, obscene underside – of the law, or the ideological 'good'.

On a number of counts *Lord Jim* anticipates what has since become a tradition of revisionist rewritings. The master narrative it 'writes back' to is not a specific text but a legend with the narrative form and imprecision of a myth. Its manifestations include those popular novels of heroic adventure that preceded Conrad's novel. *Lord Jim* substitutes contemporary events for the light literature that fed Jim's adolescent fantasies. Conrad himself, of course, had once experienced a boyish desire for the world to be an 'enchanted place'. Like his fictional other, Marlow, he too had gazed at a map in a shop window and vowed that one day he would go to the source of the Congo River (*Last Essays* 16–17; *Heart of Darkness* 52).[3]

Brierly's dog: the retrieval of lost honour

Homi Bhabha associates the significance of the time lags in *Lord Jim* with the 'untimeliness' produced by the asymmetries of colonialism: 'If, as they say, the past is a foreign country', he writes, 'then what does it mean to encounter a past that is your own country reterritorialized, even terrorized by another?' (Bhabha 1994: 198). *Lord Jim* clearly exemplifies the fractured temporality that causes problems for the writing of colonial history. In Jim's case, the sense of untimeliness is produced by the discrepancy between power and desire and the dream and its moment. Jim fails to achieve his desire because when he reacts to the defining events of his life the necessities of the moment elude him.

As frequently noted, various incidents that expose Jim's 'subtle unsoundness' (89) are linked to the act of jumping. His first missed opportunity occurs on the training ship when – faced by an emergency – he fails to jump to the rescue. Later, and as an officer, he literally jumps ship by abandoning the *Patna*, whereupon the glory that might have been his goes to the unassuming French lieutenant who brings it safely to port (83). To Marlow's amazement, Jim regards this moment of absolute disgrace as a missed opportunity. In analysing this central event, Jameson seizes on both its psychological import and its timing. What is for Jim a symptomatic repetition is not represented directly in the novel but is merely reported by him in a way that plays down his own agency: 'I had jumped . . . it seems' (*Lord Jim* 111; Jameson 1981: 262–5). Jim's psychological flaw is that he lives out his passions through fantasies that immobilize him. The romantic heroism he rehearses in the undisturbed and uncalibrated time of his daydreaming may well sustain him through the boring realities of his everyday life on board ship. But his fantasies also ensure that he never encounters the Real: Jim, it seems, is destined always to be too early or too late.

When he first fails to act heroically on board the training ship he is excusably young and it is a comparatively minor affair. But his jump from the stricken *Patna* is an altogether different matter, both psychologically and ethically. For as soon as the fantasist becomes an officer, his libidinal formation collides with the ideology of the merchant marine service. Before the emergency stirred him from his day-dream existence and caused him to jump to safety, his mind may well have been alive with images of chaos, futility, and reality gone crazy. What is now at stake, however, is not Jim's existential experience of the event but the 'code' itself, which (Jameson argues) encompasses much more than the seaman's code of honour. Not reducible to the written or even unwritten rules of conduct for British imperial servants, the 'code' epitomizes the more elusive and potent 'ideological cohesion of class values' necessary for sustaining the empire (Jameson 1981: 265). Once it has been highlighted and made public, what might have remained a minor incident is magnified into a premonition of great moments of betrayal in the century that would follow. Just as Jim abrogated his position of trust as a white officer on the *Patna*, in 1942 the British would finally abandon Singapore in the face of the invading Japanese. That episode ended Britain's moral authority in the East. As if to underscore the nationality of the shame involved, Conrad makes the unsung hero of the *Patna* episode a Frenchman, who calmly and methodically brings the vessel and its eight hundred pilgrim passengers safely into port.

Jameson notes in passing how the novel's Captain Brierly represents the lesser code of the 'confraternity of the sea' (ibid.: 264–5). This corresponds with Brierly's outrage that Jim's dogged insistence on facing the Inquiry will expose the whites 'out there' to the disparaging gaze of the native population in attendance. But in failing to account for Brierly's suicide, Jameson overlooks the narrator's suggestive observation that the crowd is attracted by a purely psychological interest, 'the expectation of some essential disclosure as to the strength, the power, the horror, of human emotions' (56). This motive is attributed not to the 'natives' but to the sailors in port. It excludes Brierly only because he does not put himself in the same category as other mortals. But Brierly himself provides an intriguing insight into the power of human emotions. However opaque its meaning, his suicide has extraordinary psychological and ideological implications. Certainly the novel is so preoccupied with Jim as to focus mainly on what Jameson vividly calls 'the interrogation of a hole in time' (ibid.: 264). By drawing him into the same hole, however, Brierly's suicide interrogates Jim's case in a way missed by the official Inquiry.

Brierly is linked to Jim in all sorts of ways. He comes from the upper echelons of the same social world – the 'knowable' and respectably middle-class English communities anatomized by Jane Austen and George Eliot. As he informs Marlow:

> 'I rather think some of my people know his. The old man's a parson, and I remember how I met him once when staying with my cousin in Essex last year. If I am not mistaken, the old chap seemed rather to fancy his sailor son. Horrible . . . '
>
> (68)

In the very first chapter of the novel, Jim's family home is described briefly but critically. It is located in a world which has its own 'certain' and hypocritical moral codes, designed to accommodate the class-divided community in which his father is a representative moral arbiter:

> Jim's father possessed such certain knowledge of the Unknowable as made for the righteousness of people in cottages without disturbing the ease of mind of those whom an unerring Providence enables to live in mansions. The little church on a hill had the mossy greyness of a rock seen through a ragged screen of leaves. It had stood there for centuries . . .
>
> (5)

The family link between Jim and Brierly back in the 'old country' indicates a different kind of borderline: the exact place where the fictional worlds of Austen and Conrad momentarily overlap. Austen chronicles the domestic and community life of the places that her brother, like Fanny Price's brother in *Mansfield Park*, left in order to explore the great waterways of the earth. Conrad, however, accompanies Jim on a quest that takes him away from the settled world of his upbringing to distant countries that are ethically beyond his understanding. Literary historians informed by postcolonial theory have already reassessed Austen and the tradition she quintessentially represents.[4] But in this context, it is equally important to recognize that she and Conrad face in opposite directions. One reason why Captain Brierly attracts so little narrative attention is that he remains locked in the class values of the community that produced him, and from which Jim has made a break.

This treacherous novel associates Brierly with Jim in ways that are at once obvious and insidious. They both jump overboard, for instance. But for Brierly, as captain of his ship, this is the most spectacular event in an otherwise unruffled and successful life. Whereas Jim's suicide is merely symbolic, Brierly actually jumps to his death. Even more strangely, he is also linked with Jim by virtue of a dog – or rather, two dogs.[5]

Brierly perfectly exemplifies dedication to the code of the service – or at least to a 'certain standard of conduct' associated with it. His career has been a masterpiece of effective commitment, and he has lived a version of the fanciful style of male greatness popularized in those novels of adventure that prompted Jim's own fantasies:

> He had never in his life made a mistake, never had an accident, never a mishap, never had a check in his steady rise and he seemed to be one of those lucky fellows who know nothing of indecision, much less of self-mistrust . . . He had saved lives at sea, had rescued ships in distress, had a gold chronometer presented to him by the underwriters, and a pair of binoculars with a suitable inscription from some foreign Government, in commemoration of these services.
>
> (57)

Unlike Jim's imaginary heroics, Brierly's actual accomplishments are dryly itemized, and read like a biographical note on an achiever unaware of the poetry of his own life. He enters the novel as he leaves it, almost unnoticed. *Lord Jim* typically infiltrates significant new characters when the reader's attention is fixed elsewhere. As a result of this strategy, Brierly's entrance lures readers into participating in the hermeneutic difficulties of the characters themselves. Unheralded and unnamed, in the earliest description of the Inquiry Brierly is identified only by the quasi-heroic phrase, 'big assessor'. This glancing and indeterminate reference is introduced revealingly at that point in the Inquiry when Jim, giving his version of the events that led him to abandon the *Patna*, remarks (as evidence of his seaman's expertise): 'I knew then there must be a big hole below the water-line' (29). But the 'big assessor' cuts Jim short 'with a dreamy smile', while 'his fingers played incessantly, touching the paper without noise'.

What are we to make of this response which remains opaque even with the knowledge of hindsight? The problem is not that it conceals its meaning, but that it allows for too many interpretative possibilities. Here the secret allegiance of the text is not with Brierly and the Inquiry but with Jim's impossible pursuit of true meaning, in all its intangible details and nuances. The Inquiry, we are told, dealt merely with essential facts. The ethical tensions that pervade *Lord Jim* resemble those endless slippages of meaning that drive *Heart of Darkness*. Both attest to the impossibility of naming the supposedly 'redeeming idea' that lies behind 'certain standards of conduct' on the one hand and mercenary greed on the other. Brierly cannot bear either the public shame of the collapse of

British moral authority in the East or the fact that Jim is 'one of us'. Confronted with the abyss of relativity, his world-order breaks down.

Yet from the perspective of Brierly's own standards of conduct, his suicide is arguably more shameful than the behaviour by Jim that triggers it. Brierly's father excises all memory of his son after his suicide (64). By the time Marlow meets him, Brierly's world is beginning to unravel, and his affinity with Jim has strengthened. This development supports Jameson's claim that what is at stake in the *Patna* affair is 'the ideological cohesion of class values' that sustains the empire (Jameson 1981: 265).

Brierly's loyal dog is a noble Retriever, which perfectly matches its master's ego ideal. Like his own given name, this thoroughbred dog symbolizes Montague Brierly's upper-class status within the social world he shares with Jim. In contrast, at a turning point in the narrative plain Jim is associated with a 'yellow cur' jumbled up among the motley crowd of 'natives' who attend the hearing to witness his shame. When Marlow draws attention to this apparently unlovable dog, Jim confusedly believes it is himself who is being disparaged. Brierly, on the other hand, is so genuinely concerned that his loyal dog might follow its suiciding master overboard that he has him locked away. Yet even at this delicate moment, Conrad's ironic verbal play results in a subdued and macabre joke that prevents too solemn a reading of the tragedy. A pedigree Retriever, loyal to its master, is precisely not the sort of dog Brierly wants in attendance after he has decided to throw himself irretrievably into the sea.

Despite the impressive calm of Brierly's death – which is of a piece with the hollow perfection of his life – it is Jim who rouses Marlow's keener moral and psychological curiosity, and eventually what amounts to a kind of love. Like Kurtz, Jim exposes both the powerful agency and the fragility of the fantasies that feed imperial greatness. As truly Conradian heroes, they oblige us to reconfigure the grounds on which ethical judgements are made. Their lives reveal undiscovered depths in the human psyche, which is why the crowd of white spectators at the Inquiry expected some kind of revelation. What exactly is revealed cannot be named. Rather, Jim's case instigates a seemingly endless pursuit after meaning, which generates Marlow's project and is in turn the driving force of Conrad's novel. The cynical and racist Brierly frankly admits to Marlow that he doesn't 'care a snap for all the pilgrims that ever came out of Asia . . . ' (68). But this discourse of down-to-earth toughness emanates from an increasingly evasive and confused Brierly, who shortly afterwards commits suicide. By contrast, Jim – with the romantic goal of an heroic destiny entrenched among his fantasies – proves to be the more resilient. The paradox encodes a political insight: the empire is sustained by nostalgic daydreaming and the supposedly debilitating fantasies of popular culture, rather than by Brierly-like shows of intransigence.

Group psychology and the desire of the subject

When Conrad embarked on *Lord Jim* he put aside the half-finished but stalled third novel of his Malay trilogy, *The Rescue*. Even in the earliest draft of what would become *Lord Jim* Conrad maintained his investment in the Malay world of the earlier novels, as is most apparent in his Patusan story. But the compulsion to shift locales completely and write *Heart of Darkness* was irresistible. Having changed tack once, Conrad put aside *Lord Jim* and revisited his very different experiences on the Congo journey. *Heart of Darkness* signals a revolution in his beliefs as well as in his writing, which in turn influenced the composition of *Lord Jim*. Together they constitute a qualitative advance from Conrad's earlier fiction.

Although works of fiction cannot be equated with forms of knowledge *per se*, at a moment of discursive uncertainty they can play a 'progressive' role by opening the way for new discourses to appear. This median positioning of Conrad's fictions is vividly illustrated by the psychological interest in Jim's case. In this respect the language of *Lord Jim* derives partly from nineteenth-century psychological models. From our own perspective, however, Conrad's novels equally appear to anticipate certain aspects of Freudian and Lacanian psychoanalysis.

It is now important to distinguish the Jim/Brierly connection from other kinds of pairing that almost obsessively pervade Conrad's fiction, and of which 'The Secret Sharer' (1912) is the prototype. This tale explicitly explores the idea that the main character is shadowed by a sinister twin or 'other'. Numerous examples appear in novels and tales written before and after 'The Secret Sharer'. In *Lord Jim*, for instance, Gentleman Brown represents the disabling return of Jim's repressed guilt. In *Heart of Darkness*, the bonding of Marlow and Kurtz is a well-known instance of 'secret sharing'. The comparable character linked to Heyst in *Victory* is the doppelganger-like Mr Jones. Jim himself could be said to function as Marlow's own secret sharer. All of these doubles expose the 'obscene dark underside' or seed of corruption in the hero.[6] In 'The Secret Sharer', the Captain and Leggatt are both described as 'Conway men', because they share a value-system and training that one of them has transgressed. *Lord Jim* as a whole appears to be structured by several such doublings. That is why it is important to distinguish the spectral apparitions of Leggatt or Jones – which originate in quasi-metaphysical notions of the doppelganger – from other pairings established by textual links dependent on the reader's ability to notice them. On the other hand, it is equally important to separate those half-developed insights which Conrad's text makes available to acute readers from interpretations that invoke the psychoanalytic unconscious, a category which did not exist at that time. The uncanny premonitions of what we might now identify as operations of the unconscious are instances of literature's capacity to intimate what later becomes codified in new discourses of knowledge.

The link between Jim and Brierly is illuminated by two distinct modes of psychological inquiry. One is outlined in Freud's 1921 essay, 'Group Psychology and the Analysis of the Ego', which explores in psychoanalytic terms how individual psychology may relate to behaviours that characterize groups (*SE* XVIII: 67–143). The other is demonstrated in a powerful chapter of Lacan's *Seminar XI* on 'The Unconscious and Repetition' (Lacan 1977: 17–64).

In part, 'Group Psychology' is Freud's response to the patriotism that led hundreds of thousands of young men to be 'willing' to die for their country in the Great War. By focusing on the kind of institutional loyalty commanded by the Catholic Church or the army, Freud distinguishes between what Edward Said would call 'filiative' and 'affiliative' ties. Filiative ties are based on 'natural' connections, such as family, and can be investigated by psychoanalysis. Affiliative ties, on the other hand, are created by socially constructed formations, such as nationhood, religion or even sport (Said 1983: 16–25). Because the kind of behaviour they manifest has been produced collectively as well as individually, they reveal the need for a group psychology. Freud's attention to the psychology of those who command such groups anticipates the notorious appearance of charismatic leaders in uprisings of extreme nationalism between the wars. In advocating total allegiance to the national good, these men came to embody the community's deepest wishes. This context prompted Freud to develop the concept of the ego ideal. Linked to the superego in the form of a moral imperative, it coerces the individual subject during the process of psychic formation to identify powerfully with a cause or a creed – or, in the case of *Lord Jim*, a code.

Although little attention is paid to the intricacies of Brierly's motives, his sudden breakdown is clearly related to his allegiance to the code. His case enables us to understand that the object of Jim's own loyalties is not exactly the same as Brierly's. For whereas Brierly's shame over the *Patna* affair is caused by the public nature of the scandal, Jim's sense of failure derives from an older and pre-nationalistic code of honour, which makes his case much more complicated. Brierly conforms to a comparatively crude notion of British superiority, partly internalized in the process of growing up, and partly codified as a way of dealing with social and racial inferiors. However intellectually languid it may appear, his total identification with the group that thinks of itself as born to rule underwrites his success. Jim is in search of something else.[7]

Jim's sense of honour does not absolutely exclude the code whose various manifestations are totally embraced by Brierly. For example, in seeing his disgrace as something more than a 'lost opportunity', Jim accepts – with whatever mental reservation – the authority of the Inquiry he faces. But both he and Marlow agree that there is more to the matter than the questions that the Inquiry is concerned to adjudicate. Whereas Marlow is interested in what the narrative of Jim's life might reveal of human psychology, Jim is transfixed by his boyhood ambition to become a hero. This is something else that arouses Marlow's curiosity: the revival of the heroic in a nation that buried it long ago under the compromises of history. From an individualist perspective, Jim's ambitions are part of his immaturity, and reveal his unregenerate adolescence. Collectively, however, his dreams are the very 'seed of commonwealths, the germs of empires' (*Heart of Darkness* 47). Whereas Brierly cannot exist when his blind faith is threatened, Jim pushes on with his quest.

Hegel's discussion of 'romantic honour' in his *Lectures on Fine Art* breaks down its different locations in literature. Traditionally, he argues, honour was a public and social matter in a world that esteemed individual self-sufficiency. 'Romantic honour', on the other hand,

> is of a different kind. In it the injury affects not the positive real value infringed, i.e. property, position, duty, etc., but the personality as such and its idea of itself, the value which the individual ascribes to himself on his own account. This value at this stage is just as infinite as the individual is infinite in his own eyes . . .
>
> [I]n every case the man of honour always thinks first of himself . . . thus he may well do the worst of things and still be a man of honour.
>
> (Hegel 1975, vol. 1: 558–9)

For the Brierlys of this world, the ego is so committed to the abstract service of an ideal that the two become commensurate. Jim's ego–structure, by contrast, maintains its integrity because it is grounded in early desires imprinted as sensuous and definite images: 'he *saw himself* saving people from sinking ships . . . ' (6; my emphasis).

Yet Jim too falters. Why he does so is illuminated by Lacan's analysis of the pathology associated with repetition, which begins by separating *tuché* from automaton, happening from structure, text from form, and difference from repetition:

> We have translated [*tuché*] as *the encounter with the real*. The real is beyond the *automaton*, the return, the coming-back, the insistence of the signs, by which we see ourselves governed by the pleasure principle. The real is that which always lies behind the automaton, and it is quite obvious, throughout Freud's research, that it is this that is the object of his concern.
>
> (Lacan 1977: 53–4)

Since Lacan regards confrontations with the real as always and necessarily 'missed encounters', he shares with Conrad a certain kind of pessimism. Both the universality of Jim's quest and the certainty of his failure are indeed as the novel describes them: there can be no 'clean slate', because 'the initial word of each our destiny' is 'graven in imperishable characters upon the face of a rock' (186). Jim appears to be truthful in asserting that the fear of death does not concern him. 'He was not afraid of death perhaps', Marlow adds, 'but I'll tell you what, he was afraid of the emergency' (88). Jim's most vivid perception in those last moments on board the *Patna* is of the chaos and futility that result from an absurd attempt to survive. Given what Jim was ready to face heroically, the whole situation was meaningless. He saves his own life not out of a fear of death but to preserve the possibility of encountering the 'real' differently, and in a way that will not be just another missed opportunity. Patusan offers him a life commensurate with his boyhood fantasies. Seeing that those dreams were fostered in 'light literature', their fulfilment is expressed in the form of a tale of adventure.

The afterglow of heroic tales

Jim gets his opportunity for redemption when Stein presents him with Patusan, because it answers to his need to gain honour by his own efforts. Although Conrad's complex narrative style continues to present Jim's buried existence skilfully through scattered 'sightings', the Patusan section is not marked by time shifts and verbal duplicity. Conrad here attempts to write a modern-day romance that resonates with the history of the White Rajahs of Sarawak. This apparent lapse into romance is offset by a strain of realism which acknowledges that such happy outcomes occur only in the fantasy world of fiction: hence the novel's tragic dénouement.

The character of Stein is based largely on the famous orientalist, Alfred Russel Wallace, whose monumental study of the Malay Archipelago provided abundant source-material for Conrad's early fictions as well as the Patusan section of *Lord Jim*.[8] Like Stein, Wallace lived in an era that combined science with adventure, and which Conrad – writing in gloomier times – regarded as both admirably amateur and idealistic. Wallace was a friend and house guest of the legendary James (or 'Rajah') Brooke, the man who was known as the benevolent protector of the Dyak peoples of Sarawak, and who founded the dynasty which ruled them for a hundred years. Brooke thus lived out in real life what was but a flawed dream for Jim. That Conrad's attitude to the controversial Brooke was not only uncritical but even sentimental is evidenced by this eulogy from the opening chapter of *The Rescue*:

The adventurers who began that struggle have left no descendants. The ideas of the world changed too quickly for that. But even into the present [i.e. nineteenth] century they have had successors. Almost in our own day we have seen one of them – a true adventurer in his devotion to his impulse – a man of high mind and of pure heart, lay the foundation of a flourishing state on the ideas of pity and justice. He recognized chivalrously the claims of the conquered; he was a disinterested adventurer, and the reward of his noble instincts is in the veneration with which a strange and faithful race cherish his memory.

Misunderstood and traduced in life, the glory of his achievement has vindicated the purity of his motives. He belongs to history . . .

(3–4)

The nostalgic cadences of this 'tribute' reveal Conrad's tendency to see the generation that immediately preceded his own as the final phase of a lost Golden Age,[9] when steamships had not yet displaced sail and undiscovered places on the world's maps enticed the adventurous into authentically exotic careers. The abolition of the Atlantic slave trade briefly enabled imperialism to wear an ethical mantle, and high ideals began to command respect. The fact that Conrad saw the possibilities of that era as surviving into his father's lifetime, but not his own, may have some minor Freudian significance. The colourfulness of that yesteryear lingers on in Conrad's earliest writing as both nostalgic memory and untimely presence. As an emotional rather than intellectually tested viewpoint, it accounts for the recurrence of certain blind spots in Conrad's less rigorous writings, which include those novels from which *Lord Jim* and *Heart of Darkness* decisively break.

In presenting the Patusan story as a tragedy, Conrad finally reveals that Jim's 'flaw' was permanently disabling. The stronger line of development in the novel, however, concerns his survivability and the seemingly interminable analysis of both his desire and his disgrace. The Tuan Jim/Rajah Brooke motif evokes the afterglow of romantic desire for an imaginary lost world where 'glamour' is still possible. 'The time was coming', says Marlow, 'when I should see him loved, trusted, admired, with a legend of strength and prowess forming round his name as though he had been the stuff of a hero' (175). Although Jim turned out to be not quite a hero, Conrad's own desultory hold on the possibility of heroism lasted until the final years of his life. After completing *The Rescue* for publication in 1920, Conrad received a warm letter of appreciation from a reader who was indubitably well positioned to read both it and *Lord Jim* 'inwardly': the 'Ranee' Margaret Brooke. Wife of the second White Rajah of Sarawak, Sir Charles Brooke (who was nephew and heir of the first Rajah, Sir James Brooke), she wrote with deep local knowledge when describing *Lord Jim* as 'the best book ever written about the islands of the East Indies' (Payne 1960: 171). Whereas Charles' reign was contemporaneous with Conrad, James had lived in the 'age of adventure' that preceded it. Long estranged from her husband and finally widowed, Margaret Brooke became in her mature years the London friend and patroness of the most famous literary men of the day. Conrad replied:

> I am immensely gratified and touched by the letter you have been good enough to write to me. The first Rajah Brooke has been one of my boyish admirations, a feeling I have kept to this day strengthened by the better understanding of the greatness of his character and the unstained rectitude of his purpose. The book which has found favour in your eyes has been inspired in great measure by the history of the first Rajah's enterprise . . .
>
> (ibid.)

The extra-textual pairing of a fictional 'Tuan' Jim with Rajah Brooke, who 'belonged to history', adds yet another layer of irony to *Lord Jim*. Sir James Brooke, like his nephew and successor Charles, was probably closer to Mr Kurtz than to Jim, and 'flawed' in ways that Conrad may not have known. For this White Rajah did not maintain his power over the Dyaks by patiently weaning them off their 'savage' ways in order to clear the seas of piracy and the forests of cannibalism. He did it by joining them on head-hunting raids. Brooke's methods – like Kurtz' – were 'unsound', although none of his family appears to have suffered a breakdown from remorse.[10]

More immediately pertinent to *Lord Jim* is a passage in Conrad's late essay on 'Geography and Some Explorers' (1924), which recalls the moment on his Congo journey when he reached the place of his own childhood dream:

> Everything was dark under the stars. Every other white man on board was asleep. I was glad to be alone on deck, smoking the pipe of peace after an anxious day. The subdued thundering mutter of the Stanley Falls hung in the heavy night air of the last navigable reach of the Upper Congo, while no more than ten miles away, in Reshid's camp just above the Falls, the yet unbroken power of the Congo Arabs slumbered uneasily. Their day was over. Away in the middle of the stream, on a little island nestling all black in the foam of the broken water, a solitary little light glimmered feebly, and I said to myself with awe, "This is the very spot of my boyish boast."
>
> A great melancholy descended on me. Yes, this was the very spot. But there was no shadowy friend to stand by my side in the night of

the enormous wilderness, no great haunting memory, but only the unholy recollection of a prosaic newspaper 'stunt' and the distasteful knowledge of the vilest scramble for loot that ever disfigured the history of human conscience and geographical exploration.

(*Last Essays* 17)

This place of childhood wonderment was situated near an Arab slave-trading camp. But the fact that 'their day was over' brings no joy to the lonely and melancholy observer. For Stanley Falls was named after a more recent explorer, who had been the willing subject of King Leopold's unholy 'newspaper stunt', and was thereby complicit in the vileness of the subsequent 'scramble for loot'. The feeling of metaphysical isolation evoked by this passage accords with the 'music' Conrad sought in *Heart of Darkness*: 'a sinister resonance, a tonality of its own, a continued vibration that, I hoped, would hang in the air and dwell on the ear after the last note had been struck' (vii).

8 *Nostromo*

The anti-heroics and epic failures of Empire

'The totality of the action'

This is not a quotation from Georg Lukács, who was sometimes parodied for reifying the Hegelian concept of 'totality' and making it the distinctive feature of 'great realism'. The phrase comes instead – and perhaps surprisingly – from *The Great Tradition*, in which Leavis declares *Nostromo* not just Conrad's 'most considerable work', but 'one of the great novels of the language'. Comparatively free here of his customary insularity, Leavis acknowledges that the strengths of *Nostromo* derive partly from French and even Flaubertian influences which encouraged in Conrad 'a serious and severe conception of the art of fiction'. 'Luxuriant in its magnificence', *Nostromo* is 'Conrad's supreme triumph in the evocation of exotic life and colour'. But the key to its achievement is its 'rich and subtle but highly organized pattern' (Leavis 1948: 190–1).

This move takes Leavis inadvertently into Lukácsian territory, and leads him to talk of 'the different strands that go to the totality of the action' (ibid.: 196). The phrasing is not merely coincidental, because Leavis is grappling here with the kinds of aesthetic problems that Lukács addressed in 1937 in his exhaustive study of European realism, *The Historical Novel* (1962). These include the fact that, just as the exotic setting of *Nostromo* is more than 'background' material, the figures in its vast 'gallery' of characters were not chosen randomly. In general terms, Lukács carefully analyses and illustrates not only the differences between the novel as represented by nineteenth-century European realism and drama (classical tragedy), but also their common links to epic. More specifically, he attempts to define both the differences and shared ground between Homer's epics, Greek and Shakespearean tragedies, and the novels of Tolstoy. Like Leavis, he frames such differences in terms of artistic form (Lukács 1962: 89–170). In focusing on the 'totality of the action', both seek to determine how the individual lives of so many characters can be properly understood only in relation to a greater design. They concur in the view that convincing characterization is not an effect of naturalism's 'true-to-lifeness', but arises instead from the way in which each character contributes to the aesthetically structured 'totality of the action'. However movingly presented, the 'inner' lives or tragedies of individual characters are fully intelligible in relation to those broader social movements of which they are representative types.

Unlike *Lord Jim*, *Nostromo* is best approached not through popular culture, but in relation to some of the greatest European writers, and seen as an instance of how realist fiction achieves the perspective of epic. The epic status of *Nostromo* is rarely discussed at length, although it is by common consent the one novel by Conrad – and one of the few novels written in English – which can be compared plausibly with the *Iliad* or *War and Peace*, on account of its qualities as well as its generic affinities.[1] I return to the traditional topic of literary genre in order to ask an untraditional question of it: what kind of political knowledge becomes possible from the perspective of epic? Before attempting to answer it, however, I want to look briefly at some general problems I raised at the beginning of this study. I will do so by showing how one particular 'textual' moment – comprising character, theme and interpretation – progresses over time and in different kinds of writing.

The hermeneutic problem I started with involved two related questions. First, from what perspective – and with what potential distortions – do we read older literary texts, encrusted as they are by interpretative histories that began with their original readers? And second, how do the texts we classify as 'great literature' relate to other forms of knowledge, including those that sustain our interpretative activities? Such problems – which also provide heuristic opportunities – are of course not confined to Conrad. The kinds of knowledge they stimulate themselves have histories that (as Michel Foucault demonstrates) are partly institutional. And they bear upon the question of whether we can 'read back' into that Shakespearean moment which antedates our current discourses of knowledge. How can we 'catch' the originary moment of Shakespearean *écriture* as experienced prior to its constitution as an object of knowledge? Eighteenth-century writers, for example, saw Shakespeare as living in barbarous times from which their own had only recently emerged. In 1765, when Samuel Johnson published his annotated edition of Shakespeare, he defended the far-fetched and fairy-tale opening scene of *King Lear*. At the same time he used Shakespeare's defensible ignorance of historical and cultural differences as evidence in support of his assumption that the Elizabethan age was far more 'primitive' than his own:

> [I]f we turn our thoughts upon the barbarity and ignorance of the age to which this story is referred, it will appear not so unlikely as while we estimate *Lear*'s manners by our own. Such preference of one daughter to another, or resignation of dominion on such conditions,

would be yet credible, if told of a petty prince of *Guinea* or *Madagascar*. *Shakespeare*, indeed, by the mention of Earls and Dukes, has given us the idea of times more civilised, and of life regulated by softer manners; and the truth is, that though he so nicely discriminates, and so minutely describes the characters of men, he commonly neglects and confounds the characters of ages, by mingling customs ancient and modern, *English* and foreign.

(Johnson 1908: 160)

By revealing that his cultural presuppositions both inform and are buttressed by his reading of Shakespeare, the blindness of Johnson's insight impresses upon us the difficulty of removing ideological filters from our transactions with the past. His final chiasmus (ancient/modern: English/foreign) exposes the grand narrative of European progress at an early stage, and suggests that the complicity between Shakespearean criticism and European colonialism has a venerable pedigree.

King Lear itself anticipates this process of relative evaluation by positioning Lear's world against an even more barbarous one. In cursing Cordelia, he tells her that

The barbarous Scythian,
Or he that makes his generation messes
To gorge his appetite, shall to my bosom
Be as well neighbour'd, pitied, and reliev'd,
As thou my sometime daughter.

(I, i, 115–19)

The hyperbolic juxtaposing of 'barbarous' familial cannibalism and Christianly virtues evoked in 'neighbour'd, pitied, and reliev'd' represents the excesses of a disturbed mind. But by Johnson's time they have become matters of academic speculation. Nowadays, however, they reveal that the racist assumptions that divided England from its others in the early modern period had already been internalized as unproblematic.

If Johnson was untroubled by racist passages in *King Lear*, he was devastated by the torture scene in which the extrusion of Gloucester's eyes is enacted on stage (III, vii). In a critical consensus that became entrenched in the nineteenth century, Shakespeare's theatrical boldness in this scene is relegated to its proper place.[2] The growing reluctance to countenance sadistic acts on stage parallels the demise of criminal torture and protracted executions as public spectacles and the concomitant growth of new modes of punishment and incarceration (Foucault 1977). But it also indicates that Europe rarely imparted its self-civilizing refinements to its colonies, where the slave trade persisted for centuries.

To register such concerns, however, is to substitute historical realities for aesthetic choices and practices. After all, Johnson was addressing the efficacy of theatrical conventions; and in the case of *Nostromo*, the politics that concerns us is a matter of representation and genres. The persistent concern over 'explicit' violence in art applies equally to 'explicit' sex: the arousal caused by simulated or real sexual behaviour is dangerous because it collapses that distance between life and art on which aesthetic understanding depends. The new problem this raises – namely, that live theatrical representation is more frightening than 'mere' imagination stimulated by suggestive writing – is hard to fathom. For both writing and stage performances maximize their expressive power by similar means, and often avoid explicitness. Writing about sexual allure, for example, Roland Barthes asks:

> Is not the most erotic portion of the body *where the garment gapes*? In perversion (which is the realm of textual pleasure) there are no 'erogenous zones' (a foolish expression, besides); it is intermittence, as psychoanalysis has so rightly stated, which is erotic: the intermittence of skin flashing between two articles of clothing (trousers and sweater), between two edges (the open-necked shirt, the glove and the sleeve); it is this flash itself which seduces, or rather: the staging of an appearance-as-disappearance.
>
> (Barthes 1975: 9–10)

As with the erotic, so with cruel violence. The most powerful scene of torture in *Nostromo* is arguably not the one that leads to the appalling death of Hirsch after Sotillo puts him to the 'strappade' (446–9). Rather it is the understated account of the torture of Dr Monagham during that nightmare of history when the dictator Guzman Bento was in power. Instead of describing exactly what took place, Conrad meditates obliquely on how one might go about torturing someone without the aid of medieval instruments of torture:

> A piece of string and a ramrod; a few muskets in combination with a length of hide rope; or even a simple mallet of heavy, hard wood applied with a swing to human fingers or to the joints of a human body is enough for the most exquisite torture.
>
> (373)

Thus Conrad positions his readers simultaneously as torturers and the tortured. Yet while the description engages readers with discomforting intimacy in the violence, the full force of this defining episode of Monagham's life is that it illuminates the core of his self-mistrust, the sardonic distance he maintains from idealists and egotists alike, and his passionate devotion to Emilia Gould. It thus links the horror of a moment in his personal history to the public narrative punctuated by the horrendous regime of Guzman Bento.

Whether we think of torture, young love or high adventure, *Nostromo* shares with the great epics and tragedies of the Western tradition a seemingly limitless capacity to include all the personal, social, political and historical aspects of human experience. Individual lives and destinies are consistently linked to larger issues. They are controlled by an artistic economy that insists upon relevance while remaining open to the 'totality' of experience. Time-shifts and other techniques disturb the comfort provided by a single narrator, whether fictional or authorial, and contribute to Conrad's achievement of what Leavis describes as 'outsideness' (Leavis 1948: 190). Most readers of *Nostromo* discover that it gains from a re-reading. By re-engaging with particular characters and their experiences we perceive more clearly the emerging and shaping structure that contains their lives. This dynamic 'totality' comprises the novel's plenitude of meaning.

To link aesthetic form with political significance by associating both with the 'private' lives of individuals caught up in the great movements of history is by no means an original move. More than any other literary historian, Lukács insisted that what we now call genre is imbricated fundamentally with political knowledge. That overlap makes classical epic a significant antecedent of both tragedy and the novel. '[T]ragedy and great epic – epic and novel – present the objective, *outer* world', he declares; 'they present the inner life of man only insofar as his feelings and thoughts manifest themselves in deeds and actions, in a visible interaction with objective, outer reality'. And while '[t]ragedy and great epic both lay claim to portraying the totality of the life-process', he finds it 'obvious in both cases that this can only be a result of artistic structure' (Lukács 1962: 90–1). By 'totality' Lukács means artistic form rather than a vast 'content'. He therefore thinks it important to analyse precisely how these different but closely related genres work, and how their insights into historical processes yield different kinds of knowledge.

In order to distinguish tragedy from epic, Lukács instances *King Lear*, which embodies the 'problematicalness and break-up of the feudal family' in a dramatic and conflictual model. The function of 'psychological richness' in this play, he notes, is to exhaust 'all the possible attitudes to this collision' (ibid.: 93–4). Following Hegel, Lukács thinks that tragedy represents those moments of world-historical change which people experience as the clash between an old world order and its emergent successor. This explains not only why great tragedy appears so rarely but also why it represents only those aspects of individual lives that contribute to an understanding of the major social changes it depicts. Tragedy omits such matters as the 'entire life surroundings of parents and children' and 'the material basis of the family, its growth, decline etc.', and does so because its principal concern is 'the inner, objective dialectic of the collision itself' (ibid.: 94, 95). The representation of life in all its detail is the business of epic and the novel.

But just as Greek tragedies share some common ground with their Homeric antecedents, novels share with both the desire to represent in full the lives of their characters. As a more expansive and eclectic genre than epic, the novel was able to re-invent that ancient and totalizing form, and by doing so became the epic of modernity. To test this idea, I want to explore why, in only a few years, Conrad's preoccupation with imperialism took him from the tightly focused colonial fable of *Heart of Darkness* to the density and narrative grandeur of *Nostromo*. What produced the change in narrative mode that coincided with Conrad's decision to take for his subject matter the Americas instead of British and European colonialism? *Heart of Darkness* and *Lord Jim* both move outwards from the metropolitan imperial centre of London to colonial peripheries. *Nostromo*, however, operates on a very different axis.

Conrad and America

Conrad made several voyages to the French Antilles when scarcely out of his teens, claiming to have glimpsed South America and to have been briefly in Venezuela.[3] Only in the year before he died did he set foot in the United States. Although his relations with the Old World were somewhat equivocal, he was European enough to distance himself from the New. Without being exclusively Polish or French or British, he created in his writings a pan-European perspective on the interconnections of its empires. Arguably the first internationalist novelist, Conrad thought the old European colonialism was dying. But unlike D. H. Lawrence, he did not detect in the world around him the dawn of a new order. On the contrary, his diagnosis of the *Zeitgeist* – before, during and after the Great War – corresponded roughly with his description of the crowd gathered at Schomberg's in Surabaya, as 'camped like bewildered travellers in a garish, unrestful hotel' (*Victory* 3).

Conrad's earliest journey to 'the Americas' was literary and resulted in his masterpiece, *Nostromo* (1904). The epic scope and detached narrative perspective of what was at that time the least personal of his novels involved a great deal of self-distancing. He set *Nostromo* in an imaginary Latin American republic. According to Conrad's Author's Note of 1917, it was assembled out of a few personal memories from his time in Marseilles (1874–8) and much reading.[4] While writing a novel that marginalizes British imperial power, Conrad himself was taking up permanent residence in the heartland of middle-class England. Set in what is strictly speaking a *post*-colonial Latin America, *Nostromo* describes new forms of imperialism created by multinational capitalism and reveals how the demise of European colonialism does not prevent Empire from perpetuating itself. Long before the colonialism of the Old World had run its course, it descries on its furthest horizon the outlines of a global economic system dominated by American capital.

The social and political realities of Costaguana are delineated in terms that go beyond the dualistic modelling of relations between colonizer and colonized. In 1823, President James Monroe had not only advised Congress to remain aloof from Europe's colonial wars but also insisted that Europe stay out of the Americas.[5] The long-term effect of this policy was to authorize the United States to 'manage' Latin America. *Nostromo* catches that history on the very cusp of change, when American intervention in Panama happened to coincide with the construction of the canal (1904–14). That event opened the way to more 'new' worlds. In the period in which *Nostromo* is set, the United States had neither completed the canal nor established its Canal Zone, although both events were shortly to happen. Situated on the Pacific side of South America, Costaguana is thus doubly removed for a little longer from the 'mainstream' of history.

Early in the novel, Charles Gould observes that '[t]here's a good deal of eloquence of one sort or another produced in both Americas' (83). The critical edge of his remark can be felt once we recall Conrad's endemic mistrust of 'eloquence' in Kurtz' infamous Report. A more immediate referent, however, is the humanitarian rhetoric of the millionaire businessman, Holroyd:

> 'Now, what is Costaguana? It is the bottomless pit of 10 per cent. loans and other fool investments. European capital had been flung into it with both hands for years. Not ours, though. We in this country know just about enough to keep indoors when it rains. We can sit and watch. Of course, some day we shall step in. We are bound to. But there's no hurry. Time itself has got to wait on the greatest country in the whole of God's Universe. We shall be giving the word for everything: industry, trade, law, journalism, art, politics, and religion, from Cape Horn clear over to Smith's Sound, and beyond, too, if anything worth taking hold of turns up at the North Pole. And then we shall have the leisure to take in hand the outlying islands and continents of the earth. We shall run the world's business whether the world likes it or not. The world can't help it – and neither can we, I guess.'
>
> (76–7)

Several generations after the Monroe Doctrine had laid down a blueprint for future American imperialism, Holroyd's discourse reads like a cross between the evangelism of Graham Greene's 'quiet American' and Hegel gone mad. From our present vantage-point, the mild fanaticism of this genially quixotic and polite Christian businessman sounds a more foreboding note. Conrad's satirical distancing of this new type of global exploiter is accompanied by the illuminating insight that the developments envisioned by Holroyd lie beyond the control of even 'the greatest country in the whole of God's Universe'. Holroyd anticipates something we now have: a self-regulating global system that no individual or national agency can constrain. Its most recent and alarming manifestation is the inability of an all-powerful United States to take moral responsibility for its interventions. *Nostromo* also contains the seeds of what was to become world-systems analysis and subsequently globalization theory.[6] Conrad remained sceptical of America for the rest of his life. In October 1922, for example, he told Bertrand Russell – who had just published a book on *The Problem of China* – that his deductions 'strike a chill into one's soul especially when you deal with the American element. That would indeed be a dreadful fate for China or any other country' (cited in Russell 1975: 396).[7]

Political discussions of *Nostromo* often repeat the familiar criticism of *Heart of Darkness*: namely, that it is unclear where Conrad 'stands' on the question of imperialism, and where his sympathies lie. Even one of his greatest admirers, the late Edward Said, criticizes *Nostromo* for 'embod[ying] the same paternalistic arrogance of imperialism that it mocks in characters like Gould and Holroyd' (Said 1993: xx). What Said objects to – the idea that native Latin Americans have no culture of their own, and are incapable of governing themselves or even of responding to any form of governance – is certainly a disabling prejudice. But it is not Conrad's. Said attributes to Conrad himself a *bon mot* of the legendary liberationist, Simón Bolívar: 'governing them, [Conrad] says, quoting Bolívar, is like ploughing the sea' (ibid.: xviii). Taking this remark to characterize Conrad's general attitude towards non-European peoples, Said here mis-remembers the passage he had cited more carefully some twenty years earlier in his major essay on *Nostromo*:

> The heritage of South America is, "as the great liberator Bolivar had said in the bitterness of his spirit . . . 'America is ungovernable. Those who worked for her independence have ploughed the sea'."
>
> (Said 1975: 111; *Nostromo* 186)

Said is not alone in attributing Bolívar's utterance to Conrad. It is not the narrator but the sceptical Martin Decoud who quotes the 'Liberator', and his reflection follows an intense argument with his beloved Antonia, Costaguana's quintessential 'patriot'. In other words, Bolívar's remark is rendered rhetorically and dramatically and its exact political meaning is to be found not in the words themselves but in the context.

The question of what Conrad 'himself' might have thought of these matters is perfectly reasonable. But before it can be put, the context of any observation attributable to Conrad needs to be borne in mind. In the one mis-remembered by Said, the disparaging and racist sentiment that emanates from Bolívar is enclosed within Decoud's meditation, which in turn is enclosed within Conrad's own novel. The critical distancing achieved by this framing device is both a function of *Nostromo*'s acknowledged breadth of vision and a warning that superficial analyses will not reveal the complexity of Conrad's politics. But instead of trying to extricate those politics directly (as it were) from *Nostromo*, I want to compare its panoramic political vision with that of traditional epic.

'The artist of the whole matter'

Conrad received this accolade from Henry James in 1906. Their literary relationship is hard to pin down. James' own masterpiece, *The Golden Bowl*, was published in the same year as *Nostromo* (1904), and it too is transnational in scope. A different kind of visionary from Conrad's Holroyd, James' Adam Verver sets himself the task of buying up the great art works of Europe in order to display them in America. In his idealism and untold wealth, Verver envisions a kind of high-cultural Disneyland. Perhaps James felt that his own trans-Atlantic perspective was narrow in comparison with the younger novelist's extra-European experiences. His letter to Conrad emphasizes that totality of vision ('the whole matter') is the key to Conrad's authority as a writer, and something that 'no-one has approached' (James 1987: 368). It is hard to believe that this does not refer, at least in part, to Conrad's most recently published novel. James' carefully chosen words go to the epic fullness of *Nostromo*'s depiction of a world at a significant turning point in human history. Novels of that scope were a long way from James' own aesthetic preferences. Those 'large loose baggy monsters' he disapproved of included *War and Peace* (James 1934: 84); and, when reviewing George Eliot's monumental *Middlemarch* (1873), he had asked: 'If we write novels so, how are we to write History' (Haight 1965: 87). All of this makes even more intriguing his praise of Conrad as the novelist of totality.

Fredric Jameson similarly associates the grandeur of *Nostromo*'s narrative design with Conrad's authoritative knowledge. He might even be considered to answer in the affirmative James' rhetorical question about *Middlemarch*, since Jameson regards *Nostromo* as both an epic novel and a model for writing history. His reading of *Nostromo* keeps to the terms of an undeclared argument with his English Marxist counterpart,

Terry Eagleton, about the question of form. Eagleton thinks that all of Conrad's novels, including *Nostromo*, are marked by a 'central absence':

> As the determining structure of which the novel's characters are the bearers (the true protagonist of the book, as Conrad commented), the silver is the unifying principle of the entire action; but since that action has for Conrad no coherent historical intelligibility, it is a principle which must of necessity be dramatically absent. It is precisely in these absent centres, which 'hollow' rather than scatter and fragment the organic forms of Conrad's fiction, that the relation of that fiction to its ideological context is laid bare.
>
> (Eagleton 1975: 138–9)

Eagleton's analysis of *Nostromo* is unusually perfunctory. He finds its non-linear and de-centred narrative structure symptomatic of a writer determined to 'speak' (but unable to 'know') the ideological contradictions within which he is trapped. By choosing a form that foregrounds actions and concrete details, while at the same time exposing certitude to 'corrosive negation', Conrad produced a text devoid of 'coherent historical intelligibility'. The ideological upshot of such exclusions and self-cancellations is to leave things precisely as they were.

Jameson, on the other hand, sees refusal of closure as the key to *Nostromo*'s method. This is what enables it to transcend the cognitive limitations of *Lord Jim*, whose deepest insights into the politics and ideology of imperialism can be recovered only from the text's unconscious. '[I]t is well, in conclusion', Jameson continues, 'having shown all the things which Conrad chose not to see, to show what he *could see* in a demanding and ambitious effort of the social and historical imagination' (Jameson 1981: 269; [my emphasis]).

Nostromo's non-linear and de-centred narrative structure gives it greater access to history. Its first reference to the success of the Monterist rebellion – the sad Ribiera's escape by donkey – is often taken to show how sceptical Conrad was about all forms of political hope. A sense that political idealism is ultimately futile, combined with Conrad's supposed counter-revolutionary tendencies, is said to be the final 'message' of *Nostromo*. But the Ribierist failure is never dramatized. Like that other central event, Jim's jump from the *Patna*, it is anticipated and later recorded as having happened, and 'is therefore present/absent in the most classic Derridean fashion' (ibid.: 272). The most momentous event in *Nostromo* is glimpsed only through the interstices of temporal and spatial narrative shifts of the opening section. It brings into being a consciousness of history inaccessible to classical realism, which belongs to a different historical moment. In recompense for that partial loss,

Jameson argues, its textual absence results in an altogether different kind of 'grand narrative': 'this hole at the centre of the narrative is itself but an external emblem of the greater one around which the gigantic system of events of the novel pivots as on some invisible axis' (ibid.).

Nostromo thus answers the question of how to represent, in the inherited forms of prose fiction, that collective and de-centred process perceived retrospectively as the coming of capitalism to Latin America. Individual lives are shown as relative to collective developments; all ideals and life-choices are absorbed into an impersonal History. Narrative traces of earlier realism (discernible in both character and action) persist like the bourgeoisie's collective memory of its heroic past, as described in Marx's *Eighteenth Brumaire of Louis Bonaparte* (1852). One of their functions is to parody the pretensions of Costaguana's chief citizens, who aspire to historical fame as founders of a new political order. The 'absent-centredness' of *Nostromo*, then, is not (in Eagleton's word) a 'hollow' which engulfs the conflictual terms of political struggle. On the contrary, it creates a perspective with its own specific insights into contemporary (and even future) realities.

The problem of writing about them is the centrepiece of Jameson's account. The 'resonance' of *Nostromo*, he declares, 'springs from a kind of unplanned harmony between this textual dynamic and its specific historical content' (ibid.: 280). Its greater understanding is revealed also in its content and political stance. Jameson states that 'Conrad never went further politically than in [his] portrayal of the nationalist-populist ideal' in Garibaldi (ibid.: 274). The ideal honoured in the memory of Garibaldi would no doubt include Conrad's appraisal of his own father's political stand. Yet in the same context, Jameson notes 'counter-revolutionary' elements in Conrad (ibid.: 270–1). In neither case, however, does he base his appraisal of *Nostromo*'s political and historical insight on its author's personal choices and attitudes. Instead, he focuses on the novel's total vision, which contains but is not contained by such elements. That is why he calls the harmony of meaning and form that it achieves 'unplanned'.

'For life to be large and full'

These words appear in Emilia Gould's melancholy meditation some years after the central event in *Nostromo*. Staged at a time when (as Captain Mitchell might have said) everything hung in the balance, it is placed at the end of the chapter that follows the unnoticed suicide of the novel's most intellectually trenchant character, Martin Decoud, and immediately before the high melodrama of Nostromo's death, which is the stuff of grand opera. 'It had come into [Mrs Gould's] mind', we read, 'that for life to be large and full, it must contain the care of the past and of the future in every passing moment of the present' (520–1). Her interior monologue brings to a close her long exchange, Chekhovian in mood, with Dr Monagham. The disappointment of her hopes leads to her bleak judgement on those 'material interests' that her husband's finer ambitions rested upon. Almost routinely, her private tragedy is taken to represent Conrad's own 'final' judgement on the politics of modernity, the capitalist world order, and all forms of human idealism and endeavour. The problem with this interpretation is that it disproportionately privileges not only Mrs Gould as a character but also the world of private and family relationships. That move is disallowed by the novel's broader perspective. It is true that the 'private' world of both family and personal relationships is a focal point of nineteenth-century English fiction, often at the expense of the public world of politics and nation building, and an interest in how the historical process unfolds. This is not to say, however, that narrative detachment is ubiquitous in *Nostromo*: indeed, some of its most intimate scenes are shot through with passionate investments. But to privilege even the most poignant personal tragedy in this novel is to distort the 'totality' to which it is subordinated.

Nostromo's world-view is no more deterministic than Marx's, with which it has some remarkable affinities. After his revolutionary hopes were defeated in 1848, Marx posed as a paradox the problem of the interplay between free will and determinism. 'Men make their own history, but not of their own free-will', he wrote, 'not under circumstances they themselves have chosen but under the given and inherited circumstances with which they are directly confronted'. And he went on to add that 'the tradition of the dead generations weighs like a nightmare on the minds of the living' (Marx 1973: 146). This looks as if it might well have served as an epigraph to *Nostromo*, given its themes. Surprisingly, however, it could not, because Marx's aphorism is far more pessimistic than Conrad's novel.[8] While it usefully reminds us that the historical process is driven by a dynamic interplay between social forces and individual desires, it corresponds only with the judgements of Emilia Gould or Martin Decoud. It does not summarize the totality that is *Nostromo*.

Nevertheless, the characters in *Nostromo* are certainly hierarchized, and some carry more authority than others. Furthermore, the judgements of many of them – Mrs Gould, Dr Monagham, Martin Decoud – are collectively bleak, while the last stages of other important characters – Don José Avellanos and his daughter Antonia, or Nostromo himself – evoke feelings of intense sadness. Emilia Gould becomes progressively disillusioned about her marriage and the disappearance of those youthful aspirations that she once seemed to share with Charles. The significance of her experience, moreover, is not just personal, because Conrad's careful patterning incorporates it into the novel's assessment of history and modernity. But to call her life a 'tragedy', as

Leavis does (Leavis 1948: 191), inflates its importance and is generically confusing. For one thing, it overlooks the fact that she and Charles perceived things differently from the start, even at the time when they felt they were embarking on a project that united them in spirit. At that pristine moment Charles is obsessed with an idea, while Emilia is so much in love that she is almost literally 'swept off her feet' (60–3). Their 'closeness' in this scene of their courtship hides from each of them what the other is thinking and feeling. We acquire this insight not from either of them but from the novel. When they come to engage with the financiers and other political supporters of Charles' plan to revive the Gould Concession, their differences gradually emerge. The narrative of the gulf that widens inexorably between them is presented with the same astringent detachment discernible in the story of Dr Monagham's torture or Decoud's lonely days on the island before his suicide. In its muffled resentment against her husband's insensitivity, Dr Monagham's sympathy for Emilia is presented compassionately. But the narrative as a whole assesses the situation differently by showing us that Charles – with whatever qualifications – has more political *nous* and even self-knowledge than Emilia. Her story, on the other hand, embodies something he doesn't recognize: that a life based on 'material interests' comes at a personal price. The full meaning of the Goulds' marriage, however, lies in the tensions explored between Emilia and Charles, and in the network of attitudes and actions that enmesh them. The only literary genre that is commensurate with Emilia Gould's desire that 'life be large and full' – and that it 'contain the care of the past and of the future in every passing moment of the present' – is epic.

British imperialism's failure to achieve epic status

Unlike ancient Rome, with which British imperialists liked to compare it, Britain failed to inspire a literary monument to commemorate its achievement. Although *Nostromo* does not focus on England, it is the only English candidate from the great age of European imperialism to rival Vergil's official paean to Augustan Rome, the *Aeneid*. Salman Rushdie's comic epic, *Midnight's Children* (1981), touches majestically on the imperial theme, but Britain's imperial greatness is considerably reduced in its story of Indian Independence. A member of two worlds, and familiar with both postcolonizers and the postcolonized, Rushdie was able to write a counter-epic to the grand narrative of Empire. Another plausible contender, E. M. Forster's *A Passage to India* (1924), begins with a truly impressive sweep across the divided terrain of British India. But it finally becomes locked into the personal needs and dramas of its characters, and fails to distance itself from specific viewpoints – including its own disturbed humanistic faith – to be able to comprehend suprapersonal forces that structure human destinies. Paul Scott's *Raj Quartet* (1966–75) adopts some of the trappings of epic. His story of the last days of the British Raj certainly contains the requisite historical ingredients for a narrative to rival Homer on the Trojan War or Vergil on the origins of Rome. But it aspires to something other than epic 'fullness' by opening up the story of Empire to the feminine world of memsahibs, and other unsung heroines who didn't occupy the centre stage of the imperial drama. Their inclusion relegates history to background.

This is a curious lacuna in Victorian literature, especially as there always seemed to be sufficient nationalist sentiment and imperialist exultation to create the desire for such a project. Like the story of its demise, the heroic period of British ascendancy on the sub-continent could have provided the content for such a narrative. Robert Clive's military and administrative achievements alone are on a scale suitable for epic treatment, especially if spectacular and horrific events – such as the 'Black Hole of Calcutta' or the extension of British struggles against French power to Indian conflicts – were to be included. But Britain never fully 'owned' its colonial achievements. A succession of impressive individuals – such as Warren Hastings and Clive himself – helped to fashion India into the 'jewel' in the British crown. But both men ended their days somewhat disgraced, back 'home' in England. Middle-class contempt for 'nabobs', stretching back to the beginning of the nineteenth century, helped to judge their mixed achievements. Acquisition of wealth in the colonies – and the supposed vulgarity that attended it – sullied their acquired social and economic status, and so much so that British India didn't quite cut the mustard for epic treatment by a talented laureate. It was with a sense of historical irony that the Bengali intellectual, Nirad C. Chaudhuri, tried to redress this imbalance in his biography of Clive written from an Indian perspective:

> Clive has not had a better deal at the hands of his biographers than the Empire has had from its historians. The fact is that, so long as it lasted, it never moved into the light of history, but remained subject to polemics, for or against. The polemical approach has not been given up, though the Empire has disappeared.
>
> (Chaudhuri 1975: iv)

Conrad was never even an unofficial 'prose laureate', despite being once dubbed as such (Sherry 1973: 61). The only laureate recalled in his imperialist novels is Vergil, who, having a dark side, was chosen by Dante as a guide through his own underworld. Like *Heart of Darkness* (which echoes both Vergil and Dante) and Conrad's other colonial classics, the *Aeneid* is 'Conradian' in being more touched by the 'tears of things' than impressed by Augustan triumphalism. In so far as its most memorable passages describe the human costs of the imperial ideal, it reads less like an act of homage than a critique of imperialism's crimes and moral contradictions. Despite such affinities, however, the narrative closest to the epic perspective of *Nostromo* is by Homer and not Vergil.

'I sing of Silver and the Mine, and the man . . . '

I can best explain this comparison by revisiting Hegel's distinction between so-called 'primitive' epics and 'artistic' epics (Hegel 1975, vol. 2: 1093–1100). Primitive epics, such as Homer's *Iliad* and *Odyssey*, were thought to be somehow closer to the 'real thing'; they seem to have arisen spontaneously out of the folk culture of the worlds they depict, and appear 'absolutely national and factual' (ibid.: 1098). 'Artistic' epics, such as Vergil's *Aeneid* or Milton's *Paradise Lost*, are by contrast more obviously and self-consciously fictional. The 'real thing' Homer represents is the heroic world of the Aegean warlords in the Bronze Age, whose power and exploits predated any social organization resembling the modern state. 'Sufficient unto themselves', in Hegel's phrase, they are memorialized culturally as a literary 'type': the larger-than-life hero on whom a whole community depends (Hegel 1962: 98–112). The *Iliad* records their most famous wars and the deaths of their greatest warriors. The aftermath of that heroic struggle is described in the *Odyssey*, which tells of a precarious attempt to restore the old world order and recreate the fullness of life that passed away on the plains of Troy. One problem ignored by this classification is that the Homeric epic poems – which developed from oral traditions – were not written down until almost half a millennium after the historical events they purport to describe. Just how close they are to 'real history' remains a moot point.

But heroic self-sufficiency is not the Homeric feature echoed in *Nostromo*. The old Garibaldino, Georgio Viola, certainly looks back to moments of heroic struggle under his legendary leader, just as Conrad sometimes meditated on the Napoleonic era as a time when heroic adventure coincided with the making of history. The Blancos of Costaguana similarly remember their 'Liberator', the legendary Bolívar. That kind of retrospectivity colours the treatment of *Nostromo*'s eponymous hero:

> Nostromo slowly crossed the large kitchen, all dark but for the glow of a heap of charcoal under the heavy mantel of the cooking-range, where water was boiling in an iron pot with a loud bubbling sound. Between the two walls of a narrow staircase a bright light streamed from the sick-room above; and the magnificent Capataz de Cargadores stepping noiselessly in soft leather sandals, bushy whiskered, his muscular neck and bronzed chest bare in the open

check shirt, resembled a Mediterranean sailor just come ashore from some wine or fruit-laden felucca. At the top he paused, broad shouldered, narrow hipped and supple, looking at the large bed, like a white couch of state, with a profusion of snowy linen, amongst which the Padrona sat unpropped and bowed, her handsome, black-browed face bent over her chest.

(252)

Conrad's descriptive method here is reminiscent of Homer's. In the narratives of some of Nostromo's other exploits the tone resonates even more closely with particular scenes in Homer. One such describes Odysseus, who (like Nostromo) when exhausted by the great swim that brings him to the land of the Phaiákians, discovers a safe hiding place where he sleeps peacefully.[9] In *Nostromo* that kind of description appears in contexts mostly alien to Homer's world. Like the breathless narrative of Nostromo's rescue of the silver in the darkness of the Golfo Placido (certainly the high point in all of Conrad's narrative descriptions) they come to be seen at best as things of the past – or as characteristic of literature. Nostromo himself recognizes ruefully that his saving of the silver was less significant to his betters than he wanted it to be. In the novel's broader context, the description of him entering the room of the dying Teresa Viola reads like pastiche. Echoes of a lost heroic code produce such a distancing effect that Conrad's novel ends up analysing the absence of the heroic rather than the thing itself. Like the painting of Garibaldi, or Antonia Avellanos' pious attendance at the plaque to commemorate Decoud's contribution to the birth of the new Occidental Republic, their function in the novel is to emphasize the fact that the world now coming into being is decidedly un-heroic.

This suggests that Conrad's ancient literary ancestor is not so much Homer but Sophocles, whose *Ajax* is also markedly post-Homeric. In taking as his tragic hero one of the greatest of the Akhaians, Sophocles accentuates the distance between his own Ajax and Homer's. Tragic heroes are more problematic versions of the heroic figures they recall. A significant cultural phenomenon separates the writing of the *Iliad* in about 800 BCE from the staging of Sophocles' 'Homeric' play in the fifth century BCE: the practice of Hero Cults, which ritualistically honoured such legendary heroes as Ajax, who was a cult figure on his native island of Salamis. The first half of Sophocles' play narrates Ajax's disgrace and subsequent suicide; the second describes the debates among the Greek chieftains over his body culminating in a formal recognition of his great achievements at Troy. The play can be read as a dramatic narrative of how Ajax's imagined exploits on the plains of Troy were at first negated by the contemptible and petty behaviour that characterized his demise, but eventually subsumed into history, memorialized and monumentalized. As Lukács plainly saw, the intertextual implications of this reading raise questions both of literary form and of cultural change.

The artistic practice of self-conscious distancing, however, also features strongly in the *Odyssey*. Like *Nostromo*, the poem announces its legendary theme before immediately baffling its readers by deferring the main story and complicating both plot and chronology. It begins, in fact, not with the heroic but with the hero's absent presence. Like his imagined audience, Homer inhabits a world remote from the events described. But so too does the poem's eponymous hero. At a turning point in his epic journey, Odysseus is received hospitably by King Alkinous of the Phaiákians, and at a feast in his honour, listens anonymously to his own deeds being recalled by the minstrel Demodokos. The 'real' Odysseus weeps in response to the moving account of himself and his companions transformed into a poem only a few years after the events it describes took place (VIII, 510–626). The literary self-consciousness that differentiates the *Odyssey* from the *Iliad* is such that the complexity of this episode is further enhanced when the King of the Phaiákians comments on the proleptic relation of history to poetry:

> Tell me why you should grieve so terribly
> Over the Argives and the fall of Troy.
> That was all gods' work, weaving ruin there
> So that it should make a song for men to come!
> (VIII, 617–20)

But while the *Odyssey* is in many ways a post-*Iliad* poem, both *Iliad* and *Odyssey* emanate from a world culturally remote from the kind of events they describe.

Nostromo is likewise self-conscious about its status as writing, which in turn determines its representation of history. It affects the tone of its recollections of past greatness, and not only in the allusions to Garibaldi. It is evident also in other forms of memorializing and monumentalizing such as the tone-deaf myth-making of Captain Mitchell and the pious chronicling by Don José Avellanos of *Fifty Years of Misrule*. In rendering events as simultaneously past, present and future, its narrative strategies result in that 'unplanned harmony' of form and content that links it to the Homeric perspective of the *Odyssey*. Despite its dramatic intensities, *Nostromo* orders the hierarchy between major and minor characters, and enables it to include both public and private, family and nation, Blanco politicians, mine owners and ordinary Costaguaneros. This does not mean that it ignores differences of value: on the contrary, judgements are made, stimulated or simply allowed throughout the novel, both in specific cases and in the overall trajectory of the narrative. But in *Nostromo* Conrad subsumed his personal preferences, attitudes and beliefs – supposing these to be capable of articulation in the first place – into a representation of the impersonal processes of history as manifest in one historical episode.

The greatest modern change from the social conditions which produced the conventions of ancient Greek and Roman epic is that military achievement is no longer regarded as the pre-eminent human virtue. Nostromo craves something like Homeric *arété*, or 'honour', although he is not even a soldier. In the novel's perfunctory anti-climax, the drunken General Barrios saves the day not by his valour or prowess but because his troops have superior modern rifles. The efficacy of Nostromo's 'famous ride' to Cayta is trivialized by Captain Mitchell in his new-found role as tourist guide for visitors to the new Costaguana. And Nostromo himself – re-incarnated as Captain Fidanza – has decided to 'grow rich very slowly' on his ill-gotten treasure (503).

Lukács recognized that while 'great realism' – exemplified in Tolstoy's novels – could achieve the perspective of classical epic, considerable adjustments of form and artistic methods were needed in order to accommodate 'the greater complexity' of our own times. As the possibility of finding a military leader comparable to Achilles or Odysseus became increasingly implausible, new types emerged to occupy central or at least key positions in modern historical narratives. That empty space could be filled effectively, however, only by a collective representation. The new type in *Nostromo* is the intellectual, who has some distant affinities with Odysseus. No previous English novel so confidently represents characters who are both highly intelligent and trenchant in their analyses of the political and historical struggles they are caught up in. That is why Nostromo cannot occupy convincingly the central place he is put in by the title of Conrad's novel. Although *Nostromo* concentrates on an essentially male world, its new heroes are no longer distinguished for their physical exploits. Acutely intelligent, and yet internally divided both in themselves and from one another, they include Gould, Decoud and Monagham. The creation of such characters is one of the most significant advances Conrad made over his earlier fictions.

9 *Victory* (1)
Valedictory to the old colonial order

Beyond politics and after colonialism

In one familiar account, Conrad's potency as a writer was interrupted in 1910 by a major breakdown in health, followed by a steady decline in his creative powers. A biographical detail often overlooked in this narrative is that in that same year Conrad re-visited (as if by way of convalescence) that period of his life and area of the earth which had inspired almost all his early novels and tales: the Eastern world of the Malay Archipelago. The great works that followed – 'The Secret Sharer' and 'Freya of the Seven Isles' (1912), *Victory* (1915) and *The Shadow-Line* (1917) – likewise involved revisiting those early and decisive experiences provoked by his first encounter with non-European people in Asia.

Moser (1957) and Guerard (1962) both imposed on Conrad an 'achievement and decline' template, which contributed significantly to the uneasy status of *Victory* and produced a restrictive view of both Conrad and politics. This familiar North American version of the Conrad canon regards *Victory* as 'patchy' at best but more commonly as evidence of final etiolation. Even Jameson's discussion of Conrad reinforces the narrative. While the mind-blowing pluralism of Jameson's writing creates a feeling of excitement and liberation, his work, Eagleton quips, 'resembles nothing quite so much as some great Californian supermarket of the mind' (Eagleton 1986: 70). His *tour de force* of postmodern appropriation displays the characteristically encyclopedic erudition of North American academic discourse, and reminds us that Jameson's colleagues at Yale included Harold Bloom and Paul de Man. *The Political Unconscious*, after all, does not seriously disturb the North American Conrad canon. A post-*Nostromo* and 'antipodean' Conrad can emerge only when one frees oneself from established assumptions and broadens one's sense of the political. This is the Conrad I shall now attempt to discover by re-reading his unsteadily canonical and resolutely anti-political high romance, *Victory* (1915). As his only major colonial novel after *Nostromo* that returns to the exotic East of his earliest fictions, it unexpectedly represents his final and most far-reaching insight into the meaning of late imperialism. In arguing this case, I shall use Jameson's hermeneutics to discover a Conrad who was responsive to historical forces that Jameson neglects.

Conrad's Surabaya and the island of Samburan are so far away from European centres of power that *Victory* appears unlikely to yield much to a Marxist reading of imperialism. As a kind of middle-aged *Lord Jim*, its opening 'strategy of containment' is to reverse the Marxist privileging of political and economic forces over personal and private lives. As such it already appears to belong among those literary developments that Jameson considers *post*-Conrad. 'After the peculiar heterogeneity of the moment of Conrad', he writes, 'a high modernism is set in place . . . [and] the political[,] . . . relentlessly driven underground by accumulated reification, has at last become a genuine Unconscious' (Jameson 1981: 280).

Yet *Victory* baffles traditional forms of materialist and other political criticism. As if to avoid those themes on which Marxist analyses thrive, Conrad places at the centre of his novel a paradoxical figure who is antithetical to the collective life of the polis and at the same time the ultimate product of civil society. Quietly puffing on a cheroot, Axel Heyst is at once a hermit and the last word in 'consummate politeness'. Alone in the silence of his lonely island, he meditates on the futility of action. Both the business of colonialism and its effects on the colonized 'natives' are banished to the periphery of the text, which contemplates instead an individual life paralysed at a very early stage and henceforth committed programmatically to non-action. Jameson has shown how Jim's adolescent daydreams result from aestheticizing processes whose function is to distance the world of work; *Victory* presents a modified version of what Jameson calls 'Jim's *bovarysme*' (ibid.: 211). Heyst's most decisive commitment is an existential affirmation of deliberate will-lessness, 'I'll drift' (92). But whereas the aestheticization of Jim's life does not prevent him from acting, Heyst's is of a different order: 'He suffered. He was hurt by the sight of his own life, which ought to have been a masterpiece of aloofness' (174). Responding to the aporia that crowned his father's philosophical and political career, Heyst the adolescent has decided to break down all 'illusion'. In his last work, the older Heyst 'claimed for mankind that right to absolute moral and intellectual liberty of which he no longer believed them worthy' (91). In a striking linguistic gesture, the cadences of both the younger and older Heyst are described as 'finished' – an ambiguous term meaning 'completed' or 'exhausted', on the one hand, or 'polished', on the other. It encompasses the debilitating split between thought and feeling in both their lives as well as the attenuated civility of the son's discourse. It marks Europe's moments of both revolutionary hope and imperialist enthusiasm as already past possibilities.

Failed realism or timeless allegory?

The novel opens with a commentary on a failed capitalist adventure: Axel
Heyst's quixotic incursion into the world of 'hard facts' and wild
speculation. Simultaneously trenchant and facetious, its very first
paragraph touches deftly on 'commodities', 'wealth', 'property' and
'finance', but in a tone calculated to deflect attention away from such
matters (3). Its discourse – the stuff of expatriate island gossip – is the
ideological fare of Schomberg's hotel. This noncommittal opening issues
in the highly centred and character-bound narrative of Axel Heyst, so
that *Victory* appears to perpetuate older realist practices instead of
moving towards the modernism of which Jameson's Conrad represents
the penultimate stage. Scholars such as Palmer (1968) and Secor (1971),
who wanted to redeem *Victory* from its classification as failed realism,
began by recuperating its allegorical mechanisms, and treating textual
traces of older narrative traditions as clues to the meaning of the novel.
Its apparent carelessness then became a sign that the novel should be
read not for its truth to everyday reality but as some sort of allegory.
Unashamed of either its allegorical modes or its affiliations with popular
culture, *Victory* could still be valued as a mode of psychological realism
that openly displays its origins in older genres. Besides, as Jameson has
argued, realism is not a new genre but a development that signals the end
of genre: in this respect, it is a processing apparatus rather than a
discrete literary form. But if *Victory* resorts to some of the earliest types of
fictional narratives, it does so from the standpoint of 'bewildered
travellers in a garish, unrestful hotel' (3), an image that James Clifford
takes as emblematic of the contemporary condition of Western man and
consequently a challenge to Western ethnographic authority.[1]

Far from providing a reliable guide to the meaning of *Victory*, these
vestiges of older narratives do little more than play with readerly desires
for coherence. The story of Heyst and Lena can be read plausibly either
as melodrama (the aristocratic seduction of an innocent working girl) or
– antithetically – as a modern version of the fairy-tale rescue of a poor
girl by a Prince Charming. Although the moral meaning of each
interpretation virtually cancels out the other, textual evidence can be
found to support either reading. From a longer perspective, *Victory* might
also be seen as a rewriting of the biblical story of Adam and Eve, the Eden
of this novel being the tropical island of Samburan. It is a suitable
location for any of these plots, partly because islands are traditionally
sites of romance and enchantment, and partly because the colonized East
is a good place for 'going native', which means investing libidinally in its
transgressive and guilt-inducing excitements.[2] The repressed themes of
sin and sexuality, which are either pushed to the edges of the text or
transmuted into melodrama, enable the Genesis story of flawed
innocence to be fused with nineteenth-century tales of exotic adventure.

Generic confusion, then, is a distinctive feature of *Victory* and needs to be accepted as such: the novel's most interesting insights are generated not by the search for some imaginary artistic or hermeneutic unity but through its crazy *dis*-order.

Victory is best approached as a comic novel. What militates against reading it that way is not only its sometimes solemn and portentous tones but also the temptations it holds out for allegorical or archetypal reading. These can have the effect of subordinating Conrad's novel to what Eagleton calls (apropos Hardy) 'the immobilizing perspectives of myth' (Eagleton 1975: 131). One such invitation emanates from Heyst himself when, at a pivotal moment of the novel, he declares: 'There must be a lot of the original Adam in me, after all' (173). Descended from that 'first ancestor' – who in turn was descended from/made by his father, God himself – Heyst exercises the Adamic prerogative of naming his woman Lena. Like those non-Europeans who arrive late at the scene of modernity, Heyst is spoken of as a 'later' arrival. Historically belated, he is sired by a father he thinks of as having the kind of mythic dimension that we might imagine Apollo had for Conrad. At one level, the memory of his father dominated Heyst's whole existence; at another, his paternity was 'purely a matter of hearsay' (175), a phrase which uncannily evokes the after-effects of Conrad's own early orphaning. The elder Heyst gloomily bequeathed to his son an unshakeably negative interpretation of life even before the young Heyst had much experience of it. Like Adam, Heyst is told what to avoid; like Adam, he succumbs to the temptation of a woman and therefore must relive the myth of the fall on his paradisiacal island. Readers wary of identifying Heyst too closely with his author should remember that Conrad himself first raised that possibility. In the Author's Note for the novel, he writes of the 'nearness of the book, its nearness to me personally, to the vanished mood in which it was written' (ix). And, as in Conrad's case, Heyst's orphaning did not *cause* his migratory existence, during which he felt neither completely rooted in his enchanted circle of islands at the outskirts of the colonial world nor sufficiently liberated to escape from it. Both the deracination experienced on becoming an orphan and his later wanderings in exile are simply seen as two variations of the basic paradigm of separation and loss. This complex pattern of deracinated existences is what gives *Victory* its modern feel, making it a postcolonial novel for postcolonizers as well as the postcolonized. But it is also for those who, while living in neither group, still experience fractured memories as a result of migration.

The adverse judgement of *Victory* as failed realism was only partially redeemed by those archetypal readings for which it appears to provide abundant evidence. The reason why none of them quite adds up is that the 'clues' which support one reading are often at odds with or cancel out those adduced by another. These trailers are rather like that self-contradictory yet loosely apposite list of nicknames scattered through the opening chapters as we are first getting to 'know' Axel Heyst: 'Enchanted Heyst', 'Hard Facts Heyst', 'the Utopist', 'the Spider', 'the Enemy' and 'the Hermit'. These names are the residue of island gossip. None of them, we discover, describes Heyst adequately, for the novel's own habit of caricaturing is at odds with the mission of realism. A Jamesonian 'strong' reading of *Victory*, which seeks political rather than allegorical meanings, must begin by recognizing that the planting of mythical allusions in the text is a narrative strategy whose effect is to obfuscate rather than illuminate the whole. Yet even without such metacommentary, the novel ambushes readers in pursuit of allegory. Take, for example, the idea that its mastercode is the Biblical Eden. Since *Victory* is a post-Victorian novel (whose delicate eroticism distances it from the Victorian ethos),[3] its use of the Genesis Creation myth is shadowed by the equally potent counter-discourse of Darwin's theory of evolution. Is Ricardo the tempting serpent in the Garden, or simply a lower form of life, whose 'suffering soul of savagery' (288) is hell-bent on achieving a higher state of existence through Lena? Has Pedro properly come down from the trees? Such complications make it impossible to sustain even more clever and complex versions of archetypal reading. For with his incipient class-consciousness, Ricardo might just as well be taken to represent (in a somewhat lumpen form) the miseries of the proletariat. In this reading, his *ressentiment* burgeons into class solidarity with Lena. She may well see him as 'the embodied evil of the world' (298); but he surely touches a sore spot with his invitation to get out from under the class-dominated world of 'yporcrits' and escape their common exploitation as 'wage-slaves' (296). 'What do you think a fellow is', he asks Lena: 'a reptile?' (300). With that passionate cry, the allegorical cat is again out of the bag.

The anti-political *Victory*

The mainspring of *Victory*'s narrative development, then, is not politics but the psychological drama of Axel Heyst. And even if we find a moral fable in the allegorical burden of Heyst's fall and the novel's sad didactic conclusion that he had got it all wrong, this reversal of Heystian commitment to non-action is but a faint echo of Marx's mighty eleventh thesis on Feuerbach: learning to 'trust in life' may be a timid first step towards action, but that still leaves Heyst a long way from the horizon that includes changing the world.[4] If Jameson is right to think that *Nostromo* marks the limits of Conrad's exploration of politics, this moderately progressive reading of *Victory* keeps it within a dialectics that would have to have been resolved before the narrative of *Nostromo* could even be set in motion. Exposed to political interrogation, and evincing

Conrad's struggles with both realist conventions and political meanings, *Victory* appears an oddly recidivist novel to have been published in England in the first year of the Great War. By reducing the activities in Southeast Asia at that time to a merely exotic setting, it reads almost like a counter-revolutionary tract.

Before going that far it is worth noting that in one respect Conrad's perspective on late imperialism intersects with the analyses of Hilferding and Lenin among others. All of them record a shift in the economic structure from 'banking finance' (as represented, for example, by the capitalist individualism of Holroyd in *Nostromo*) to 'finance capital'. By enabling the metropolitan bourgeoisie to engage in colonialist expansion, this produces what Lenin called 'the highest stage of capitalism', which is also the moment of high imperialism (Lenin 1917).[5] The story of Heyst's abortive career as a colonial capitalist repeats, in a different key, the demise by bankruptcy of 'the great De Barral' in Conrad's previous novel, *Chance* (1913). The narration of these court proceedings moves with a Zen-like detachment:

> [I]t was discovered that this man who had been raised to such a height by the credulity of the public was himself more gullible than any of his depositors. He had been the prey of all sorts of swindlers, adventurers, visionaries, and even lunatics. Wrapping himself up in deep and imbecile secrecy he had gone in for the most fantastic schemes: a harbour and docks on the coast of Patagonia, quarries in Labrador – such-like speculations. Fisheries to feed a canning factory on the banks of the Amazon was one of them. A principality to be bought in Madagascar was another. As the grotesque details of these incredible transactions came out one by one ripples of laughter ran over the closely packed court – each one a little louder than the other. The audience ended by fairly roaring under the cumulative effect of absurdity. The Registrar laughed, the barristers laughed, the reporters laughed, the serried ranks of the miserable depositors watching anxiously every word, laughed like one man. They laughed hysterically – the poor wretches – on the verge of tears.
>
> (81–2)

Dickensian in tone, this passage seems merely to remind us that human folly is ineradicable. But in fact it heralds the arrival of a new global menace in the form of a new wave of European expansion. Heyst's efforts on behalf of the Tropical Belt Coal Company show a business flair similar to De Barral's speculations. And if that company fails to be a 'great stride forward for these regions' – as Heyst put it in his managerial heyday, enthusiastically mouthing the crude rhetoric of progress that characteristically accompanies such invasions (6) – neither does it appear to do much harm. In *Victory*, however, there is a more important shift of perspective. The scandal of joint stock running amok is seen from the point of view of the people affected by it in places that Europeans consider 'remote'. It is Europe that is now marginalized and curtly judged to be 'removed' – remote – 'from the world of hazard and adventure' (23). Even so, the antipodean perspective thus promised is kept carefully contained: the indigenous life of the region becomes a mere 'play of shadows' in a novel centred on a seedy bunch of enervated expatriates (167).

While these narrative strategies recall Jameson's *Lord Jim*, *Victory* distances its material much more thoroughly. In this respect, one of its minor characters, 'poor Morrison', is a typical product of the novel's transvaluations. Far from epitomizing colonial exploitation, Morrison comically becomes the exploited: his power to 'squeeze' the villagers in his debt is poignantly reduced to furious but ineffectual memos scratched in his pocketbook (10–11). Similarly, the 'good Davidson' is the humble white servant of a paternalistic Chinese boss. Finally, Heyst's pathetic encounter with the world of hard facts ends rather bleakly when the man he provides for – a waif like himself, the Chinese 'coolie' Wang – rewards him by playing a part in his demise. In this late novel of Conrad's, serious analysis of European imperialism at a critical moment of its history is effectively repressed by whimsy, comedy and the absurd. The forestage is occupied by a tragic love-story, while the Dutch colonial masters are barely mentioned.

In Jameson's reading of *Lord Jim*, the will-to-style is a way of repressing consciousness of the waterways of empire as sites of work: it results in the language of 'romance and daydream, of narrative commodity and the sheer distraction of "light literature"' (Jameson 1981: 213). Set in the same outlands of empire, *Victory* imagines a very different fictional geography. Its seas do not appear to link the islands it is dotted with. Instead, their wide empty spaces exist in a blank uniform glare. Samburan is redolent of a Shakespearean fantasy-island surrounded by endless uncharted seas and populated by 'calling shapes and beckoning shadows dire'.[6] The self-generating *écriture* of *Lord Jim* is replaced in *Victory* by a narrative voice whose distinctive tone is self-conscious detachment. In Part I it mediates the casual island gossip through which Heyst's doings are filtered, and against which his peculiar intensities stand out in comic relief. The shift in Part II to a more intimate and coherent account of Heyst's affairs resembles the sequence from one 'movement' to another in a classical symphony, and could seem a somewhat gratuitous change of perspective. But by being unannounced it often goes unremarked, because the novel consistently uses one kind of detachment or another. This binds into an apparently seamless tale not only the novel's slow and mimetic reproduction of a will-to-realism but also its deliberate frustration of that will in the quasi-allegorical melodrama of the dénouement. The shift from dispersed point-of-view in Part I to the more focused omniscience of Part II involves this process. The ironic point-of-view in *The Secret Agent* (1907) generates what Conrad in the Author's Preface describes as both 'inspiring indignation and underlying pity and contempt' (viii). But in *Victory* irony operates through a mobile play of voice: consistently and disconcertingly detached, one of its functions is to prevent the readers from ever having a fixed attitude towards Heyst. If *Victory* is to be valued for its political insights or postcolonial critique, we should expect to find such features in that narrative voice which produces the characteristic tone of this novel, rather than in transparent statements about imperialism. This is the textual 'slope' that Jameson opposes to narrative structure, and which he treats either as style or the 'sentence-by-sentence life of the narrative text' (Jameson 1981: 257).

Conrad's postcolonial unconscious

The elder Heyst offers rich possibilities to allegorizers who favour an Oedipal reading of the novel. What its deceptive strategies conceal, however, is that the role played by this father of mythic proportions, who is the dominant power in the novel's deep memory, resembles that of another revolutionary and national hero, Garibaldi. Like *Nostromo*'s Garibaldi, the elder Heyst is present in *Victory* only as an image on the wall. This political echo from *Nostromo* enables us to get beyond treating the elder Heyst as the allegorical key to *Victory*, and to see him instead as signifying a precise moment in history, which predates the time in which the novel's events take place. He is not a mythical figure but an embodiment of that mythopoeic impulse which originates in our desire for myth and burdens history with it. The elder Heyst might thus be seen to represent a specific stage in Europe's gradual movement to what we have come to know as 'late capitalism'. In marking the change from a passionate belief in reform to its passionless dying, he prepares the way for his son's near total estrangement from anything but negative convictions. If Heyst's story, in this account, begins to look like a historical allegory, the ground is yet to be cleared for a truly political reading of the novel. What motivated Conrad to relocate a moment of European impasse in the exotic setting of oriental romance, and to narrate it in the form of a love-story?

One way of opening up these perspectives and further scrutinizing the textual processes of repression and recuperation which shape *Victory* is again to compare it with *Lord Jim*, this time in terms of narrative structure. To reveal how Conrad organized the complex tension between the positive and negative poles of activity and value in *Lord Jim*, Jameson made use of Greimas' semiotic rectangle.[7]

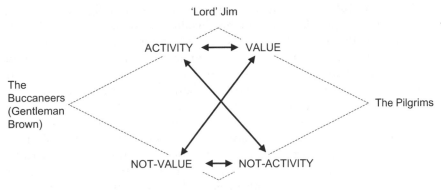

The close affinity between the two novels becomes apparent when *Victory* is inserted into Jameson's diagram for *Lord Jim*. Moving clockwise with Jameson from the right hand side, an embarrassing slot (on the cosmopolitan and imperialist stage occupied by Conrad's novels) is the first conjuncture of 'value' with 'non-activity'. An available European occupant is Heyst himself, or at least his project of fashioning his life as a 'masterpiece of aloofness'. Unlike 'Lord' Jim, however, Heyst remains a genuinely Lukácsian problematic hero who might occupy equally convincingly any of the four slots. His failure to defeat the sadly defeatable 'Evil trio' allocates him to the 'not-value/not-activity' category. 'Activity' associated with 'not-value' characterizes perfectly that comic parody of Western development in the embryonic Third World, the Tropical Belt Coal Company. Even the final 'complex term' – the resolution of contradictions between activity and value – can be glimpsed in Heyst's rescue of Lena, at one of the novel's crossroads. It points to a potential outcome of their relationship which, when the strangers intrude into their island existence, is shown to have a chance of delivering Heyst from his father's philosophy of negation.

I will not place Heyst, then, in what (in the colonial world at least) is the un-European category of value attaching to not-activity. Instead, as Jameson did with *Lord Jim*, I shall allocate the Asian elements in the novel to this slot. These include shadowy half-presences like those native fishermen who go about their business while impeding no one, and least of all the narrative ambitions of Conrad's text. Another component is the dignified servant 'John' in Schomberg's hotel, who witnessed the shameful brawl between two white men, Schomberg and Zangiacomo, but refuses to gossip about it. And above all there is Wang, whose existence, like that of the pilgrims in *Lord Jim*, seems motivated by forces and directed to goals inaccessible to a European consciousness.

The second slot, or 'neutral term', in Greimas' paradigm is far easier to fill. *Victory*'s equivalent of those briefly-alluded-to 'deck-chair sailors' in *Lord Jim* is the clientele of Schomberg's hotel, the people Ricardo wonderfully calls a 'bloodless lot of animated cucumbers' (149). These include the 'hail-fellow-well-met' crew of expatriates who soak up Schomberg's gossip, join Mr Jones' gambling circle, or take advantage of the 'entertainment' provided by Zangiacomo's orchestra. Passive and parasitic on a social order established by those heroic adventurers who preceded them, they comfortably occupy the neutral axis of 'non-activity/non-value'. Significantly, their gossip constitutes the narrative restlessness of Part I of *Victory*, which begins in a spirit of negation and neutrality. They have a structural role in the novel's attempts to plot and resolve the contradictory tensions between action and value. At least one of them, Davidson, is pleasant. More ambiguous is the shadowy narrator-as-character, whose presence in the novel is confined to the occasional Hitchcock-like appearance. Collectively, they influence the novel's predominant mood and characteristic style. By containing this group and its discourse to just one segment in a greater whole, the Greimas rectangle shows a way beyond receiving the world passively as the always already known. Ethically, it teaches us that Schomberg's self-amusing gossip is in fact dangerous. Not surprisingly, the next slot in Greimas' rectangle – the collocation of action with non-value – is somewhat over-subscribed. Central to Jameson's reading of late-nineteenth-century fiction, this is the realm of Nietzschean *ressentiment*. Schomberg has a slave's mentality as well as dark passions, the obscene residue of victimizing his scrawny wife to whom he is bound by habit and twisted respectability. Both beget their counterparts in Heyst's double, the renegade gentleman Mr Jones, and his criminal entourage who represent one version of Nietzschean *ressentiment*. With his father's library in tow, Heyst typifies the other product of *ressentiment* spawned by the reifications of late capitalism: the disaffected intellectual, whom Jameson takes to be the focus of George Gissing's novels. This thematic pattern is sufficiently complex to justify Jameson's description of Conrad as the 'epic poet' of *ressentiment* (Jameson 1981: 268) – provided we remember that Conrad always makes it a part of much wider processes, and that it is developed far more subtly in *Victory* than in the earlier novels.

The puzzling affirmation of Conrad's title suggests a candidate for the final space on Greimas' rectangle, the 'complex term' or 'ideal synthesis of the two major terms of the contradiction'. That 'last word' which Conrad wrote of the novel, however, wilfully forecloses the hopes his readers may have that the personal impasse between Heyst and Lena will be resolved. It is therefore appropriate to regard *Victory* as culminating in an act of Brechtian estrangement rather than adhering to realism. Ironically, the victory seems to be given to Lena, so that her Supreme Act enables her to occupy – uneasily – the final space in the grid. As in the case of *Lord Jim*'s 'impossible hero', our acceptance of this dated performance of self-sacrifice by the heroine of *Victory* involves what Jameson calls a 'lowering of our reality principle' (ibid.: 256). Yet the seriousness of Conrad's intention here ought not to be minimized. On the one occasion when Conrad was cajoled, like Dickens, into giving public readings in the United States, he wrote to his wife how his well-to-do audience had reacted to his rendition of the crowning episode in *Victory*: 'There was a most attentive silence, some laughs and at the end when I read the chapter of Lena's death, audible snuffling' (Karl 1979: 889).

Once Lena has played the role that culminates in this *coup-de-théâtre*, the subtle psychological and ethical drama between the lovers, enacted above all on their long walk to the mountain, recedes in significance. Together with the scene in which Heyst first meets Lena, the lovers' conversation on the walk represents the high point of realism in *Victory*. Its purely dramatic action is achieved by means of dialogue uninterrupted by either narratorial intrusions or interpretative gestures. Conrad never wrote anything as intimate as this scene in which a gap between chapters is used to curtain off a moment of private sexual intensity between the violent and erratic passions which precede their encounter and the radical calm that follows it (215–16). As if in answer to Heyst's philosophical dilemma, this incomplete but nevertheless ongoing and embodied experience will either threaten or resolve the Heystian dilemma. More than just a love romance is interrupted by the arrival of the 'external world' to the island: with this visitation, the rich vein of psychological and (unexpectedly in Conrad) sexual realism explored on the mountain walk is phased out of the text.

The island-romance theme, which delicately explores Heyst's sexual relationship with Lena, is just one term in a novelistic experiment that demands rapid shifts of attention by its readers. Its results are not necessarily negated by the introduction of a new variable in the form of 'the world' or 'evil'. Seen in this way Conrad legitimately chooses to break one kind of narrative contract in the interests of another. In order to politicize the reading of *Victory*, I think we should not dwell on what the novel may have lost as a result of Conrad's failure to develop the love relationship further. On the contrary, we should ask what narrative quest was refused in the first place by moving away from politics towards love romance and psychological drama. The initial comic belittling of the Tropical Belt Coal Company yields to the high seriousness of the Heyst–Lena story. The mechanistic and psychological links between these two aspects of Heyst's engagement with the world mask the apparently arbitrary though predictable choice of setting a love-story in the exotic 'East'. After all, the love-story in *Victory* is not even inter-racial. It does not develop those stories of 'going native' that Conrad had explored in his earliest novels, which are also set in the Malay Archipelago.

Lena is to Heyst a 'script in an unknown language' (222). 'Her tone betrayed always a shade of anxiety', we are told, 'as though she were never certain how a conversation with him would end' (186). Their close relationship involves an encounter with language that, in Heyst's case, dismantles the 'finished' courtesy that shields him against the world. We are positioned to read their verbal misunderstandings with a sympathy that comes from a wider perspective than they themselves have on the seemingly random shifts of their dialogue. Although they appear completely safe from external threats, Heyst and Lena experience a mutual distress that has originated in nothing but words. The text is organized in such a way as to obscure for us too the question that Lena had once put casually to Heyst, and to which their meandering conversation intermittently returns: 'Why are you here?' (194). The nearest Heyst comes to a direct answer is to reiterate his life-story: his father's influence, the meeting with Morrison, what happened at Schomberg's hotel, and so forth. Heyst's re-reading of what we already know is not only fascinating in itself but a clear indication of the small but significant space that separates him from his author. It indicates the intimacy of identification which characterizes many of Conrad's references to *Victory*, while maintaining a critical distance from Heyst's inability to answer directly Lena's profound and simple question: 'Why are you here?'

The seriousness of Lena's innocent question is fully manifest when the boat-load of strangers arrives on the island. What disturbs Heyst is that they are white men. Why are *they* here, he might well ask. He suddenly experiences, without recognizing it as such, the lost originary moment of a history of imperialism written by the vanquished: the shock of something like the premonitory fear felt by 'the natives' on seeing Europeans for the first time.

> [T]heir apparition in a boat Heyst could not connect with anything plausible. The civilisation of the tropics could have had nothing to do with it. It was more like those myths, current in Polynesia, of amazing strangers, who arrive at an island, gods or demons, bringing good or evil to the innocence of the inhabitants – gifts of unknown things, words never heard before.
>
> (227–8)

Confronted by these visitants half-dead in their boat, Heyst fails to ask them the question that Lena had asked him, and which might have devastated immediately their designs on his supposed riches: 'Why are you here?' When Wang steals his revolver, Heyst misrecognizes the situation so badly as to feel more threatened by Wang than by the 'amazing strangers'. His assessment of the situation is pathetically colonialist: 'Wang would hardly risk such a crime in the presence of other white men' (257).

In failing to negotiate Lena's fundamental question, which lies at the heart of all colonialisms, Heyst has less difficulty with its curious 'why' than the non-referentiality of its deictic 'here'. For both Lena and the 'enchanted' Heyst, these islands and waterways are a nameless non-place, a simple setting for life's romantic adventures. The lovers inhabit only one side of the island. On the other side – barricaded from them by a symbolic 'jungle' – live villagers engaged in an island economy that lies beyond the ken of the former manager of the Tropical Belt Coal Company. Heyst and Lena are sympathetic characters only for as long as *Victory* remains a love-story. As soon as it moves on to the suppressed narrative of colonialism, they must be unmasked, unfortunately, as among other things unconscious racists incapable of relating to the place where they live.

Their profoundly Eurocentric world-view, which appears only fleetingly in inconsequential snatches of dialogue, is exemplified in Heyst's brief explanation to Lena of Wang's presence on the island:

> "He has been tidying the place in this labour-saving way," explained Heyst, without looking at the girl, whose hand rested on his forearm. "He's the whole establishment, you see. I told you I hadn't even a dog to keep me company here."
>
> Wang had marched off towards the wharf.
>
> "He's like those waiters in that place," she said. That place was Schomberg's hotel.
>
> "One Chinaman looks very much like another," Heyst remarked. "We shall find it very useful to have him here . . . "
>
> (182)

The important point here is not that Conrad presents Heyst and Lena's racism as 'benign' but that he positions his readers in such a way that they barely notice it. But at this moment of crisis for Heyst, our narrative assumptions are profoundly destabilized. Wang, who formerly has been observed 'under Western eyes' and labelled unobtrusive, suddenly emerges as a person in his own right, with a consciousness whose history is non-European:

> His Chinaman's mind, very clear but not far-reaching, was made up according to the plain reason of things, such as it appeared to him in the light of his simple feeling for self-preservation, untrammelled by any notions of romantic honour or tender conscience. The graves of

Wang's ancestors were far away, his parents were dead, his elder brother was a soldier in the yamen of some Mandarin away in Formosa. No one near by had a claim on his veneration or his obedience.

(307)

From this point on, the text treads a more delicate line in its representation of Wang. His reinvention as something other than an object of the colonial gaze highlights *Victory*'s radical departure from Conrad's earliest novels. These may innocently have colonized for fiction the indigenous life of the Malay Archipelago by incorporating the daily life of its inhabitants into a pre-existent European realism. By distancing the 'natives', the sea novels gained considerably in authenticity. But, by being unaware of the politics first exposed by Edward Said in the colonizing mission of Orientalist learning, they invite the further charge of ignoring the prior inhabitants of subsequently imperialist lands. The transformation of Wang from a stage Chinaman into an active participant in the real world reveals enough of his life to show us by contrast the fatal limitation of Heyst's world-view. That new world opened up so significantly, however, cannot be completely assimilated. Readers now encounter a sympathetic point of view that is damningly critical of Heyst's very existence, and witness with embarrassment the bizarre drama on the white man's side of the island. More importantly – and partly through Wang's eyes – the narrative paradigm revealed by Greimasian analysis also changes significantly. By reason of his supposed Asiatic passivity, Wang could suitably be allocated to the category of 'value/not-activity'. But once the stereotypical mask is removed, he evacuates that space which henceforth remains vacant. Having disarmed the white man and thrown in his lot with the Alfuro villagers, he now serves the diagnostic purpose of showing that Heyst's dreamy existence on Samburan is based on deeply racist assumptions. He proves that he himself (and not Mr Jones) is the true challenger to Heyst's Adamic mission. Like Jones, he is also Heyst's double. With the graves of his ancestors far away, his parents dead, and no one nearby (apart from one woman) with any claim on his veneration or his obedience, he lives out on the island a more authentic version of Heyst's orphaned life as a migrant. The vanishing burden of the sad white man is to populate a world which, he has not noticed, is already populated. Its melodramatic finale is played out in the breathless scene of Lena's great sacrifice, and in Wang's more modest contribution to the debate over action and value by shooting Pedro. Wang becomes the shadowy pretender ready to materialize alongside Lena on that difficult-to-fill empty chair. The ideal resolution of the tensions that the novel has negotiated so boldly will only become possible in a postcolonial world that properly belongs to 'the poetry (of) the future' (Marx 1973: 149).[8]

Unlike *Nostromo*, *Victory* no doubt underestimates the power of economic forces in sustaining European imperialism. But by recognizing that the racism in imperialist ideology lies also at the heart of exotic fiction, it insinuates a resonant discord into the 'innocent' and 'feminine' discourse of popular romance. Focusing on Europe's (un)consciousness of its protracted historical trespass, *Victory* masterfully deploys and finally abandons the modes of classical realism. In doing so it signals a terminal crisis for both imperialist ideology and literary colonization. At a time when the majority of colonial novels were still to be written, it marks the end of the genre. Meanwhile, the intriguing glimpses we are given into that other world which Wang represents anticipate new opportunities for English-language fiction in a postcolonial world.

10 *Victory* (2)

Postcolonial Conrad

Emerging from the ruins

In a spirit of respect and exasperation, D. H. Lawrence once described Conrad as one of the 'Writers among the Ruins' (Lawrence 1962, vol. 1: 152). While Lawrence's agenda as a writer was radically different from Conrad's, the comment is apposite, particularly to the European author of those great and gloomy counter-revolutionary classics, *The Secret Agent* (1907) and *Under Western Eyes* (1911). The political futility they embody has greatly influenced assessments of Conrad's politics. Their 'structure of feeling' also plays a part in *Victory* (Williams 1980: 20–7), an ambivalently titled novel completed on the eve of the Great War and published in 1915, when talk of endings was becoming so commonplace that even Lawrence himself sometimes chimed in. 'When I drive across this country', he wrote to Lady Ottoline Morrell,

> with autumn falling and rustling to pieces, I am so sad, for my country, for this great wave of civilisation, 2000 years, which is now collapsing, that it is hard to live. So much beauty and pathos of old things passing away and no new things coming . . . the past, the great past, crumbling down, breaking down, not under the force of the coming birds, but under the weight of many exhausted lovely yellow leaves, that drift over the lawn, and over the pond, like the soldiers.
> (Lawrence 1962, vol. 1: 378)

This elegiac note reminds us that Lawrence, like Conrad, was a contemporary of those very English composers, Delius and Vaughan Williams, whose music evokes a leisurely and vanishing England experienced through a softening haze: a poignant world (sharply contrasted with the present) of finer feelings, yearning for things lost. This prevailing Edwardian sensibility, merging with the sentimentalities of wartime, constitutes the evanescent beauties of their music, which is so different in spirit from the more ebullient patriotism of their older contemporary Elgar.

A pivotal moment in *Victory* similarly evokes a sombre relationship with the European past. Very near the centre of the novel, Axel Heyst is found literally 'among the ruins' of the Tropical Belt Coal Company, 'meditating'. The narrator comments: 'A meditation is always – in a white man, at least – more or less an interrogative exercise' (173). This observation introduces a chapter that is itself a kind of meditation – and not just of the white man's kind. Its scenes, which emanate from dispersed times and locations, are as vivid – and elusively connected with one another – as in a dream. Heyst leaves the amazing situation he finds himself in at present – living with a woman on a desert island – and revisits a moment of desertion in the past, when he bemusedly superintended the demise of the Tropical Belt Coal Company.

The first half of this chapter is dominated by the remembered scene of his father's death; the second, by his meeting with Wang. The death of the father takes place in the heart of London, whose 'houses began to look like the tombs of an unvisited, unhonoured, cemetery of hopes' (174). His father is memorialized as 'the silenced destroyer of systems, of hopes, of beliefs' (175). The sad and lonely room where they had the last of their many talks is contrasted with the anonymous and amorphous street below. The unheeding 'begrimed shadows of the town' recall the London of *The Secret Agent* with its crowded, impersonal intensities. They contrast with Axel Heyst's barren grief: in the austere and refined atmosphere of the dying man's room

> [a] few slow tears rolled down his face. The rooms, filling with shadows, seemed haunted by a melancholy, uneasy presence which could not express itself. The young man got up with a strange sense of making way for something impalpable that claimed possession, went out of the house, and locked the door. A fortnight later he started on his travels – to "look on and never make a sound."
>
> (176)

Heyst, as we know, did not find it quite so easy to shut the door on his past. His attempt to become a settler on Samburan coincides with the expiration of the lease on his father's London house. When Heyst transports the 'objects familiar to his childhood' to the tropical island where he now lives, he becomes a man 'among the ruins' not only of his father's library but also of the intellectual traditions it embodies. Yet by disconnecting past from present, Heyst's emigration has changed the terms of his existence. His enduring but ambiguous presence on Samburan prompts island gossip, although it also evinces one sympathetic response in the form of Davidson's discreet and solicitous visitations to the island. Conrad's estranging deployment of time and place captures Heyst's ambivalence:

> The manager of the Tropical Belt Coal Company, unpacking [his father's belongings] on the verandah in the shade besieged by a fierce sunshine, must have felt like a remorseful apostate before these relics. He handled them tenderly; and it was perhaps their presence there which attached him to the island when he woke up to the failure of his apostasy.
>
> (177)

Heyst's 'apostasy' is his inability to remain aloof, his failure to fulfil his father's wishes. His residual touch of humanity (the 'original Adam' in Heyst) is the loose thread that eluded the nihilistic system of his dying father. The elder Heyst's bitter philosophy of negation fed on the failure of his own youthful aspirations in a now vanished world. Manifesting themselves finally as Schopenhauerian negation, they had once included the revolutionary nationalist hopes and romantic heroism of a Garibaldi or a Mazzini – not to mention Conrad's own father, Apollo Korzeniowski. Their traces linger in *Nostromo* as the tender memories of an impossible dream of the old Garibaldino, Georgio Viola. But in *Victory* they have become a deadly legacy bequeathed to the younger Heyst. Conrad's life-long fascination with Napoleon, prototype of the romantic heroic, was equally ambivalent. Long after the cult worship of Napoleon had faded, Conrad continued to be fascinated by this man he scorned, which is why scholars express surprise at how easily he dismissed Napoleon in his major essay on European politics, 'Autocracy and War' [1905] (*Notes on Life and Letters* 83–114). The Napoleon who had once come to the assistance of an embattled Poland had also (at the behest of the Pope) ended Garibaldi's proud occupation of Italy under the banner of revolutionary nationalism. Although the political significance in Costaguana of the 'old Garibaldino' is presented as purely archival, it is portrayed with loving respect and is an important clue to Conrad's political values. His complex loyalties include fidelity to his father's heroic moment.

At the funeral of Apollo in Cracow, the young Conrad himself had 'walked at the head of the procession, inconsolable according to his grandmother' (Karl 1979: 77). In the year *Victory* was published Conrad described that mournful scene in an essay printed by the *Daily News* and entitled 'Poland Revisited' [1915]. The declaration of war in 1914, Conrad recalled, had cut short that visit:

> In the moonlight-flooded silence of the old town of glorious tombs and tragic memories, I could see again the small boy of that day

following a hearse; a space kept clear in which I walked alone, conscious of an enormous following, the clumsy swaying of the tall black machine, the chanting of the surpliced clergy at the head, the flames of tapers passing under the low archway of the gate, the rows of bared heads on the pavements with fixed, serious eyes. Half the population had turned out on that fine May afternoon. They had not come to honour a great achievement, or even some splendid failure. The dead and they were victims alike of an unrelenting destiny which cut them off from every path of merit and glory. They had come only to render homage to the ardent fidelity of the man whose life had been a fearless confession in word and deed of a creed which the simplest heart in that crowd could feel and understand.

It seemed to me that if I remained longer there in that narrow street I should become the helpless prey of the Shadows I had called up. They were crowding upon me, enigmatic and insistent, in their clinging air of the grave that tasted of dust and of the bitter vanity of old hopes.

(*Notes on Life and Letters* 169–70)

Like Conrad, Heyst is a haunted man. These brief, quiet scenes of the deaths of two powerful fathers signify among other things the failure of revolutionary hope in the nineteenth century. Nineteenth-century literature is replete with stories of strong fathers who bequeath to over-sensitive sons their stern but ambivalent messages of continuance. Conrad stands directly in that line.[1]

* * *

Wang 'materializes' from the ruins of the Tropical Belt Coal Company. One of the Chinese 'coolies' brought in to set up the enterprise, he alone has decided to stay on with Heyst. His first appearance in the novel hints at how important he will become for defining Conrad's responses to imperialism: 'Of the crowd of imported Chinese labourers, one at least had remained in Samburan, solitary and strange, like a swallow left behind at the migrating season of his tribe' (178). Psychologically, Wang appears to be totally different from Heyst, even though he too lives on the island with a woman. While respecting both the secrets of Wang's nuptials and his 'strong personal views as to the manner of arranging his domestic existence' (180), Heyst regards his Chinese 'boy' as someone totally removed from his own experience. The Chinaman's intensity of purpose amazes him: '[L]ooking silently at the silent Wang going about his work in the bungalow in his unhasty, steady way, Heyst envied the Chinaman's obedience to his instincts' (181). Whether or not Conrad intended the 'victory' in the novel to be Wang's, its narrative structure allows that possibility. Wang remains on the island with his 'native' wife after the various European principals and their entourages have safely departed. His commitment to the traditional inhabitants of Samburan suggests that Asian solidarity has outlasted the excesses of European adventure and romance. In dismissing Western 'material interests' such as the Tropical Belt Coal Company, Conrad certainly includes their quixotic tendencies:

> Company promoters have an imagination of their own. There's no more romantic temperament on earth than the temperament of a company promoter. Engineers came out, coolies were imported, bungalows were put up on Samburan, a gallery driven into the hillside, and actually some coal got out.

> (24)

In their ambiguous relationship with one another, similarities between Heyst and Wang are more important than differences. Shifting affiliations between individual characters and groups of people make it difficult to determine the exact nature of Conrad's colonial politics. In this case, for example, Wang's 'victory' is not that of the colonized over the colonizer, because Conrad does not construct the Malay Archipelago in those binary terms. Wang's own history before coming to Samburan makes him as much an intruder there as Heyst. In marrying a local woman – 'Catchee one piecee wife', he explains to Heyst (179) – he encounters some hostility from the Alfuros, who had been 'frightened by the sudden invasion of Chinamen' (179). Part of the great Chinese diaspora of the past two centuries, Wang is a displaced person whose migrant experience links him to Heyst. In Memmi's paradigm, the colonizer and the colonized are bound together by 'a relentless reciprocity' (Memmi 1965: xxviii) in a binary structure broken finally by the violent struggles for national liberation. But that does not match Conrad's understanding that imperialist power operates by means of complex doublings bound to neither certain origins nor predetermined outcomes.

Although Conrad told Bertrand Russell that he did not know much about the Chinese, he was nevertheless attuned to their provisional and transitory status in Southeast Asia.[2] In 1922, when Russell published *The Problem of China*, Persia Crawford Campbell, a scholar at the University of Sydney, went to London and wrote a different kind of book, on the overseas Chinese (Campbell 1923).[3] Her history of one particular group within the world structured by European imperialism found a belated readership in the 1970s among a generation becoming aware of the complexities of diasporic uprootedness in a postcolonial world. Her analysis exposes the legitimated processes of indentured labour which, thriving on the unimaginable poverty of late-nineteenth-century South China in particular, were enacted under the aegis of Pax Britannica, in conditions and on terms comparable to those of the Atlantic slave trade. Conrad's fictions glimpse intriguingly and sympathetically into the world created by what Campbell was to call *Chinese Coolie Emigration to Countries within the British Empire*. In *Victory*, for instance, the rootless Wang seeks permission from his boss, Axel Heyst, to stay on in Samburan when the Europeans and 'coolies' are leaving. That opens the way for a different story from among the ruins of a failed European quest for tropical coal. Postcolonial discourse seeks to articulate that other story, and discover what it might be like to read Europe's grand narrative from a non-imperial perspective.

That is why postcolonial studies has altered the meaning of Conrad's earlier tale, *Typhoon*, and some of his other fictions. Mulhern (1990) uses this story to expose the narrow chauvinism of F. R. Leavis, who had stressed the order symbolized by the British seaman, Captain MacWhirr, and neglected those narrative strands which undermine it. When reminiscing on how *Typhoon* originated in a real-life episode at sea, Conrad remarked that the 'interest' for him in this tale was 'not the bad weather but the extraordinary complication brought into the ship's life at a moment of exceptional stress by the human element below her deck' (v). That 'human element' consisted of two hundred 'coolies' returning to China after years spent working in the mines of Southeast Asia. 'Every single Celestial of them was carrying with him all he had in the world' (7), the narrator remarks, including, he adds laconically and unemotionally, meagre savings accumulated from their hard labour as 'seven-years'-men' (12).

In *Typhoon* the genial Jukes has his own way of relating to the Chinese. Bewildering Captain MacWhirr by referring to them as 'passengers', he displays a consequent concern for their comfort, and genuinely tries to make contact with their dignified interpreter by concocting a completely opaque version of pidgin (13). Although some might consider Captain MacWhirr certifiably insane, he is the man who slowly perceives the justice of returning to the coolies their money scattered by the force of the typhoon. The Chinese – impassive to European eyes and glimpsed below deck as a bleeding and maimed tangle of pig-tailed bodies washed about horizontally and vertically by the typhoon's irresistible force – become the silent beneficiaries of MacWhirr's responsible accountancy.

Campbell's historical reconstruction helps to remind us of the humanity ignored by the principal actors on board the *Nan-Shan*. It enables us to see that the tunnel vision of that dutiful servant of empire, Captain MacWhirr, is not just amusing but a serious matter for ethical and political critique. It again exposes some of the human consequences of that 'sordid enterprise' served by the honourable codes of the merchant marine service. In the early tale *Typhoon*, as much as in the later masterwork *Victory*, such meanings are partially obscured by the initial marginalizing of non-European characters. From a different angle, by creating an ironic gap between the narratorial manner and the people it describes, Conrad establishes an authenticity of modesty as the ground on which to redraw both narrative and historical contracts. His new contract with the reader involves subverting and eventually cancelling others that legitimate both caricatures of non-Europeans and silence about them. This way of accounting for the political and ideological mission of Conrad's fictional discourse borrows heavily against a future so far beyond colonialism that terms such as 'mimicry' and 'hybridity' will have lost the pejorative associations it conferred on them.

It is hard to say what would have become of Wang. His relationship with his Alfuro wife appears far more solid than does poor Heyst's with Lena. His role in protecting the community against the invading white men may have helped to erode the suspicion with which the Alfuros first treated him. A Chinese in what would later become the modern nation of Indonesia, Wang and his descendants would probably have retained their ethnic identity; but, unlike their numerous compatriots who went to Malaya as indentured labourers, they would have remained a small and threatened minority. Three hundred years of Dutch rule in the East Indies would be interrupted first by the Japanese occupation, then by the short-lived return of the Dutch, and finally by wars of national liberation. The Emergency of 1965 would no doubt have brought Wang's descendants under suspicion of being Communist, and potentially with horrifying consequences. With luck, on the other hand, the family market-gardening business might still be thriving quietly on the island of Samburan, which (apart from one brief affair) is more renowned among literary critics than among imperialistic invaders.

Conrad's encounter with feminine sexuality

Jameson (1981: 269) describes *Nostromo* as an 'advance' on *Lord Jim*, because Conrad never got further than that novel in his understanding of themes present only in the unconscious of *Lord Jim*: namely, the politics of imperialism and the spread of global capitalism. In these terms, *Victory* amounts to a complete withdrawal from politics. My reason for 'elevating' the significance of Wang is to counteract the idea that Conrad was crudely Eurocentric. Unfortunately this is made at the expense of another character Conrad's novel gives a voice to: Lena, Heyst's lover on the island. She represents the farthest point Conrad reached in exploring that other 'dark continent', female sexuality.[4] Having the greatest claim to that empty space on the Greimasian rectangle, she at once resolves the novel's deepest narrative tensions and embodies

Conrad's late and unexpected encounter with the feminine, love and sexuality. In its understanding of what D. H. Lawrence called 'the great relationship between men and women', *Victory* is to *Heart of Darkness* as *Nostromo* is to *Lord Jim*, in Jameson's rank-ordering of Conrad's fictions. Its direct negotiation of 'the woman question' is a major advance on Conrad's earlier treatment of female characters.

To justify this claim, I will begin with the belated arrival of feminists in Conrad studies. Although Conrad sanctified the male world of action and adventure by turning it into the stuff of high literature, his writings avoided the negative fall-out from feminist readings that began in the 1970s. Lawrence – who was sometimes said to understand women better than they did themselves – was the writer whose reputation was fatally damaged by feminist charges of phallocentrism.[5] Having speculated polemically about female sexuality while simultaneously flirting with repugnant and dangerous notions of male supremacy, Lawrence was no doubt a more obvious target for feminist critique. Conrad, by contrast, probably seemed so irrelevant to second-wave feminists that his writings could be safely ignored. But given the political attention he received in that period over his attitude to race and his representation of colonized peoples, and in view of the fact that even the Greek tragic poets attracted intensive scrutiny from academic feminists, Conrad's comparative sequestration in this regard is remarkable. And in two recent books Conrad is even shown to be positively sympathetic in his representation of women and the roles he assigns to them.[6]

In challenging the ways in which female characters are represented in *Heart of Darkness*, the gendered criticism of Conrad encountered problems. Invoking the reasonable criteria of sympathetic and fair representation, sporadic feminist attacks stumbled as other forms of political critique had done over the indeterminate nature of the text and its consequent refusal to be pinned down. The ensuing debates – deferred almost until the 1990s and still unresolved – have produced new interpretations by generating new analytical paradigms of political critique.

Women certainly play significant roles in *Heart of Darkness*, even though they occupy only a marginal place in the narrative. Both Marlow's journey and the narration of it are generically masculine quests. His desire to encounter Kurtz entails excluding 'the women', who must be kept out to preserve the 'goodness' he attributes to them. Inadvertently mentioning 'the girl', he reflects: 'Did I mention a girl? Oh, she is out of it – completely. They – the women I mean – are out of it – should be out of it. We must help them to stay in that beautiful world of their own, lest ours gets worse' (115). In the final scene of the novel, Marlow follows up this initial allusion to Kurtz' 'Intended' by protecting her from the truth about him. His compassionate lie not only keeps the

Intended in the dark about what happened but does so for the spurious purpose of preventing the male world of action from appearing even worse than it is. That feminist attention to this episode came so late is certainly surprising.[7] Marlow's listeners on board the *Nellie* unquestionably belong to an exclusively male club.

The 'strong' feminist reading of *Heart of Darkness* by Nina Pelikan Straus (Straus 1996: 48–66) was among the first to break the polite silence of feminine unease about Conrad. New combinations of theoretical approaches are needed, she argues, to grasp this complex problem. Straus thinks that the 'chivalrous' sexism of the novel cannot be attributed solely to its narrator. Even if the attitudes expressed represent the masculine limitations of Marlow as narrator – and are thus (like Marlow's equally benevolent racism) subject to criticism by Conrad as author – there is still no space for the female reader *as woman*:

> Even if the sexism of Marlow and Kurtz is part of the 'horror' that Conrad intends to disclose, the feminist reader cannot but consider that the text is structured so that this horror – though obviously revealed to male and female reader alike – is deliberately hidden from Kurtz's Intended.
>
> (ibid.: 49)

While conceding the notorious 'undecideability' of the text, Straus defends her feminist critique against the rejoinder that this episode should be read as dramatizing a still further 'horror' in the masculine world of Kurtz and Marlow's Congo: namely, that Conrad deliberately shows Marlow's 'redeeming' idea to be based on a lie to the Intended. And even if her argument does not cover every interpretative possibility, it is unproductive to go on invoking textual undecideability in defence of the novel. Feminist criticism at this point exhumes a problem deeply buried in Conrad's verbal duplicity, which makes the academic question of whose interpretation is correct no longer the most important one to ask. It might be said that Straus can be faulted for not acknowledging the extraordinary ability of Conrad's text to ward off such directly political criticisms as its failure to recognize how uneasy it makes female readers feel. Nevertheless, her theoretical framework produces an admirably lucid reading of the peculiarly homosocial nature of the bond between the 'good' Marlow and the 'satanic' Kurtz. To reject her analysis on the former grounds can amount to resorting to theoretical correctness in defence of 'our author' – perhaps even replicating the self-protective male freemasonry that Straus identifies in Marlow's lie to the Intended. What she challenges is the basis of masculine authority – whether colonial or academic – and the collusion needed to preserve it from scrutiny.

In the cultural arena where these polemics are contested, feminist 'mis-readings' of *Heart of Darkness* are easily dismissed, as Straus reveals in her deft use of Gayatri Spivak's anecdote about an authoritative academic putdown at a feminist conference. The subject was a paper on Dante's *La Vita nuova*:

> The paper took no stand on the brutal sexism of the tradition within which that text is situated. A woman in the audience asked at the end of the hour: "How can a woman learn to praise this text?" Before the speaker could answer, a distinguished woman present in the audience said, with authority: "Because the text deconstructs itself, the author is not responsible for what the text seems to say."
>
> I was deeply troubled by that exchange. Here is male authority, I thought, being invoked by a woman to silence another woman's politics . . . When used in this way, the slogan seemed to fit only too well into the dreary scene of the mainstream pedagogy and criticism of literature in the United States – hedged in as it is by the "autonomy of the text," "the intentional fallacy," and, indeed, "the willing suspension of disbelief."
>
> (Spivak 1987: 15–16)

This is not the place to deal at length with Spivak's challenge to those conservative formations which enabled the American academy to assimilate so comfortably the scandal of Derridean deconstruction. But it is certainly relevant to the masculinist production of 'safe' readings of *Heart of Darkness*. Spivak and Straus are more concerned to show how such institutionally sanctioned ploys inhibit the responses of women, both as academic and private readers. Traditional criticism asks whether the novel deliberately criticizes or otherwise 'places' Marlow's desire not to reveal his secret knowledge of Kurtz to women. (I believe it does both, and thus opens a space for more radical understandings of what is at stake.) Feminist criticism asks whether Conrad himself or his dramatized narrator Marlow is responsible for the benign sexism that silences the female voice while continuing at the same time to distinguish the ungovernable sensuality of the African woman from the civilized purity of the Intended. (This is surely part of Kurtz' nightmare and his problems with women: he fails both his Intended and his African mistress.) But neither question identifies the nature of the darkness at the heart of the novel or determines how far *Heart of Darkness* dares to go in exposing its anxiety about the bonds between men. There is no place for woman's desire in the determinedly masculine perspective of Conrad's narrative. That signals a tragic moment for Conrad himself: the old truths appear ready to crumble, but as yet some of the new ones are not even discernible. Something more complex is at stake than the question of whether Conrad sits on the fence when it comes to political commitment.

Unlike the women in *Heart of Darkness*, *Victory*'s Lena is no stereotype, nor is she a neat and well-rounded character. At least three distinct Lenas result from her being put to different uses in three different phases of the narrative, each defined by her relationship to Heyst. Founded on Lena's physicality and Heyst's sexual attraction to her, their relationship remains a constant thread throughout the novel despite their jarring differences. When Heyst 'falls in love' with Lena, and almost immediately plans to rescue her by taking her to live with him on his island, she is given the unconvincing accent of a working-class Londoner. Sounding like a waif abroad, she is depicted as barely educated. Heyst, on the other hand, is the quintessence of European sophistication: located intellectually somewhere beyond both Schopenhauer and Nietzsche, he epitomizes philosophical existentialism.[8] By the time we encounter the lovers virtually alone in their new life on the island, Lena's stage-cockney accent has disappeared and been replaced by a lucid and direct form of speech that cuts across Heyst's controlling humour, distancing ironies and self-disparaging evasions. This Lena emerges fully on a long walk in the heat, during which the strains of their attempts at understanding and knowing one another both progress and complicate the erotic and emotional bonds between them. At this delicately balanced moment of the novel, Lena finds her voice and declares her desire. Unlike the Intended, she is not denied full and intimate access to her lover and then left with a barren and mythical account of him. The purpose of Lena's final role as heroine of high melodrama is to secure Heyst's love and commitment by a more conventional act of self-sacrifice. Although the plot calls for this operatic closure, there is no bathos in Conrad's presentation of either the intensity of Lena's need or Heyst's pathetic recognition of his life's failure.[9]

Well before the scandal of *Lady Chatterley's Lover*, Conrad described Lawrence's later development as a descent into 'filth' (Karl 1979: 730). In keeping with his time and status, Conrad himself appears to have maintained an austere attitude towards sexual behaviour. His frank presentation of Heyst and Lena's relationship is in this respect surprising. But *Victory* is something other than a modest protest against Victorian censorship, which in any case was already on its last legs, despite the fact that *The Rainbow* was prosecuted for obscenity about the same time as *Victory* was published. Its principal break-through is rather that it is Conrad's final encounter with female sexuality and desire, as mediated through Heyst's failed encounter with both.[10]

The 'problem' of female sexuality left over from Freud occupied the first hundred years of the psychoanalytic tradition.[11] If Conrad can be said to participate in 'the moment of Freud', the question of understanding Lena's desire is best approached by recalling a premise I began with: namely, that psychoanalysis is not a readily available and stable system for interpreting literary texts. Equally to the point is the degree to which 'the poets' (among whom Freud includes all creators of 'literature') anticipated what would become categories in the new science of the unconscious. Bearing these things in mind, it could be said that *Victory*'s presentation and analysis of Heyst and Lena uncannily predicts psychoanalysis instead of waiting for it to explain the novel's meanings.

Lena first appears in *Victory* as the object of Heyst's gaze (65–76). In this respect, Conrad's approach to romance seems purely conventional: his hero falls in love at first sight. Furthermore, the stress on visual effects at moments of high drama is a hallmark of this writer whose professed aim was 'above all, to make you *see*' (*The Nigger of the 'Narcissus'* x). The intensely visual nature of the encounter, however, is also consistent with Lacanian observations on the beam of desire. The Imaginary (or visual) apprehension of reality precedes the insertion of the embryonic subject into the Symbolic order of language and the Law and is thus more 'primal'. When the beloved object is gone, our most poignant recollections are images rather than speech – a perception widely exploited by film directors. The appropriate medium for creating the traumatic moment that will eventually destabilize Heyst's sense of reality and completely destroy his composure is thus the (Lacanian) Imaginary. For Lacan, both the gaze and sexuality belong to the field of the drive, whose power Heyst experiences at the moment of seeing and falling in love with 'Lena' (Lacan 1977: 187–200). That fateful gaze brings the drive into play: this – rather than a surprising manifestation of the 'old Adam' – is what precipitates Heyst's fall from aloof detachment. We are told that his impulse towards the woman he comes to call Lena is identical with his 'rescue' of Morrison. Her capture of his gaze on the stage in Schomberg's hotel gives the image an uncomfortable density: 'he was the same man who had plunged after the submerged Morrison whom he hardly knew otherwise than by sight' (77). Heyst's emotional gesture of rescue is more interesting at this moment than his moral irresponsibility. From the very start, his movement towards Lena is marked by a compulsion whose unconscious operation is revealed by Lacan and which Freud associated with the death drive.[12]

Lena's beauty intersects the trajectory of Heyst's desire in a way that recalls Lacan's analysis of Sophocles' *Antigone*. The power of this drama, he says, derives from the effect of Antigone's beauty on desire (Lacan 1992: 247–9). The beauty in question, needless to say, is not just those attractive attributes that Antigone may be imagined as having, and which would be difficult to communicate in a masked Greek drama. Nor is it simply (as they say) 'in the eye of the beholder'. Rather it resides in the potency of the total visual effect produced within the kind of drive Heyst is now caught in. The power – or what Lacan calls the 'splendour' – of Antigone's image emanates from the place she has come to inhabit by virtue of opting for death. In the case of Lena, on the other hand, her youthful womanliness – set against her drab surroundings, and attached to the icon of a creature in distress – proves irresistible to Heyst. The spectacle she presents evokes his father's bleak advice: that if 'a full and equable contempt' for beliefs was beyond him, he should at least 'cultivate that form of contempt which is called pity' (174). Heyst's father had seen the 'weakness' in his son that would erode an otherwise perfect commitment to indifference:

> She had captured Heyst's awakened faculty of observation; he had the sensation of a new experience. That was because his faculty of observation had never before been captured by any feminine creature in that marked and exclusive fashion. He looked at her anxiously, as no man ever looks at another man; and he positively forgot where he was. He had lost touch with his surroundings. The big woman, advancing, concealed the girl from his sight for a moment. She bent over the seated youthful figure, in passing it very close, as if to drop a word into its ear. Her lips did certainly move. But what sort of word could it have been to make the girl jump up so swiftly? Heyst, at his table, was surprised into a sympathetic start.
>
> (71)

The reader's gaze is controlled by Heyst's own line of sight, which is governed by the pace and ordering of his subjective experience, whose unconscious object is Lena. At this point in the novel, the male (anti-)hero dominates the narrative: as yet, this is still *his* story. But the primacy of the visual in awakening desire is not the only intimation that anticipates Lacan. This deceptively simple passage shows how Lena's beauty, Heyst's gaze and the history of his subjectivity form the narrative trajectory of Conrad's novel. It also clearly differentiates male from female positions in such a story, and above all articulates Heyst's anxiety. His response is the primal angst of a man drawn into the orbit of the feminine. This occasions a barely discernible apprehension, which is inaccessible to reason and corresponds with the Freudian castration anxiety. It contains the fear of death.

In first approaching the woman, then, *Victory* tracks the experience of the man. And that positioning is not immediately reversed in scenes set on the island. The men – Jones, Ricardo and Heyst (Pedro doesn't really qualify as a man) – see Lena as an abomination to avoid, an object of lustful fantasy, or in Heyst's anticipation of Freud's dark continent, 'a script in an unknown language' (222). The focus begins to change during Heyst's long walk with Lena. Ruminating aloud (his preferred style of conversing with Lena), Heyst comes to be perceived gradually through the way his words affect her. Our interest in his intriguing psychology is accordingly quickened. But it becomes more critical when Lena's desire for intimacy founders on his ingrained and sophisticated defences. His mysterious altruism and humane response to a girl in distress are not experienced as generosity of spirit. Instead, they reveal a stubborn core in his being that renders him incapable of recognizing the other, let alone admitting it. Heyst simply cannot bear the intimacy of exposure and trust that Lena needs. Whereas in *Heart of Darkness* women were successfully excluded from the preserve of male self-deception, the emotional crisis of *Victory* requires that Heyst admit Lena:

> "You should try to love me!" she said.
>
> He made a movement of astonishment.
>
> "Try!" he muttered. "But it seems to me – " He broke off, saying to himself that if he loved her, he had never told her so in so many words. Simple words! They died on his lips. "What makes you say that?" he asked.
>
> She lowered her eyelids and turned her head a little.
>
> "I have done nothing," she said in a low voice. "It's you who have been good, helpful and tender to me. Perhaps you love me for that – just for that; or perhaps you love me for company, and because – well! But sometimes it seems to me that you can never love me for myself, only for myself, as people do love each other when it's to be for ever." Her head drooped. "For ever," she breathed out again; then, still more faintly, she added an entreating: "Do try!"
>
> These last words went straight to his heart – the sound of them more than the sense. He did not know what to say, either from want of practice in dealing with women or simply from his innate honesty of thought. All his defences were broken now. Life had him fairly by the throat. But he managed a smile, though she was not looking at him; yes, he did manage it – the well-known Heyst smile of playful courtesy, so familiar to all sorts and conditions of men in the islands.
>
> "My dear Lena," he said, "it looks as if you were trying to pick a very unnecessary quarrel with me – of all people!"
>
> She made no movement. With his elbows spread out he was twisting the ends of his long moustaches, very masculine and perplexed, enveloped in the atmosphere of femininity as in a cloud, suspecting pitfalls, and as if afraid to move.
>
> (221–2)

At the novel's dénouement, Heyst fails to deal directly with the physical threat to both his own and Lena's life. More the outcome of his inability to trust than the mere loss of his revolver, it results in a melodramatic playing out of his impasse with Lena at the level of intimacy. Readers have been positioned to register her frustrations with this man, and to gauge both her dependency and determination to change things. She may appear to trace the traditional contours of a woman's desire for a man. But she is subjected to an analysis which not only breaks down the cliché but remorselessly exposes Heyst by stripping off his self-protecting cocoon. *Seeing* these things is the novel's true victory.

It is said that Conrad once told Edward Garnett that before he went to the Congo he was simply a 'perfect animal' (Kimbrough 1988: 195–6). *Victory* may well be the furthest point of his literary journey away from that state. It is his most intimate and tragic encounter with the radical otherness of female sexuality. In his seminar on *The Ethics of Psychoanalysis*, Lacan remarks that from the very beginning psychoanalysis has been implicated with tragedy. The desires that are proper to both analysis and its concomitant ethics, he argues, overlap with the experience of an Antigone, an Oedipus or a King Lear. These literary heroes and heroines are driven by an ineluctable desire to *know*, wheresoever their journey takes them: replicating the norms of middle-class values is not on their agendas.

The confluence in *Victory* of lines of force constituted by desire, choice and tragedy encourages us to read Conrad *with* Lacan. Such a project would certainly not be exhausted by its deployment in this particular instance. In assuming no hierarchical priority between literary text and psychoanalytical theory, it would enable Conrad's subtle love story and Lacan's difficult attempts to understand the nature of desire and its connection with tragedy to be brought into a reciprocally illuminating relationship. And it would be another humbling reminder that the interpretative process knows no closure.

Epilogue
Conrad and the new world order

Conrad with Lacan[1]

Conrad regarded the sinking of the *Titanic* as an instance of human fatuity on a tragic scale. The essay he wrote shortly after the disaster is a strange mixture of sobriety and mania. Alternating between comic and tragic tones, he writes as though he had seen the whole catastrophe in advance. But there is nothing 'knowing' about his stance. The story, of course, did not end with the 'event' itself – the sinking of the great ship – or even the Inquiry that followed. In fact, it did not even begin with these events.

Ironies still cling to the *Titanic*. The Hollywood movie made about it in 1997 sought epic status by matching the ship's claim to be the biggest event of its time. The film's narrative introduces a Conradian motif in the form of a (fictitious) diamond (falsely) believed to have sunk with the ship, which inspires a contemporary crew of scientists to probe once again the mystery of the *Titanic*. Like the renegades in *Victory*, who venture to Heyst's island in quest of non-existent treasure, those in search of the fabulous diamond fail to recognize its true identity at the heart of the romantic love-story. One 'gem' which did go down with the real-life *Titanic* was the manuscript of Conrad's tale, 'Karain: A Memory', en route to its American buyer, John Quinn (Najder 1983: 377). Quinn's purchases at the time helped Conrad to resolve some of his chronic financial difficulties, for which the author was grateful. Quinn subsequently sold his collection of Conradiana for a fortune. As we have seen, the afterlives of written works of fiction take various and unpredictable forms.

Writing about the *Titanic* some years before the Hollywood extravaganza, Slavoj Žižek discovered a different kind of irony: the Teiresian powers of prophecy in a world beyond the limitations of temporality. Žižek uses the 1983 account of a novel that tells how an ocean-liner called the *Titan*, almost identical in dimensions to the *Titanic*, struck an iceberg and, like its namesake, sank 'on a cold April night'. According to Žižek's source, the novel (written by a 'struggling author' named Morgan Robertson) was published in 1898: that is, fourteen years before the real-life *Titanic* sank (Žižek 1989: 69–71). This example of life imitating art is an instance of what Žižek calls the 'sublime object of ideology'. Its significance lies 'deeper' than either the irony of its false status as icon of its time or its readily available metaphorical meaning. For Žižek, the horror of the *Titanic* is that it becomes 'a Thing in the Lacanian sense: the material leftover, the materialization of the terrifying, impossible *jouissance*'. The 'tragic' insight immanent in this repetition is that the 'real-life' wreck is nothing less than 'a form in which society lived the experience of its own death'. It therefore derives its uncanny force not from articulatable meanings and narrative detail but by occupying the place of the unrepresentably sublime object. Žižek here alludes to the discussion of *das Ding* in Lacan's *The Ethics of Psychoanalysis*, on which I based my own discussion of the nameless 'horror' in Conrad's *Heart of Darkness*.

We have our own equivalent of this uncanny moment: the planes crashing on 11 September 2001 into both the Pentagon and the twin towers of the World Trade Center in New York, which instantly became known as 'the events of nine-eleven'. Lived in advance in numerous science fiction movies as an unrepresentable horror – at once terrifying and thrilling – this highly televised but real-life 'event' rendered immediately obsolete both the fantasies of the genre and the most vividly imagined fears of the Other. These events gave everybody the opportunity to encounter that Lacanian Real which lies beyond representation and to catch an appalling glimpse of the Thing.

Political criticism

Žižek's own politics here remain hard to identify, especially when 'translated' from their specifically European seedbed. While disconcertingly admitting to charges of blatant revisionism and eclecticism, he has accepted the challenge to label the component parts of his political agenda. He claims to be still 'unashamedly Marxist in [his] insistence on the need to repoliticize the sphere of the economy' (Žižek 1999: x), but can do so only by relativizing Marxism. '[I]f one is to save [Marxism's] legacy', he writes,

> one has to renounce its crude 'economic essentialism' (the notion of the class struggle, the role of the proletariat, socialist revolution, etc.), and maintain just the empty messianic emancipatory promise – the new social order should not be 'ontologized', but should remain an elusive democracy *à venir*.
>
> (ibid.: ix)

While renouncing Marxism's absolutist reliance on a particular grand narrative of historical necessity, Žižek is equally careful to avoid turning Lacan into the new master signifier for transcending every interpretative impasse. Instead, he uses Lacan as 'a privileged intellectual tool to reactualize German Idealism' (ibid.). He thus disperses the idea that Lacan or psychoanalysis can be the ultimate horizon of meaning – even when Lacan is read within a revisionist version of Marxism. He unequivocally declares that Lacan is best understood in the tradition of German Idealism that culminates in Kant and Hegel. But in Žižekian dialectics, Lacan is always used – like the movies of Alfred Hitchcock, psychoanalysis, popular culture or philosophy – strategically and opportunistically. This freedom enables Žižek in his own practice to liberate more dispersed kinds of methodological manoeuvring.

Žižek's explosive entry into the Western academy in the aftermath of other 'events' in Eastern Europe *circa* 1989 accelerated the development in the United States of an already emergent and psychoanalytically grounded political criticism. Mark Bracher, for example, used *Heart of Darkness* as the test case for a new model of politico-psychoanalytic cultural critique (Bracher 1993: 138–67). As an intervention in end-of-century uncertainties in the humanities, Bracher's methodology is typically eclectic. He grafts a version of reader-response criticism on to the Lacanian discourse of the subject, and enlists both for a feminist critique of Conrad. He argues that the prevalence of a 'redemptivist' response to *Heart of Darkness* reveals that something in Conrad's text – and not just in Marlow's narrative – calls it forth. That 'something' is the injunction to recoil like Marlow from the threat of those desires which destroyed Kurtz. Bracher regards this as a conservative and self-protective textual politics – antithetical to the ethical imperative of Lacanian psychoanalysis, which encourages the possibility that 'the way things are might be susceptible to change' (ibid.: 144). Readers of *Heart of Darkness* are 'coerced to choose between, in Marlow's terms, restraint and lack of restraint, with no option of compromise or transformation of either drives or ideals' (ibid.: 147). The emancipationist agenda that Bracher attributes to Lacan undoubtedly makes his critique useful for certain kinds of feminist politics. What it risks occluding, however, is the fact that Lacan refuses to yoke his analytical procedures to any kind of personal or political 'liberation'.

It remains politically important to explore ways of bringing together these two bodies of writing. My way has been to read Conrad's fictions in conjunction with Freud's exploration of those tragic contradictions that inhere in the idea of selfhood. Like Conrad, Freud explored the relationship between the goals of civilization and man's inability to emancipate himself from both primitive drives and a remorseless Law. Brought together in this way, they reveal an eminent domain that can be no more appropriated by psychoanalysis than by aesthetics, sociology, feminism, Marxism, postcolonialism, or even the most inclusive or eclectic cultural studies. That is why Žižek both invites and resists being situated institutionally.

I have also used psychoanalytic insights to interrogate Leavis' too lucid interpretation of *The Shadow-Line*. The exposure of systematic repressions in the practices of that formidable critic reveals how *misrecognition* can open up more comprehensive ways of reading. Modestly emancipatory, if only at the level of hermeneutics, it might be the best that the humanities can offer to political practice: a depth and precision in the interpretation of difficult texts that does not prescribe specific agendas. This activity induces habits of mind that are essential if politics is to avoid the disastrous blind spots that disfigure history.

Leavis began by addressing E. M. Forster's declaration that Conrad's work suffers from a 'central obscurity', a failure to deliver the promise of 'some general philosophic statement about the universe' (Leavis 1948: 173). Conrad was inclined to collude with such a perception of his work by attributing its elusiveness to his 'Polishness'. My response to this line of critique is to relocate Conrad in the discourse of tragedy rather than realism. Leavis demanded a higher degree of specificity in novels than in Shakespearean tragedy, which he admired for what he felicitously called its 'poetic-creative' use of language. One of his touchstones was a passage from an essay written in 1935 by his fellow-Scrutineer, the psychologist D. W. Harding, on the First World War poet, Isaac Rosenberg:

> Usually when we speak of finding words to express a thought we seem to mean that we have the thought rather close to formulation and use it to measure the adequacy of any possible phrasing that occurs to us, treating words as servants of the idea. 'Clothing a thought in language', whatever it means psychologically, seems a fair metaphorical description of much speaking and writing. Of Rosenberg's work it would be misleading. He – like many poets in some degree, one supposes – brought language to bear on the incipient thought at an earlier stage of its development. Instead of the emerging idea being racked slightly so as to fit a more familiar approximation of itself, and words found for that, Rosenberg let it manipulate words almost from the beginning, often without insisting on the controls of logic and intelligibility.
>
> (Harding 1963: 99)

This description looks back to the period in which Conrad moved away from realism and Freud wrestled with language to explain a previously unformulated idea. Both writers sought help from poetry and myth. Leavis himself was neither chary of risking an imperfectly formulated thought nor immune from the dangers of 'adjectival insistence' – a muffled expression matched by his appeal to the emptiest category in *The Great Tradition*: its central term, 'moral'. Had he pursued his deeper insights in more philosophical terms, his unexamined departure from normal uses of this word might have made a different kind of contribution. In his late essay on Conrad's short story, 'The Secret Sharer', Leavis tries to specify the kind of ethics he thinks characteristic of great literature. He argues for the necessity – in certain circumstances – of responding to a categorical imperative that might threaten the 'code', the greater good of society, or the Law itself. Recalling Kant, such an ethics resembles the one advocated by Lacan. Leavis glimpsed its subversive power only in the resistances it produced – and not least in himself. His own 'adjectival insistence' in *The Great Tradition* invited derision. There the 'moral' is constantly gestured towards and always deferred, adumbrated by empty signifiers – sometimes borrowed from D. H. Lawrence, such as 'a reverent openness towards life'. Yet like his 'misreading' of *The Shadow-Line*, whose stress on communal solidarity masks something closer to its opposite, this undisclosed meaning partly explains why Leavis was seen in his time as dangerous. The closest he comes to facing that subversive slope is in his unstable late essay on Tolstoy's classic novel of adultery, *Anna Karenina*, which awkwardly attempts to negotiate D. H. Lawrence's (equally awkward) championship of desire as opposed to the Law (Leavis 1967: 9–32).

Conrad's journey into 'dark' and ambivalent places is the opposite of mystical. Instead of embracing new superstitions, he puts on the agenda of human knowledge hitherto unknown areas of experience. An emphatic testimony to this aim is his impatient rejection of the idea that *The Shadow-Line* contains supernatural traces:

> I could never have attempted such a thing, because all my moral and intellectual being is penetrated by an invincible conviction that whatever falls under the dominion of our senses must be in nature and, however exceptional, cannot differ in its essence from all the other effects of the visible and tangible world of which we are a self-conscious part. The world of the living contains enough marvels and mysteries as it is; marvels and mysteries acting upon our emotions and intelligence in ways so inexplicable that it would almost justify the conception of life as an enchanted state. No, I am too firm in my consciousness of the marvellous to be ever fascinated by the mere supernatural . . .
>
> (Author's Note v)

Conrad's writing occupies a space that separates the mysteries of the tangible world from the 'mere supernatural'. It is not unlike the space evoked by Freud and Lacan and designated as the unconscious. Radically other than the world of consciousness, which is the traditional domain of cognition, it stubbornly claims to be an object of knowledge rather than of faith. For over a century now, psychoanalysis has been consolidating and extending the insights of its founders. The knowledge achieved by Conrad sits at the very brink of that development, and is different again. What Conrad knew he was often terrified to commit to language. A certain terror accompanies even his most lucid insights and is one of their constituent ingredients. Political theory and cultural critique now demand the inclusion of terror.

Notes

Introduction

1 To use Fredric Jameson's distinction, a contradiction is capable of resolution, whereas an antinomy represents absolute difference (Jameson 1994: 1–2).
2 As a result of Said's radical suggestion, postcolonial readings of Jane Austen became so fashionable in the 1990s that they threatened to displace more traditional readings and establish a new orthodoxy. See, for example, Park and Rajan (2000).
3 The two classics of mid-century literary criticism I have in mind are Leavis (1948) and Williams (1973). While neither pays detailed attention to Austen, Williams' book is – among other things – a historicist revision of Leavis' version of English literary history. Their different approaches to Austen point to an important shift in literary studies, particularly in Britain. A roughly comparable generational shift in America is epitomized by differences between the liberal humanist assumptions of Trilling (1951) and the 'New Historicism' of Greenblatt (1980). Interest in the political dimensions of Conrad's novels was initiated somewhat earlier in the United States, by Howe (1957).
4 The sense in which Leavis' criticism can be considered 'idealist' will be explained in Chapter 3.
5 The movie, and these scenes in particular, are discussed in detail by Wiltshire (2001: 135–6).
6 For an egregious example of this widespread conservative response, see Bloom (1994).
7 In both Conrad and Jameson, a strain of pessimism and a habit of solitariness signal that loss for which, in both cases, the activity of writing partially compensates.
8 English historians generally refer to this event as a 'mutiny', Indian ones as a 'rebellion'.
9 I am here distinguishing between texts which endure by surviving the so-called 'test of time' and texts which travel (i.e. move from one context to another, taking on something of the newness they encounter there). 'Iterability' is an especially apposite term to apply to Conrad, given his associations with various cultural locations and the equally fascinating journeys of the texts he authored. Said (1983: 226–47) provides one of the best analyses of this capability, although he doesn't call it iterability.
10 A very short list of Conrad's literary heirs would include: T. S. Eliot, André Gide, Bronislaw Malinowski, Louis-Ferdinand Céline, George Orwell, Graham Greene, V. S. Naipaul, Chinua Achebe, Ngugi wa Thiong'o, Nadine Gordimer, Gabriel García Márquez, Edward Said and Bruce Chatwin.

11 The most suggestive telling of this story is by Barthes (1968).
12 Other histories relevant to the crisis as well as to Conrad include the account by Bongie (1991) of a drastic revaluation of the exotic in the art and writing of the *fin de siècle*. The change is starkly invoked by the contrasting slogans of Rousseau's 'noble savage' and Conrad's 'heart of darkness'.
13 Williams (1971) lucidly analysed Orwell's ambivalent relationship to Britain and its empire, and his commitment to England in the Second World War. There is a fine discussion of Conrad's complex national affiliations by Harpham (1996: 1–70).
14 Mulhern (1979) gives a scholarly and respectful account of the Leavises' achievement. For a much more acerbic analysis of Leavisian narrowness, see Mulhern (1990).
15 Bhabha (1994) effects a cultural reversal by appropriating the formerly offensive colonialist term, 'hybridity', and using it to articulate new speaking positions. His use of the term encapsulates not only the advantages of cultural mixing but also a recognition that the colonizer's discourse was never perfectly inscribed, but always generated new refinements of difference.
16 In the 1920s and 1930s the most powerful voice of the new feeling about imperialism was of course M. K. Gandhi. The 'Gandhi whirlwind' blasted every continuum of its history and practice. In appraising Conrad's understanding of both the British Empire and global imperialism, I shall comment on the almost total absence of India from his colonial world.
17 For an insider's account of these debates, see Williams (1980: 11–30).
18 The first American to politicize Conrad's fiction in a postcolonial manner may have been Jonah Raskin, whose book on *The Mythology of Imperialism* (1971) contains a chapter on *Heart of Darkness* and is dedicated to Ho Chi Minh. Raskin's essay 'Imperialism: Conrad's *Heart of Darkness*' was first published in the *Journal of Contemporary History*, 2 (1967: 109–27). See also Hay (1963) and Fleishman (1967), which focus largely on the *theme* of politics (traditionally understood) in Conrad's fiction. Parry (1983) subsequently problematized the meaning of 'politics' in Conrad.
19 He mounted his attack on Conrad on 18 February 1975 in a lecture at the University of Massachusetts, Amherst (Achebe 1975). In Chapter 5 I discuss issues arising from Achebe's intervention.
20 In this respect, postcolonialism resembles feminism. Originating outside the academy, both were eventually welcomed there, although more for their theoretical discourses than for their revolutionary politics. Both, however, continue to regard the academy as a suitable site from which to effect social change.
21 Among the factors that determine this difference – from English, American, French, African or Indian perspectives – is Australia's paradoxical relationship to the British Empire. Still not legally dislodged from its British heritage (the tie with the monarchy remains intact at this moment), Australia has been at different times a set of colonies, a Commonwealth superintended by British Governors General reporting to the British Crown, and – despite its ongoing state of dependency – even a quasi-colonizing power itself (in Papua New Guinea). Cultural phenomena originating in England, such as Leavisism in English studies, have had peculiar histories in Australia (Collits 1999). Even Australia's geographical remoteness may have affected the way in which Conrad has been read here, since in our dealings as colonizers with Aboriginal peoples we have our own 'hearts of darkness'.

1 Conrad in the history of ideas

1 For detailed discussions of this much-quoted letter, see Hay (1963: 12) and Harpham (1996: 150–1).
2 Another quester after things exotic, D. H. Lawrence approached the Teiresias question more directly: when writing *Lady Chatterley's Lover* he asked his wife Frieda to give him an exact account of the nature of the female orgasm. In the nature of things, the experiment was doomed: as Lacan might have put it, the discussions belonged purely to the Symbolic order, the 'experience' to another place.
3 See, for example, Clifford (1988).
4 The difficulty is exacerbated when one turns to their French 'equivalents'. For a succinct discussion of translation problems, see Faubion's introduction to Foucault (1998: xxv–xxix).
5 Not unlike both Freud and Lacan, who believed that psychoanalytic categories had been anticipated (*avant la lettre*) by poets and artists, Gadamer relates this knowledge to the realm of the aesthetic.
6 For an analysis of the nineteenth-century phase of these developments, see Gadamer (2000: 3–42).
7 The chronologies and narrative highlights I adduce to describe the crisis of humanism in the twentieth century are selected on the basis of their usefulness for tracing Conrad's twentieth-century journey. I do not claim that they take precedence over the impact of such world-historical and conscience-shattering events as the Battle of the Somme, the Jewish Holocaust, Hiroshima or the Vietnam War on the moral confidence of Western humanism.
8 On late-twentieth-century 'Endism', see Fukuyama (1992).
9 The degree of closeness between Clifford's 'experience' and the ethnographer's fieldwork 'participation' model might be suggested by these retrospective comments of Clifford:

> Joining the civil service of Malaya in 1883, at an unusually early age, it so chanced that for the best part of the two decades that followed I was stationed in some of the more remote and primitive districts of the Malayan Peninsula and, to a degree unequalled by any of my brother officers, lived among the people in almost complete isolation from men of my own race . . . I was thus afforded an insight, rarely vouchsafed to a European . . . Having acquired the vernacular in much the same effortless manner in which a child learns a foreign language; living for long periods in native huts, on native diet and in the native fashion; and in familiar daily intercourse with Malays of all classes, I emerged from the experience possessed of a very intimate knowledge of the people . . .
> (Clifford 1926: foreword)

Clifford's formidable and sympathetic knowledge of his Malays, however, sits comfortably alongside unquestioned assumptions about the 'advanced' nature of British civilization and the need for 'the intervention of Great Britain in Malaya'. That was the 'lie' which Clifford could not recognize, and which *Heart of Darkness* exposed.
10 Intimations of discursive crisis in Shakespeare include Macbeth's 'nothing is but what is not' (I, iii, 141–2), Lear's unanswered 'Who is it that can tell me who I am?' (I, iv, 229) and of course *Hamlet, passim*.

11 By now, the process we will examine in Chapter 5 of 'the empire writing back' has encompassed a reciprocal project to Said's: unearthing the ways in which during the colonial period the colonized were also busy constructing 'the West'. A recent instance of what is a broadly based scholarly endeavour in India, for example, is Vijayasree (2004), which gathers essays that explore such constructions in Indian-language texts.

12 For a trenchant refutation of Said's too easy assimilation of Marx in his Orientalism hypothesis, see Ahmad (1992: 221–42).

2   Conrad in literary history

1 See especially such essays as 'The Function of Criticism at the Present Time' and 'The Study of Poetry' (Arnold 1906: 9–34, 235–60).

2 For the prosecution, defence and judgement of *Madame Bovary*, see Flaubert (1857: 367–441). The defence's case is almost like a seminar on how to read this new kind of fiction, especially when exonerating the author from responsibility for the lyrical fantasies of his character. Conrad studies is bedevilled by the difficulties of making this dissociation.

3 I owe this term to Simon During, who in the 1980s suggested that a new ideal for criticism might be that it aspire to be 'pre-suppositionless'. With regard to *Typhoon* I have in mind Francis Mulhern's strong reading of this novella (Mulhern 1990: 250–64).

4 Lukács' Moscow connections did not prevent his authority from being contested in Marxist circles. Some of the liveliest debates took place in the 1930s, and involved subsequently famous German Marxists who were virtually unknown at that time in the non-European West: Ernst Bloch, Georg Lukács, Bertolt Brecht, Walter Benjamin and Theodor Adorno. Such delays in intellectual transmission were common until the 1980s. Their debilitating effect on an Anglophone world that denied itself access to such thinkers as Lukács and Lacan thus helped to sustain its provinciality.

5 For those debates about expressionism (i.e. modernism), see especially Bertolt Brecht's 'Against Georg Lukács' (in Adorno *et al.* 1977: 68–85). The desire for a unitary totality of knowledge did not disappear with Lukács. It is evident in the writings of Fredric Jameson and also Louis Althusser, whose influence on British Marxists such as Terry Eagleton will be examined in Chapter 4 (Althusser 1971: 221–7). By redefining ideology as the force that reproduces existing power relationships, Althusser argued that literature could not avoid being limited by the ideology it drew upon and objectified. The corollary of this is that only Marxian 'science' can go beyond ideology. Although Jameson finally rejected Althusserian hermeneutics in *The Political Unconscious*, it lingers in his desire to incorporate all heuristic systems (Freudian, structuralist, semiological) into an encompassing model whose ultimate horizon is variously named as 'Marxism', 'History', or 'the Political'.

6 Barthes may be mimicking an essay by Marcel Proust that dwells mesmerically on how Flaubert's combination of past tenses and participles constitutes a revolutionary change in the history of narrative (Paganini 1994: 83).

7 Greek tragedies themselves can be read as rewritings of the Athenians' own 'inherited traditional or sacred narrative paradigms which [were] its initial givens' (Jameson 1981: 152). The 'error' to be avoided here resembles the one made by neo-classical theorists, who perpetuated a supposedly Greek model that had little relevance to Greek theatrical practice.

8 As Reiss recognizes, in seeking the truth we are disadvantaged by both our temporal distance from the ancient Greeks and the paucity of their literary

and material remains. The dubious advantage, however, of these adverse conditions is that they facilitate general concepts about the Greeks.

9 For Nietzsche, *The Birth of Tragedy* (1870–1) is also the story of its death in failing to withstand Socratic rationalism. Nietzsche thought that Socrates never understood the profound links between tragedy and myth and the 'deeper' truths accessible in myth. Reiss thus concurs with Nietzsche in seeing discursive incompatibility at the heart of this narrative. But Nietzsche confuses tragedy with a knowledge attributed to it retrospectively. His highly influential assimilation of tragic knowledge with myth is itself a conservative conception of tragedy.

10 D. H. Lawrence invokes the common idea that tragedy is multi-levelled when discussing it in relation to the novels of Thomas Hardy: 'There is a lack of sternness, there is a hesitating betwixt life and public opinion, which diminishes the Wessex novels from the rank of pure tragedy' (Lawrence 1936: 440). George Eliot has in mind a similar hierarchy when classifying the suffering of Mr Casaubon in *Middlemarch*, as 'the pathos of a lot where everything is below the level of tragedy except the passionate egoism of the sufferer' (G. Eliot 1871–2: 423).

3 Conrad in England

1 For a very mixed bag of reminiscences, some of them hagiographic, see Thompson (1984).

2 Of the many books published in England on the rise and formation of academic English, those by Widdowson (1982), Baldick (1983), Eagleton (1983) and Doyle (1989) broadly support my emphasis on the importance of the Cambridge English Faculty in this story.

3 During (1993: 1–25) traces this lineage in a useful summary of the history of cultural studies.

4 Leavis' close attention to Dickens in *The Great Tradition* was confined to a 'note' on *Hard Times*. Dickens is said to have the genius 'of a great entertainer' and to lie 'at the other end of the scale from [the] sophistication' displayed by Henry James (Leavis 1948: 18, 19). The fierceness of these unequivocally damning assessments possibly conceals an embarrassment of affection, since a later book on Dickens by both Leavises amounts to a recantation (F. R. Leavis and Q. D. Leavis 1970).

5 In his classic essay 'On Liberty' (1859), which defends the rights to liberty of individuals in a modern state, Mill made this ominous proviso:

> Despotism is a legitimate mode of government in dealing with barbarians, provided the end be their improvement, and the means justified by actually effecting that end. Liberty, as a principle, has no application to any state of things anterior to the time when mankind have become capable of being improved by free and equal discussion. Until then, there is nothing for them but implicit obedience to an Akbar or a Charlemagne, if they are so fortunate as to find one.
>
> (Mill 1912: 16)

6 Perera (1991) analyses the ways in which consciousness of empire impinged on mainstream English novels in the first half of the nineteenth century, even when their narratives were located firmly in England.

7 T. S. Eliot took the famous utterance announcing Kurtz' end in *Heart of Darkness* ('Mistah Kurtz – he dead') as an epigraph for his 1925 poem, 'The Hollow Men'. He had earlier intended to use Kurtz' own unforgettable

epitaph on his life ('The horror! The horror!') as an epigraph for *The Waste Land* (1922). Such appeals to Conradian authority continued throughout the twentieth century, culminating in Francis Ford Coppola's epic movie of the Vietnam War, *Apocalypse Now* (1979), which adds literary density to its own filmic vision by evoking the mythic resonances of both Conrad's novel and Eliot's poetry.

8 In Chapter 6 I discuss at length Marlow's faltering desire for an 'idea' that might justify the exploitations and miseries of 'real' colonialism. On Leavis' 'Platonic' relationship with Cambridge, see below (p. 62). MacKillop's biography of Leavis presents a detailed narrative of his troubled relationship with 'establishment England' and its sad dénouement.

9 From Gide's 1924 tribute, 'Joseph Conrad' (Stallman 1960: 4). A close friend of Conrad, in 1923 Gide translated *Typhoon* into French, and later dedicated to Conrad the narrative of his own Congo journey, *Travels in the Congo* (1927). A reprint (undated) of the commemorative edition of *La Nouvelle Revue Française: Hommage à Joseph Conrad* (1924) has recently been published in France. It contains Gide's tribute as well as those of André Maurois and Paul Valéry (among many others).

10 The starkest fictional representation of such psychic splitting is Conrad's tale 'The Secret Sharer' (1912), the overtones of whose title resonate through psychoanalytic literature. Antecedent literary treatments of the alter ego appear in the writings of Melville and Dostoyevsky. The two best biographies of Conrad (Karl 1979, Najder 1983) emphasize the deracinated Conrad.

11 The first biographer to suggest that Conrad was a chronic sufferer from depressive illness was Zdzislaw Najder, who dates the first 'attack' as early as 1891, shortly after Conrad's Congo journey. Najder employs the taxonomies for classifying depression current in the 1960s and doesn't draw on psychoanalytic categories (Najder 1983: 144–5).

12 For a more exact idea of Conrad's spoken English, we have a 'first-hand' account from the young American reporter, Jane Anderson, with whom the 60-year-old Conrad is alleged to have had a brief sexual liaison (Meyers 1991: 293–309). Her transcription reads: 'I would show you . . . ze spire of ze cathedral as you would see it from the hills – but my car is broken, and we do not go. Zis will be for anuzzer time' (ibid.: 301). Conrad's habit of using broken or accented English to record the speech of (usually unsavoury) characters might lead us to reconsider either his alleged personal 'sensitivity' on this matter or the value-assumptions in his textual play with voices and hybrid nationalities. These matters are discussed exhaustively by Harpham (1996: 137–83).

13 The writing of this tale for publication in 1915 involved an even more literal return to an earlier moment in Conrad's life. The idea for it seems to date back to the time when he was writing *Heart of Darkness* and *Lord Jim*. Originally entitled 'First Command', it was taken up several times in the intervening years (Karl 1979: 477).

14 The reading I am proposing deliberately eschews poststructuralist or other theoretical discourses remote from Leavis' own practice. It is more akin to the different interpretations that conductors elicit from the score of a musical work, without one 'interpretation' cancelling the possibility of another.

15 In 'The mirror stage as formative of the function of the I' (Lacan 1977a: 1–7) Lacan argues that the child's first intimations of a unitary self occur when it sees its own holistic image in a mirror. Because this happens at a time when it experiences no equivalent sense of motor control or power of agency, its recognition is in fact a misrecognition. Lacan calls this stage in the growth of subjectivity 'imaginary' because it is founded on an 'image'. For Conrad's

captain, the image reflected in the table is uncannily disconcerting. As such, it partially reverses Lacan's schema. The dis-concert experienced by the young man in that image of 'himself' involves a subliminal awareness of psychic disturbance that he cannot fully recognize at this moment of change. From this perspective, to regard Conrad's tale as a psychological case study is no less valid than to read it as an exemplary moral fable.

16 *The Shadow-Line* inspired one of the finest of many translations of Conrad novels into film (the first one as early as 1919). This was the 1976 version of the great Polish director, Andrzej Wajda. I can recall the initial feeling of estrangement that the film occasioned by virtue of the fact that this familiar story was peopled by actors who were Polish, so that all traces of Britishness were effaced. That does not mean, of course, that Wajda's film can therefore claim higher authenticity than Leavis' reading, on the grounds that the 'original' for the hero of the novel was indeed a Pole. For a detailed discussion of Wajda's film, see Miczka (1997). For an excellent discussion of Conrad's foreignness, see Harpham (1996) whose book is ironically titled *One of Us*.

17 For a strongly pro-Casement analysis of this relationship, see Taussig (1987: 3–36).

18 Symptomatic of Shakespeare's 'postcolonial moment' in the 1980s were the re-readings of both *Othello* and *The Tempest* in terms of early European colonization. Examples include Thomas Castelli's 'Prospero in Africa: *The Tempest* as a colonialist text and pretext' and Karen Newman's ' "And wash the Ethiop white": femininity and the monstrous in *Othello*' (both in Howard and O'Connor 1988: 99–115, 143–62). These, along with many related pieces both earlier and after, are indebted to decolonizing uses of *The Tempest*, one by the West Indian novelist, George Lamming (1960), and the other by Jacques Lacan's psychoanalytic colleague, the Madagascan Otto Mannoni (1990).

19 Mulhern's reading of Leavis' reading of Conrad's *Typhoon* is a model of the critique I am here attempting (Mulhern 1990: 255–6).

20 In his biography of Leavis, Ian MacKillop modifies the common view that Leavis was nostalgic for a lost rural world of 'organic community' by pointing out that the 'golden world' described in Leavis' doctoral thesis 'is a brief urban one, that of the post-Restoration London of John Dryden and Robert L'Estrange, with the coffee-house a nerve-centre of communication in which writing was for group, not market' (MacKillop 1995: 72).

21 Funes lacks the ability to select from experience on which memory depends (Borges 1970: 87). By contrast, rigorous processes of both selecting and shaping determined Proust's acts of remembering.

4 Conrad and Marxism

1 See Ashcroft, Griffiths and Tiffin (1989). The title they used for their much-read book on postcolonialism was adapted from the second 'chapter' of the science-fiction *Star Wars* movies, *The Empire Strikes Back* (1980). Since that phenomenally successful blockbuster self-consciously transformed the narrative of imperialism into a futuristic inter-galactic story of 'Empire', it is hard to determine who is 'borrowing' from whom. Quicker off the mark, and in the wake of huge race riots around England in 1981, the Centre for Contemporary Cultural Studies at Birmingham in 1982 took the exact title of the movie for a collection of essays about 'Race and racism in 70s Britain'. See CCCS (1982).

2 Eagleton has documented both his 'attack' on Williams and his 'recantation'. Neither term catches the spirit of the rift, in which each maintained great respect for the other while conducting their dispute in a tone of extraordinary

objectivity (Eagleton 1975: 21–43, 1984: 108–15). After Williams' untimely death in 1988, Eagleton delivered a finely balanced eulogy which incorporated the complex responses to his work (Eagleton 1989: 1–11).

3　The change in emphasis nevertheless resituates Williams in a Marxist tradition that includes Georg Lukács. Eagleton's remark about 'apparently standing still' uncannily repeats a common appraisal of Lukács' 'preternatural consistency'. His shifts of stance seem mainly an effect of changed political circumstances.

4　For a rich discussion of these shifts on both sides of the Atlantic during the 1960s, seen from the perspective of a 'Third-World' intellectual, see Ahmad (1992: 43–72).

5　On the terms used here see especially Wallerstein (1974) and Frank (1984).

6　For an excellent summary of the main lines of these developments, see Brewer (1980). An important intervention in British Marxism by Warren (1980) reassesses the dominant judgements about twentieth-century imperialism.

7　Said, for example, treats Marx's discussion as yet another instance of the West's incapacity to see the non-European world from any but an Orientalist perspective (Said 1978: 153–7). This position is powerfully contested by Ahmad (1992: 221–42).

8　Kant uses this term neutrally, without nosological or otherwise derogatory connotations.

9　'*Falstaff* unimitated, unimitable *Falstaff*, how shall I describe thee?', Samuel Johnson asked. But while Jameson shares with Shakespeare's character a certain 'plenitude' (Johnson 1908: 125), he is certainly not 'unimitated', given the many parodies of his extraordinary prose. For a brilliant example of the genre, see Eagleton (1986: 65).

10　An early instance of the academy's interest in *The Political Unconscious* is the Fall 1982 issue of *diacritics* which is devoted to critiquing it.

11　In the Introduction to a new anthology of his writings, Jameson (2000:1–29) illuminatingly discusses some of the influences on his intellectual formation.

12　A crude example of how a conservative academy failed to demonstrate its professed openness to new knowledge was Alan Sokal's dismissal of thinkers such as Lacan and Derrida on the grounds that they misunderstand the physics and mathematics they allude to (Sokal and Bricmont 1998). 'Le pauvre Sokal' was Derrida's lofty riposte in *Le Monde*.

13　Jameson's use of Williams here extends Lucien Goldmann's adaptation of Lukács' notion of 'totality', which divides the 'world-view' of any given moment into 'actual' and 'possible' states of consciousness (Williams 1980: 19–22).

14　Jameson also adopts Ricoeur's distinction between the desire to restore to a text the lost original meaning ('kerygma' or proclamation) and the process of demystification that results in a 'reduction of illusion' (Jameson 1981: 284–5). He makes strategic use of Gadamer's notion of widening circles of meaning revealed in an ever-extending horizon (ibid.: 75). Such widening of horizons reveals Jameson's peculiar but fundamental adaptations of both Marx's political materialism and the Freudian unconscious.

15　The ultimate source is Hegel's narrative of History mediated by Marx. In Parisian intellectual (especially Marxist and psychoanalytic) circles, Hegel was widely influential in the decades immediately before critical theory emerged in the 1960s. See Kojève (1980).

16　This is not to say that Lukács himself saw the aesthetic 'dimension' of realism simply as an 'additive'. The difference between them is that Lukács lacked what Jameson benefited from, a developed theory of language. This has some parallels with the gap between Freud and Lacan: Freud's dictum, for example, that the unconscious is structured like a language had to await Lacan's absorption of developments of modern linguistics for fuller enunciation.

17 In a discussion marked by considerable respect, Harpham (1999: 164) comments that Jameson could never be 'accused of being a winning stylist'. Eagleton, in contrast, confesses: 'I take a book of his from the shelf as often in place of poetry or fiction as literary theory' (Eagleton 1986: 66).

5 Conrad in the postcolonial world

1 The most notable contemporary scholar to go against this trend was (the late) Edward Said, whose activist role in the Palestinian struggle reinforced the sense that all his work is political in both the narrow and the full sense. Yet postcolonial studies continues to be associated principally with the academy, where most of Said's academic work can be read without invoking the Middle East as its referent.

2 One school of analysis maintains a strong opposition between (exploitative) colonizer and (oppressed) colonized. The other admits multiple stories, and by doing so effectively weakens resistance and encourages apologists for imperialism. For a lucid historical analysis of these intersecting forces, see Young (1995).

3 I am indebted to Lyn Innes for a vivid first-hand account of this exciting and scandalous moment, when the US academy was still determinedly apolitical. Achebe's robust intervention needs to be read against prevailing constructions of the novel as a timeless classic providing insights into universal human nature.

4 The principal outcomes of this position are powerfully articulated by Dipesh Chakrabarty (2000), a Subaltern Studies historian to whose work Ahmad seems surprisingly hostile.

5 A 'return to Sartre' is signalled by the recent publication of an English translation of his major writings on colonialism, first published in book form in France in 1964 (Sartre 2001).

6 Ahluwalia (2002: 184–204) analyses the problem of relations between the European 'settler' community in Australia and the indigenous peoples who had been there literally from time immemorial.

7 Sartre offended Fanon by pointing out this uncomfortable truth in response to the *négritude* movement. He argued that, whatever its immediate political efficacy, the affirmation of 'black pride' creates an 'anti-racist racism', and thereby fails to eradicate racism. Fanon (1967: 132–4) elaborates on the intellectual and political complexities involved in his exchange with Sartre on this matter.

8 This was how I actually introduced myself at a postcolonial conference at Utkal University, Orissa, India in January 1991.

9 Clearly illiterate, Pierce Collett bequeathed to his Australian descendants the misspelling which became our name: Collett > the Collett family > the Colletts > Collits. Both he and his wife Mary were natives of Kilkenny, Ireland. In a remarkable display of upward mobility, Pierce had become Sheriff of Penrith by 1810, and Mary opened the first school in the area.

10 The fact that some elements of Eagleton's autobiography replicate my own contemporaneous 'Irish Catholic' childhood a hemisphere away is a reminder that national formations are often insufficient to describe group affiliations (Eagleton 2002).

11 This exchange first appeared in *Social Text* 15 (1986) and 17 (1987), and subsequently in book form (Jameson 2000: 315–39; Ahmad 1992: 95–122). I have queried the term 'debate' because Jameson's response to Ahmad's self-styled 'comradely' aggression was brief, remarkably low-key and anything but polemical.

12 For a lucid discussion of this recent 'malaise' in postcolonial studies, see Seshadri-Crooks (2000: 3–23).

13 That is how Coleridge described it (Coleridge 1960: 44).

14 Ahmad (2000) subsequently abjured the niceties of postcolonial theory.

15 Similarly, Jameson observes apropos *Nostromo* that the 'offensive and caricatural' elements in Conrad's representation of the politics and the people of Costaguana were first made visible by Latin America's discovery of its own 'literary and political voice' (Jameson 1981: 269–70).

16 For a fuller discussion of this matter see Chapter 6 (pp.119–23).

17 Commenting on the same passage in *Arrow of God*, Thieme (2001: 18–23) argues that the Conradian echoes play a more precise role in defining Achebe's response to *Heart of Darkness*, which is 'to allow the Conradian view just enough space for its limitations to be apparent' (ibid.: 22).

6 *Heart of Darkness*: history, politics, myth and tragedy

1 I am alluding here to some of the earliest politicizing readings of *Heart of Darkness* (as opposed to studies of the political themes it contains) which began to appear in the 1970s and are usefully analysed by Hawkins (1979).

2 When Conrad's reputation was most vulnerable to negative political criticism, the French critic Jacques Darras (1982) published one of the best books on Conrad and imperialism, blending semiotics and deconstruction – with a politics informed by the *événements* of 1968 – into a complex practice of reading. My own account of *Heart of Darkness* owes much to Darras' rigorous analysis.

3 Francis Ford Coppola's *Apocalypse Now* (1979) transforms *Heart of Darkness* into a film of the 1964–75 Vietnam War. Dean (1998) makes the case for reading *Heart of Darkness* in terms of the AIDS epidemic.

4 The 'discourse of the university' is one of the 'four discourses' examined in Lacan's *L'Envers de la Psychanalyse: Seminar XVII (1969–1970)*, which has not yet been translated into English (Lacan 1991).

5 Throughout the 1990s, sustained attempts were made to link political (and especially Marxist and feminist) critique with Lacanian psychoanalysis in order to produce a more comprehensive hermeneutics. The most explosive manifestation of this trend is the work of the Slovenian philosopher, Slavoj Žižek. Other studies directly relevant to my own project include those by Bracher (1993), Seshadri-Crooks (2000), and especially Rutherford (2000), whose book has directly influenced my outline here of a 'Lacanian' reading of *Heart of Darkness*.

6 Rutherford offers a crucial caveat against misapplying the 'ethics' Lacan defines through his reading of *Antigone*:

> In *The Ethics of Psychoanalysis*, Lacan very clearly limits his ethical trajectory to the domain of psychoanalysis. When he gives the formula 'The only thing of which one can be guilty is of having given ground relative to one's desire', he is speaking to the analyst and the analysand. It is not an ethics for the public domain, nor is it an ethics that can be translated into a science of desire.
>
> (Rutherford 2000: 204)

The relationship between these two possible trajectories of ethics, one directed to society's 'good' and the other towards the end of analysis, is yet to be determined.

7 On the place of desire in the understanding of colonialism, see Young (1995), whose excellent survey is marred only by his perfunctory and dismissive references to the most important psychoanalytical theorist of desire, Jacques Lacan.

8 These observations by Lacan are uncannily similar to those of Gorgias of Leontini, whom Howard Felperin quotes as a distant avatar of 'hard-core deconstruction': 'Firstly . . . nothing exists; secondly . . . even if anything exists, it is inapprehensible by man; thirdly . . . even if anything is apprehensible, yet of a surety it is inexpressible and incommunicable to one's neighbour' (Felperin 1985: 104).

7 *Lord Jim*: popular culture and the transmission of the code

1 In his 'Thoughts on the Late Transactions respecting Falkland's Islands' (1771), Samuel Johnson saw this lonely atoll – which was even then in dispute between Britain and Argentina – as the perfect image of human futility (Johnson 1968: 60–90).

2 Perhaps the finest example of radical rewriting is Jean Rhys' *Wide Sargasso Sea* (1966), a prequel to *Jane Eyre* (1847) in which Charlotte Brontë's nameless and grotesque 'mad woman in the attic' occupies the centre of her own novel as Antoinette Cosway. Her postcolonial experience is based on Rhys' own impoverishing displacement from the once-privileged ruling class of West Indian Dominica following the emancipation of the island's slave population. Another example of the genre is J. M. Coetzee's *Foe* (1986), whose starting point is the ur-text of all European colonial fictions, Daniel Defoe's *Robinson Crusoe* (1719).

3 Hampson (2003: 33–56) discusses this 'mythologized moment' in his careful analysis of the relations between maps and the imagination in Conrad's writings.

4 See especially Park and Rajan (2000).

5 For another canine analysis of the novel, see Harpham (1996: 31–2).

6 Freud's colleague, Otto Rank, provides a fascinating survey of the complex history of this psychoanalytic concept (Rank 1971).

7 In discussing 'the possibility of a leading idea being substituted for a leader', Freud highlights how subservience is prerequisite to the take-over of a subject's individual will (*SE* XVIII: 95).

8 See Wallace (1869). In his detailed discussion of the sources for Conrad's Stein, Sherry (1966: 141–7) points out that Wallace's scientific memoir was Conrad's 'favourite bed-side book' (ibid.: 142).

9 *The Rescue* was the third of Conrad's Malay novels, the others being *Almayer's Folly* (1895) and *An Outcast of the Islands* (1896). Set aside several times while Conrad experimented with different kinds of fiction, it was not completed for publication until 1920. The sentiments quoted here are those of the pre-*Heart of Darkness* Conrad. For a detailed analysis of his development as a thinker and writer, see Watt (1979), a book trenchantly critiqued by Harpham (1996: 125–7).

10 For an Australian 'rewriting' of the Brooke story, see Pybus (1996), who notes that while both James and Charles would accompany their Dyaks on head-hunting expeditions, the nephew Charles at least appeared 'squeamish' about the beheading of women and children, and encouraged his followers to restrain themselves accordingly (Pybus 1996: 40). More recently, Godshalk (1998) focuses on the strength shown by Margaret Brooke in her strange marital existence in Sarawak.

8 *Nostromo*: the anti-heroics and epic failures of Empire

1 Tillyard (1958) was among the first to address (although not very trenchantly) the question of Conrad and epic. In his searching discussion of epic in modernist fiction, Adams (2003) gives more space to Conrad than to any other English novelist. His sense of what makes the novel 'Homeric', however, diverges from mine because he regards the *Odyssey* as a journey poem.

2 This view had become orthodoxy by the time of A. C. Bradley's *Shakespearean Tragedy*, first published, like *Nostromo*, in 1904. '[T]he mere physical horror of such a spectacle', Bradley writes,

> would in the theatre be a sensation so violent as to overpower the purely tragic emotions, and therefore the spectacle would seem revolting or shocking. But it is otherwise in reading. For mere imagination the physical horror, though not lost, is so far deadened that it can do its duty as a stimulus to pity, and to that appalled dismay at the extremity of human cruelty which it is of the essence of the tragedy to excite. Thus the blinding of Gloster belongs rightly to *King Lear* in its proper world of imagination; it is a blot upon *King Lear* as a stage-play.
>
> (Bradley 1904: 251)

3 On the basis of extensive archival research, van Marle (1991) returns an open verdict on the question of whether or not Conrad ever went to South America.

4 For a powerful and imaginative attempt to penetrate the mysteries that lie behind the scant record of Conrad's turbulent years in Marseilles prior to his English re-birthing, see Lesage (2003).

5 Arrighi (1978: 93) compares America's attitude towards European imperialism at the end of the nineteenth century with that towards China:

> An analogous role was played by the United States in Latin America, where the application of the Monroe Doctrine had effectively contained European expansionist tendencies. It is true that American policy in this area already prefigured, by its intimidating acts of intervention, the limits of its support for national sovereignty. But that did not stop the USA from presenting itself as an anti-colonialist power faithful to its image of the 'first ex-colony', or from being perceived as such on the world arena.

6 See, for example, Wallerstein (1979) and Frank (1984). Both are prominent world-systems theorists.

7 Although Conrad was averse to Americanism, North American scholarship, by contrast, served him well in the post-war period with its rigorous attention to his work. American Conrad studies has been more attentive than its British counterpart to his politics. Howe's brilliant discussion of the politics of *Nostromo* appeared in *Kenyon Review* as early as 1953–4 (Howe 1957: 76–113). The study by Hay (1963) remains among the finest of both this subject and Conrad in general, while Fleishman (1967) established the framework for future analyses of Conrad and politics.

8 In fact, Conrad chose a hopeful epigraph for *Nostromo*, borrowed from Shakespeare: 'so foul a sky/ clears not/ without a storm'. It should be noted also that while the *Eighteenth Brumaire* catches Marx's feelings at a low point it does not represent his 'final' view of history.

9 I refer throughout to Robert Fitzgerald's translation of the *Odyssey* (1961); book and line numbers are taken from the 1998 edition. The Homeric

passage referred to here is V, 474–519. The comparable moment in *Nostromo* follows Nostromo's own swim from the Great Isabel to the mainland after the desperate night rescue of the silver. Both Homer and Conrad liken their waking heroes to wild animals (*Odyssey* VI, 137–50; *Nostromo* 411–12).

9 *Victory* (1): valedictory to the old colonial order

1 This phrase and its ethnographic appropriation are discussed in Chapter 1 (see especially p. 28)
2 The theme of 'going native' (including its sexual dimension) occupies considerable space in Conrad's first two novels, *Almayer's Folly* (1895) and *An Outcast of the Islands* (1896). The island romance of Heyst and Lena can be read as a mutation of this theme. *Victory* makes no attempt to represent 'native' life; and since Lena (unlike Jim's Jewel) is English she is also, like Heyst, a European.
3 See, for example, the description of Lena (252–3). In contrast with Conrad's lightly suggestive prose, the dust-jacket of Methuen's first edition of the novel displays a lurid drawing of Heyst in pyjamas and Lena clad in a sarong (reproduced by Karl 1979: illustration following 722).
4 'The philosophers have only *interpreted* the world, in various ways; the point, however, is to *change* it' (Marx 1969: 286).
5 Lenin depends on Rudolf Hilferding's analysis of 'finance capital' or 'joint stock' as the mechanism that from *c.*1870 enabled the final and most massive development of imperialism.
6 Part of the quotation from Milton's *Comus* (1637) which forms the epigraph to Conrad's novel.
7 Jameson 1981: 46–9, 254–7; Greimas 1987: 106–20.
8 Eagleton associates 'the poetry of the future' with Jameson's 'excess of style' in *The Political Unconscious* (Eagleton 1986: 68).

10 *Victory* (2): postcolonial Conrad

1 Three famous Victorians who felt the looming presence of fathers are John Stuart Mill, Matthew Arnold and Edmund Gosse.
2 For a recent discussion of Conrad's treatment of the overseas Chinese, see Yeow 2004.
3 One of Campbell's scholarly advisers in London was Conrad's countryman, Bronislaw Malinowski. The anthropologist knew Conrad well enough to call on him in 1923, when they discussed the novelist's recent visit to Poland (Najder 1983: 483).
4 The cliché of 'darkest Africa' gained currency in the last decades of the nineteenth century. It possibly originated with H. M. Stanley's *Through the Dark Continent* (1878). An early 'reversal' of its colonial application to Africa was William Booth's *In Darkest England and the Way Out* (1890), published in the same year as Stanley's famous *In Darkest Africa*. Freud's application of the term to sexuality means that it traversed what would become, approximately a hundred years later, the central categories of 'identity politics': race, class and gender. Somewhat later than Conrad's novel, Freud quotes the phrase (in English) in a late essay, 'The Question of Lay Analysis' (1926), when considering how the sexual behaviour of boys differs from that of girls, whom he regards as less knowable, more primitive and more complicated. 'We need not feel ashamed of this distinction', he adds; 'after all, the sexual life of adult women is a "dark continent" for psychology' (SE XX: 212). Some feminists argue that in this matter, as in others, *Heart of Darkness* anticipates Freud in

linking the 'dark continent' with both women and sexuality. For a powerful and complex reading of *Heart of Darkness* in this light, see London (1990: 29–58).

5 The feminist attack on Lawrence (along with Freud, Henry Miller and Norman Mailer) was inaugurated in Kate Millett (1971) and never effectively answered by Lawrence's defenders (MacLeod 1985).

6 See Nadelhaft (1991) and Jones (1999). Although both are firmly grounded in Conrad scholarship, neither treats *Victory* as a significant departure for Conrad. I believe their arguments would have been strengthened by doing so.

7 Contributions to the critical debate about Marlow's lie are included in both versions of the Norton Critical Edition of *Heart of Darkness* (1963, 1988). None investigates the feminist implications of the fact that the lie is told specifically to a woman.

8 Conrad's main point in giving Heyst a philosophical genealogy is to show him as representing the end of a tradition that offered him nothing with which to face life's vicissitudes. For a thorough discussion of Conrad's European existentialism, see Bohlman (1991).

9 I use 'operatic' and 'melodrama' without the negative connotations they automatically carry in literary critical discourse. The last section of *Victory* strikes me as powerful 'melodrama' in the sense that the root force of that word ('sung drama') does justice to its pathos. The novel's theatricality is attested to by the fact that an operatic version of *Victory* was staged in 1970. At least seven movie versions were produced between 1919 and 1998.

10 While Heyst can disregard the moral question of their 'irregular' (because unmarried) relationship, Lena is not entirely untouched by the stigma that women of their time incurred by engaging in extramarital sex. It is a minor strain in their complex misunderstandings, mainly because she thinks it could make Heyst feel ashamed of her. The novel touches on this issue several times when it notes the 'good Davidson's' delicate responses (50, 57) and Lena's conventionality and guilt (351–3).

11 Books that document this process include Mitchell and Rose (1985), Minsky (1996) and Grigg, Hecq and Smith (1999).

12 For the analytical implications of significant repetition, see Freud (*SE* XVII: 18–23, 32–38) and Lacan (1977: 53–77), which analyses the role of the gaze in the matrix of the drive.

Epilogue: Conrad and the new world order

1 Both Lacan and Žižek enjoy the practice that Samuel Johnson attributes to the 'Metaphysical Poets' whereby 'the most heterogeneous ideas are yoked by violence together' (Johnson 1925, vol. 1: 11). In a more controlled way, I have tried to emulate that practice as a way of opening up the range of meanings accessible through Conrad's novels. My title-heading here echoes one of Lacan's most original 'yokings' of this kind: 'Kant avec Sade' (Lacan 1966: 765–90).

Bibliography

Achebe, C. (1958) *Things Fall Apart*, London: Heinemann.

—— (1964) *Arrow of God*, London: Heinemann; republished African Writers Series, 1974.

—— (1975) 'An Image of Africa: Racism in Conrad's *Heart of Darkness*', *The Massachusetts Review*, volume 18; reprinted in R. Kimbrough, editor, *Heart of Darkness*, third edition, New York and London. Norton, 1988.

Adams, D. (2003) *Colonial Odysseys: Empire and Epic in the Modernist Novel*, Ithaca and London: Cornell University Press.

Adorno, T. *et al.* (1977) *Aesthetics and Politics*, translated and edited R. Taylor, afterword by F. Jameson, London: New Left Books.

Afzal-Khan F. and Seshadri-Crooks, K., editors (2000) *The Preoccupation of Postcolonial Studies*, Durham, North Carolina and London: Duke University Press.

Ahluwalia, P. (2002) 'Towards (Re)Conciliation: The Postcolonial Economy of Giving', in D. Goldberg and A. Quayson, editors, *Relocating Postcolonialism*, Oxford: Blackwell.

Ahmad, A. (1992) *In Theory: Classes, Nations, Literatures*, London and New York: Verso.

—— (2000) *Politics in Contemporary South Asia*, London and New York: Verso.

Althusser, L. (1971) *Lenin and Philosophy and Other Essays*, translated B. Brewster, New York and London: Monthly Review Press.

Anderson, B. (1983) *Imagined Communities: Reflections on the Origin and Spread of Nationalism*, London: Verso.

Anderson, P. (1968) 'Components of the National Culture', *New Left Review*, number 50.

Arnold, M. (1906) *Essays in Criticism*, London: J. M. Dent and Sons; new edition, 1964.

Arrighi, G. (1978) *The Geometry of Imperialism*, translated P. Camiller, London: New Left Books; Verso edition, 1983.

Ashcroft, B., Griffiths, G. and Tiffin, H. (1989) *The Empire Writes Back: Theory and Practice in Post-Colonial Literatures*, London and New York: Routledge.

Baldick, C. (1983) *The Social Mission of English Criticism, 1848–1932*, Oxford: Clarendon Press.

Barthes, R. (1968) *Writing Degree Zero*, translated A. Lavers and C. Smith, New York: Hill and Wang.

—— (1972) *Mythologies*, translated A. Lavers; reprinted St Albans: Paladin 1976.

—— (1975) *The Pleasure of the Text*, translated R. Miller, New York: Hill and Wang.

Benedict, R. (1983) *Race and Racism* [1942], London, Melbourne and Henley: Routledge and Kegan Paul.

Benjamin, W. (1968) *Illuminations*, edited H. Arendt, translated H. Zohn, London: Jonathan Cape; republished Glasgow: Fontana Books, William Collins, 1973; second impression, 1977.

Bhabha, H. K. (1994) *The Locations of Culture*, London and New York: Routledge.

—— editor (1990) *Nation and Narration*, London and New York: Routledge.

Bloom, H. (1994) *The Western Canon*, New York: Harcourt Brace.

Bohlman, O. (1991) *Conrad's Existentialism*, New York: St. Martin's Press.

Bongie, C. (1991) *Exotic Memories: Literature, Colonialism, and the Fin de Siècle*, Stanford: Stanford University Press.

Borges, J. L. (1970) *Labyrinths*, Harmondsworth: Penguin.

Bracher, M. (1993) *Lacan, Discourse, and Social Change: A Psychoanalytic Cultural Criticism*, Ithaca and London: Cornell University Press.

Bradley, A. (1904) *Shakespearean Tragedy*, London: Macmillan.

Brecht, B. (1964) *Brecht on Theatre: The Development of an Aesthetic*, edited and translated J. Willett, London: Eyre Methuen.

Brewer, A. (1980) *Marxist Theories of Imperialism: A Critical Survey*, London: Routledge and Kegan Paul.

Campbell, P. C. (1923) *Chinese Coolie Emigration to Countries within the British Empire*, reprinted London: Frank Cass and Company, 1971.

CCCS (1982) *The Empire Strikes Back*, Centre for Contemporary Cultural Studies, University of Birmingham, London: Hutchinson.

Chakrabarty, D. (2000) *Provincializing Europe: Postcolonial Thought and Historical Difference*, Princeton and Oxford: Princeton University Press.

Chatwin, B. (1977) *In Patagonia*, London: Jonathan Cape; republished Picador, London: Pan Books 1979.

—— (1980) *The Viceroy of Ouidah*, London: Jonathan Cape; republished Picador, London: Pan Books 1982.

Chaudhuri, N. C. (1975) *Robert Clive of India*, Bombay: Jaico Publishing House; third impression, 1996.

Clifford, H. (1926) *Saleh: A Prince of Malaya*, New York: Harper and Brothers; reprinted Singapore: Oxford University Press, 1989.

Clifford, J. (1988) *The Predicament of Culture*, Cambridge, Massachusetts and London: Harvard University Press.

Coleridge, S. T. (1960) *Samuel Taylor Coleridge: Shakespearean Criticism*, edited T. M. Raysor, two volumes, London: Dent.

Collits, T. (1999) 'Sydney Revisited: Literary Struggles in Australia (*circa* 1965 and Ongoing)', Australian Essay in *The Australian Book Review*, number 210, May.

Conrad, J. (1946–55) *Collected Edition of the Works of Joseph Conrad*, 22 volumes, London: J. M. Dent and Sons.

—— (1983–) *The Collected Letters of Joseph Conrad*, edited F. Karl *et al.*, six volumes (to date), Cambridge: Cambridge University Press.

—— (1986) *Joseph Conrad: Selected Literary Criticism and The Shadow-Line*, edited A. Ingram, London and New York: Methuen.

Cruttwell, P. (1960) *The Shakespearean Moment*, New York: Random House.

Darras, J. (1982) *Joseph Conrad and the West: Signs of Empire*, translated A. Luyat and J. Darras, Totowa, New Jersey: Barnes and Noble Books.

Dean, T. (1998) 'The Germs of Empire: *Heart of Darkness*, Colonial Trauma, and the Historiography of AIDS', in C. Lane, editor, *The Psychoanalysis of Race*, New York: Columbia University Press.

Diacritics, volume 12, number 3, Fall 1982.

Doyle, B. (1989) *English and Englishness*, London and New York: Routledge.

During, S. editor (1993) *The Cultural Studies Reader*, London and New York: Routledge.

Eagleton, T. (1970) *Exiles and Emigrés: Studies in Modern Literature*, London: Chatto and Windus.

—— (1975) *Criticism and Ideology*, London: New Left Books.

—— (1981) *Walter Benjamin, or Towards a Revolutionary Criticism*, London: Verso.

—— (1983) *Literary Theory: An Introduction*, Oxford: Blackwell.

—— (1984) *The Function of Criticism*, London: Verso.

—— (1986) *Against the Grain: Essays 1975–1985*, London: Verso.

—— (1991) *Ideology: An Introduction*, London and New York: Verso.

—— (2002) *The Gatekeeper: A Memoir*, London: Penguin.

—— editor (1989) *Raymond Williams: Critical Perspectives*, Oxford: Polity Press.

Eliot, G. (1871–2) *Middlemarch*, London: Penguin Books 1994; reprinted 2003.

Eliot, T. S. (1932) *Selected Essays*, London: Faber; reprinted 1972.

Evans, D. (1996) *An Introductory Dictionary of Lacanian Psychoanalysis*, London and New York: Routledge.

Eysenck, H. (1971) *Race, Intelligence and Education*, New York: Library Press.

Fanon, F. (1967) *Black Skins, White Masks*; republished, with a foreword by H. K. Bhabha, London: Grove Press 1986.

Felperin, H. (1985) *Beyond Deconstruction: The Uses and Abuses of Literary Theory*, Oxford: Clarendon Press.

Flaubert, G. (1857) *Madame Bovary*; republished Paris: Garnier-Flammarion 1966.

Fleishman, A. (1967) *Conrad's Politics: Community and Anarchy in the Fiction of Joseph Conrad*, Baltimore: Johns Hopkins Press.

Foucault, M. (1972) *The Archaeology of Knowledge*, translated A. M. Sheridan Smith, London: Tavistock Publications; republished Social Science Paperback, 1974.

—— (1977) *Discipline and Punish*, translated A. Sheridan, Harmondsworth: Peregrine, 1979.

—— (1984) *The Foucault Reader*, edited P. Rabinow, Harmondsworth: Penguin.

—— (1998) *Aesthetics, Method, and Epistemology: Essential Works of Foucault 1954–1984, Volume Two*, edited J. D. Faubion, translated R. Hurley *et al.*, London: Penguin.

Foulkes, A. P. (1983) *Literature and Propaganda*, London and New York: Methuen.

Frank, A. G. (1984) *Critique and Anti-Critique: Essays on Dependence and Reformism*, London: Macmillan.

Freud, S. (1953–74) *The Standard Edition of the Complete Psychological Works of Sigmund Freud*, edited and translated J. Strachey *et al.*, 24 volumes, London: Hogarth Press; reprinted 1995.

Fukuyama, F. (1992) *The End of History and the Last Man*, London: Penguin.

Gadamer, H.-G. (1975) *Truth and Method*, translated J.Weinsheimer and D. G. Marshall, New York: Continuum; second (revised) edition, republished 2000.
—— (1976) *Philosophical Hermeneutics*, translated and edited D. E. Linge, Berkeley: University of California Press; paperback edition, 1977.
Gandhi, L. (1998) *Postcolonial Theory: A Critical Introduction*, Sydney: Allen and Unwin.
Geertz, C. (1988) *Works and Lives: The Anthropologist as Author*, Oxford: Polity Press.
Gide, A. (1924) 'Joseph Conrad', *La Nouvelle Revue Française: Hommage à Joseph Conrad*, numéro. 135, 1er Décembre.
Godshalk, C. S. (1998) *Kalimantan: A Novel*, London: Little, Brown and Company.
Goldberg D. T. editor (1990) *Anatomy of Racism*, Minneapolis: University of Minnesota Press.
Goldberg D. T. and Quayson, A. editors (2002) *Relocating Postcolonialism*, Oxford: Blackwell.
Gorky, M. (1919) *Reminiscences of Leo Nikolaevich Tolstoy*, reprinted in K. Mansfield, S. S. Koteliansky and L. Woolf, translators, *Reminiscences of Tolstoy, Chekhov and Andreev*, London: Hogarth Press 1934.
Greenblatt, S. (1980) *Renaissance Self-Fashioning*, Chicago and London: University of Chicago Press.
Greene, G. (1961) *In Search of a Character: Two African Journals*, London: The Bodley Head.
Greimas, A. J. (1987) *In Meaning: Selected Writings in Semiotic Theory*, translated P. Perron and F. Collins, with foreword by F. Jameson, Minneapolis: University of Minnesota Press.
Grigg, R., Hecq, D. and Smith, C. editors (1999), *Female Sexuality: The Early Psychoanalytic Controversies*, London: Rebus Press.
Guerard, A. J. (1962) *Conrad the Novelist*, Cambridge, Massachusetts: Harvard University Press.
Haggard, H. R. (1885) *King Solomon's Mines*; London: Puffin Books, 1958.
Haight, G. S. (1968) *George Eliot: A Biography*, London: Oxford University Press.
Hampson, R. (2003) '"A Passion for Maps": Conrad, Africa, Australia, and South-East Asia', *The Conradian*, volume 28, number 1, Spring.
Harding, D. (1963) *Experience into Words*, London: Chatto and Windus.
Hardt, M. and Negri, A. (2000) *Empire*, Cambridge, Massachusetts: Harvard University Press.
Harpham, G. G. (1996) *One of Us: The Mastery of Joseph Conrad*, Chicago and London: University of Chicago Press.
—— (1999) *Shadows of Ethics: Criticism and the Just Society*, Durham, North Carolina and London: Duke University Press.
Hawkins, H. (1979) 'Conrad's Critique of Imperialism in *Heart of Darkness*', *PMLA*, volume 94, number 2, March.
Hawthorn, J. (1979) *Joseph Conrad: Language and Fictional Self-Consciousness*, London: Edward Arnold.
Hay, E. K. (1963) *The Political Novels of Joseph Conrad*, Chicago and London: University of Chicago Press; Midway reprint with a new preface, 1981.
Hegel, G. W. F. (1956) *The Philosophy of History*, translated J. Sibree, New York: Dover Publications.

—— (1962) *Hegel on Tragedy*, edited A. and H. Paolucci, New York: Anchor Books.

—— (1975) *Aesthetics: Lectures on Fine Art*, translated T. M. Knox, two volumes, Oxford: Clarendon Press.

Homer (1961) *Homer: The Odyssey*, translated R. Fitzgerald, New York: Doubleday; republished New York: Farrar, Straus and Giroux, 1998.

Howard, J. E. and O'Connor, M. F. editors (1988) *Shakespeare Reproduced: The Text in History and Ideology*, New York and London: Methuen.

Howe, I. (1957) *Politics and the Novel*, New York: Horizon Press.

Jackson, R. (1994) *Frieda Lawrence*, London: Pandora.

James, H. (1873) 'George Eliot's *Middlemarch*', in G. S. Haight, editor (1965) *A Century of George Eliot Criticism*, London: Methuen.

—— (1934) *The Art of the Novel: Critical Prefaces*, New York and London: Charles Scribner's Sons, republished 1962.

—— (1963) *Selected Literary Criticism*, edited M. Shapira, London: Heinemann.

—— (1987) *Selected Letters*, edited L. Edel, Cambridge, Massachusetts and London: Harvard University Press.

Jameson, F. (1971) *Marxism and Form: Twentieth-century Dialectical Theories of Literature*, Princeton: Princeton University Press.

—— (1981) *The Political Unconscious: Narrative as a Socially Symbolic Act*, Ithaca, New York: Cornell University Press.

—— (1984) *Sartre: The Origins of a Style*, second edition, with new afterword, New York and Guildford, Surrey: Columbia University Press.

—— (1991) *Postmodernism, or, The Cultural Logic of Late Capitalism*, London and New York: Verso.

—— (1994) *The Seeds of Time*, New York: Columbia University Press.

—— (2000) *The Jameson Reader*, edited M. Hardt and K. Weeks, Oxford: Blackwell.

Johnson, S. (1908) *Johnson on Shakespeare*, edited W. Raleigh, Oxford: Oxford University Press; reprinted 1968.

—— (1925) *Lives of the English Poets*, two volumes, London: Dent.

—— (1966) *Johnson: Prose and Poetry*, edited M. Wilson, London: Rupert Hart-Davis.

—— (1968) *The Political Writings of Dr Johnson*, edited J. Hardy, London: Routledge and Kegan Paul.

Jones, S. (1999) *Conrad and Women*, Oxford: Oxford University Press.

Kant, I. (1993) *Critique of Practical Reason*, edited and translated L. W. Beck, Upper Saddle River, New Jersey: Prentice-Hall.

Karl, F. R. (1979) *Joseph Conrad: The Three Lives: A Biography*, London: Faber.

Keats, J. (1954) *Letters of John Keats*, edited F. Page, London: Oxford University Press.

Kimbrough, R. editor (1971) *Joseph Conrad: Heart of Darkness*, Norton Critical Edition, second edition, New York and London: Norton.

—— (1988) *Joseph Conrad: Heart of Darkness*, Norton Critical Edition, third edition, New York and London: Norton.

Kipling, R. (1964) *A Kipling Anthology*, edited W. Bebbington, London: Methuen.

Kojève, A. (1980) *Introduction to the Reading of Hegel* [1947], edited A. Bloom, translated J. H. Nichols, Jr., Ithaca and London: Cornell University Press.

Kovel, J. (1984) *White Racism: A Psychohistory*, New York: Columbia University Press.

Lacan, J. (1966) *Écrits*, Paris: Éditions du Seuil.

—— (1977) *The Four Fundamental Concepts of Psycho-Analysis*, translated A. Sheridan, Harmondsworth: Penguin.

—— (1977a) *Écrits: A Selection*, translated A. Sheridan, New York and London: Norton.

—— (1985) *Feminine Sexuality*, edited and translated J. Mitchell and J. Rose, London and New York: Norton.

—— (1991) *L'Envers de la Psychanalyse: Seminar XVII (1969–1970)*, Paris: Éditions du Seuil (not yet translated).

—— (1992) *The Ethics of Psychoanalysis: The Seminar of Jacques Lacan, Book VII, 1959–1960*, translated D. Porter, edited J.-A. Miller, London: Routledge.

Lamming G. (1960) *The Pleasures of Exile*, London and New York: Allen and Busby.

Lawrence, D. H. (1936) *Phoenix: The Posthumous Papers of D. H. Lawrence*, edited E. D. McDonald, London: Heinemann.

—— (1960) *Lady Chatterley's Lover*, London: Heinemann.

—— (1962) *The Collected Letters of D. H. Lawrence*, edited H. Moore, two volumes, London: Heinemann.

Leavis, F. R. (1948) *The Great Tradition*, London: Chatto and Windus.

—— (1962) *The Common Pursuit*, London: Chatto and Windus.

—— (1962a) *Two Cultures? The Significance of C. P. Snow*, London: Chatto and Windus.

—— (1963) '*Scrutiny*: A Retrospect', Foreword to the Cambridge University Press re-issue, in twenty volumes, of the complete *Scrutiny*, Cambridge: Cambridge University Press.

—— (1967) '*Anna Karenina*' *and Other Essays*, London: Chatto and Windus.

Leavis, F. R. and Leavis, Q. D. (1970) *Dickens the Novelist*, London: Chatto and Windus.

Leavis, Q. D. (1932) *Fiction and the Reading Public*, London: Chatto and Windus; re-issued 1965.

—— (1943) 'The Cambridge Tradition: Academic Case-History', reprinted in *A Selection from Scrutiny*, compiled by F. R. Leavis, two volumes, Cambridge: Cambridge University Press 1968.

Lenin, V. I. (1917) *Imperialism, the Highest State of Capitalism*, republished Moscow: Moscow Progress Publishers 1978.

Lesage, C. (2003) *Joseph Conrad et le Continent*, Michel Houdiard, éditeur, Montreuil-sur-Mer: IEH.

Lichtheim, G. (1971) *Imperialism*, Harmondsworth: Penguin.

London, B. (1990) *The Appropriated Voice: Narrative Authority in Conrad, Forster, and Woolf*, Michigan: University of Michigan Press.

Lukács, G. (1962) *The Historical Novel*, London: Merlin Press; third impression, 1974.

—— (1963) *The Meaning of Contemporary Realism*, translated J. and N. Mander, London: Merlin Press.

—— (1968) *History and Class Consciousness*, translated R. Livingstone, London: Merlin Press.

—— (1970) *Lenin: A Study in the Unity of his Thought*, translated N. Jacobs, London: New Left Books.

—— (1972) *Studies in European Realism*, translated E. Bone, London: Merlin Press.

Lyotard, J.-F. (1988) *The Differend: Phrases in Dispute*, translated G. Van Den Abbeele, Manchester: Manchester University Press.

MacKillop, I. (1995) *F. R. Leavis: A Life in Criticism*, London: Penguin.

MacLeod, S. (1985) *Lawrence's Men and Women*, London: Heinemann.

Mannoni, O. (1990) *Prospero and Caliban: The Psychology of Colonization*, Michigan: University of Michigan Press.

Marle, H. van (1991) 'Lawful and Lawless: Young Korzeniowski's Adventures in the Caribbean', in *L'Époque Conradienne*, volume 17.

Marx, K. (1973) *Surveys from Exile*, edited D. Fernbach, London: Penguin.

Marx, K. and Engels, F. (1969) *Marx and Engels: Basic Writings on Politics and Philosophy*, edited L. S. Feuer, Glasgow: Collins.

Memmi, A. (1965) *The Colonizer and the Colonized*, introduction J.-P. Sartre; expanded edition, afterword by S. G. Miller, translated H. Greenfield, Boston: Beacon Press, 1991.

Meyers, J. (1991) *Joseph Conrad: A Biography*, London: John Murray.

Miczka, T. (1997) 'Literature, Painting, and Film: Wajda's Adaptation of *The Shadow-Line*', in G. M. Moore *Conrad on Film*, Cambridge: Cambridge University Press, 1997.

Mill, J. S. (1912) *On Liberty, Representative Government, The Subjection of Women*, London: Oxford University Press.

Millett, K. (1971), *Sexual Politics*, London: Rupert Hart-Davis.

Minsky, R. (1996) *Psychoanalysis and Gender: An Introductory Reader*, London and New York: Routledge.

Mitchell, J. and Rose, J. editors and translators (1985) *Jacques Lacan: Feminine Sexuality*, London and New York: Norton.

Moser, T. (1957) *Joseph Conrad: Achievement and Decline*, Cambridge, Massachusetts: Harvard University Press.

Mulhern, F. (1979) *The Moment of 'Scrutiny'*, London: New Left Books.

—— (1990) 'English Reading', in H. K. Bhabha, editor, *Nation and Narration*, London and New York: Routledge.

Nadelhaft, R. (1991) *Joseph Conrad*, London and New York: Harvester Wheatsheaf.

Naipaul, V. S. (1981) *The Return of Eva Peron*, Harmondsworth: Penguin.

Najder, Z. (1983) *Joseph Conrad: A Chronicle*, Cambridge: Cambridge University Press.

Nietzsche, F. (1872) *The Birth of Tragedy*, translated S. Whiteside, edited M. Tanner, London: Penguin Books 1993.

Paganini, M. (1994) *Reading Proust: In Search of the Wolf-Fish*, Minneapolis and London: University of Minnesota Press.

Palmer, J. A. (1968) *Joseph Conrad's Fiction*, Ithaca, New York: Cornell University Press.

Park, Y. and Rajan, R. S. editors (2000) *The Postcolonial Jane Austen*, London and New York: Routledge.

Parry, B. (1983) *Conrad and Imperialism: Ideological Boundaries and Visionary Frontiers*, London: Macmillan; reprinted, 1987.

—— (1987) 'Problems in Current Theories of Colonial Discourse', *Oxford Literary Review*, volume 9, numbers 1–2, 27–58.

Payne, R. (1960) *The White Rajahs of Sarawak*, first published by Robert Hale Limited, then re-issued in paperback series in 1986, Singapore, Oxford and New York: Oxford University Press.

Perera, S. (1991) *Reaches of Empire: The English Novel from Edgeworth to Dickens*, New York: Columbia University Press.

Pybus, C. (1996) *White Rajah: A Dynastic Intrigue*, Brisbane: University of Queensland Press.

Rabaté, J.-M. (2001) *Jacques Lacan: Psychoanalysis and the Subject of Literature*, Basingstoke and New York: Palgrave.

Rank, O. (1971) *The Double: A Psychoanalytic Study*, translated and edited H. Tucker Jr., Chapel Hill: University of North Carolina Press.

Raskin, J. (1971) *The Mythology of Imperialism*, New York: Random House.

Reiss, T. J. (1980) *Tragedy and Truth*, New Haven and London: Yale University Press.

Rushdie, S. (1981) *Midnight's Children*, London: Jonathan Cape.

—— (1991) *Imaginary Homelands: Essays and Criticism 1981–1991*, London: Granta.

Russell, B. (1975) *The Autobiography of Bertrand Russell*, London: George Allen and Unwin.

Rutherford, J. (2000) *The Gauche Intruder: Freud, Lacan and the White Australian Fantasy*, Melbourne: Melbourne University Press.

Said, E. (1975) *Beginnings: Intention and Method*, New York: Columbia University Press.

—— (1978) *Orientalism*, London: Routledge and Kegan Paul; republished with new afterword, London: Penguin, 1995.

—— (1983) *The World, the Text, and the Critic*, Cambridge, Massachusetts: Harvard University Press.

—— (1984) 'Orientalism Reconsidered', in *Europe and its Others: Proceedings of the Essex Conference on the Sociology of Literature, July 1984, Volume One*.

—— (1993) *Culture and Imperialism*, London: Chatto and Windus.

—— (1999) *Out of Place: A Memoir*, New York: Alfred A. Knopf.

Salusinszky, I. (1987) *Criticism in Society*, New York and London: Methuen.

Sartre, J.-P. (1964) *Colonialism and Neocolonialism* (in French), Paris: Éditions Gallimard; new edition, translated A. Haddour, S. Brewer and T. McWilliams, London and New York: Routledge, 2001.

Sarvan, C. P. (1980) 'Racism and the *Heart of Darkness*', *The International Fiction Review*, volume 7, reprinted in R. Kimbrough, editor, *Heart of Darkness*, third edition, New York and London: Norbon 1988.

Scott, P. (1976) *The Raj Quartet*, first published as four separate novels between 1966 and 1975, London: Heinemann.

Secor, R. (1971) *The Rhetoric of Shifting Perspectives*, Pennsylvania: Pennsylvania State University Press.

Seshadri-Crooks, K. (2000) *Desiring Whiteness: A Lacanian Analysis of Race*, London and New York: Routledge.

—— (2000) 'At the Margins of Postcolonial Studies', in F. Afzal-Khan and K. Seshadri-Crooks, editors, *The Preoccupation of Postcolonial Studies*, Durham, North Carolina, and London: Duke University Press.

Shakespeare, W. (1912) *The Tragedies*, edited W. J. Craig, London: Oxford University Press; reprinted 1966.

Sherry, N. (1971) *Conrad's Eastern World*, Cambridge: Cambridge University Press.

—— editor (1973) *Conrad: The Critical Heritage*, London and Boston: Routledge and Kegan Paul.

Sokal A. and Bricmont, J. (1998) *Intellectual Impostures: Postmodern Philosophers' Abuse of Science*, London: Profile Books.

Spivak, G. (1985) 'Can the Subaltern Speak?' in *Wedge* numbers 7/8.

—— (1987) *In Other Worlds: Essays in Cultural Politics*, New York and London: Methuen.

—— (1989) 'Naming Gayatri Spivak', interviewed M. Koundoura, *Stanford Humanities Review*, volume 1, number 1.

Stallman, R. W. editor (1960) *The Art of Joseph Conrad: A Critical Symposium*, Michigan: Michigan State University Press.

Stern, F. editor (1956) *The Varieties of History: From Voltaire to the Present*, Cleveland and New York: Meridian Books; eighth printing, 1962.

Straus, N. (1996) 'The Exclusion of the Intended from Secret Sharing', in *Joseph Conrad*, edited E. Jordan, New Casebooks, London: Macmillan.

Taussig, M. (1987) *Shamanism, Colonialism, and the Wild Man: A Study in Terror and Healing*, Chicago and London: University of Chicago Press.

Thieme, J. (2001) *Postcolonial Con-Texts: Writing Back to the Canon*, London and New York: Continuum.

Thompson, D. editor (1984) *The Leavises: Recollections and Impressions*, Cambridge: Cambridge University Press.

Tillyard, E. M. W. (1958) *The Epic Strain in the English Novel*, London: Chatto and Windus.

Trilling, L. (1951) *The Liberal Imagination*, London: Martin Secker and Warburg.

Vijayashree, C. (2004) *Writing the West 1750–1947: Representations from Indian Languages*, New Delhi: Sahitya Akademi.

Wallace, A. (1869) *The Malay Archipelago*, London: Macmillan; reprinted with introduction by J. Bastin, Singapore: Oxford University Press, 1989.

Wallerstein, I. (1974) *The Modern World System*, New York: Academic Press.

—— (1979) *The Capitalist World Economy*, Cambridge: Cambridge University Press.

Warren, B. (1980) *Imperialism: Pioneer of Capitalism*, edited J. Sender, London: Verso.

Watt, I. (1957) *The Rise of the Novel: Studies in Defoe, Richardson and Fielding*, London: Chatto and Windus.

—— (1979) *Conrad in the Nineteenth Century*, Berkeley and Los Angeles: University of California Press.

Widdowson, P. editor (1982) *Re-Reading English*, London: Methuen.

Williams, R. (1970) *The English Novel from Dickens to Lawrence*, London: Chatto and Windus; republished London: The Hogarth Press 1984; reprinted 1987.

—— (1971) *George Orwell*, New York: Columbia University Press.

—— (1973) *The Country and the City*, London: Oxford University Press.

—— (1976) *Keywords: A Vocabulary of Culture and Society*, London: Croom Helm.

—— (1977) *Marxism and Literature*, Oxford: Oxford University Press.

—— (1979) *Politics and Letters: Interviews with New Left Review*, London: New Left Books.

—— (1980) *Problems in Materialism and Culture*, London: Verso.

—— (1983) *Keywords: A Vocabulary of Culture and Society*, revised and extended second edition, London: Fontana.

Wiltshire, J. (2001) *Recreating Jane Austen*, Cambridge: Cambridge University Press.

Woolf, V. (1948) *The Common Reader*, London: The Hogarth Press.

Yeow, A. (2004) 'Conrad and the Straits Chinese: The Politics of Chinese Enterprise and Identity in the Colonial State' *The Conradian*, volume 29, number 1, Spring.

Young, R. J. C. (1995) *Colonial Desire: Hybridity in Theory, Culture and Race*, London and New York: Routledge.

Žižek, S. (1989) *The Sublime Object of Ideology*, London and New York: Verso.

—— (1999) 'Preface: Burning the Bridges', in E. Wright and E. Wright, editors, *The Žižek Reader*, Oxford: Blackwell 2000.

Index